The Making of
Theatrical Reputations

The Making of

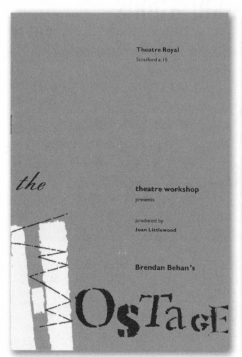

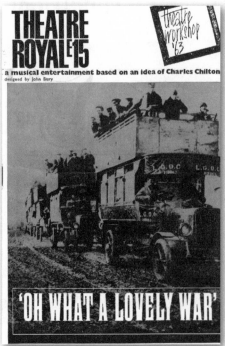

STUDIES IN THEATRE HISTORY & CULTURE

Edited by Thomas Postlewait

Theatrical Reputations

Studies from the Modern London Theatre

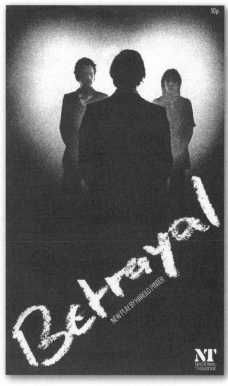

YAEL ZARHY-LEVO

UNIVERSITY OF IOWA PRESS   Iowa City

University of Iowa Press, Iowa City 52242

Copyright © 2008 by the University of Iowa Press

All rights reserved

Printed in the United States of America

Design by Richard Hendel

www.uiowapress.org

The University of Iowa Press is a member of Green Press Initiative
and is committed to preserving natural resources.

Printed on acid-free paper

LCCN: 2007940204

ISBN-13: 978-1-58729-626-0

ISBN-10: 1-58729-626-8

08   09   10   11   12   C   5   4   3   2   1

For Yeshayahu, a partner throughout

Contents

Acknowledgments

Through the long process entailed in working on this project, in which I have aspired to study an era, locale, and culture somewhat distant and different from my own, I have relied on the help and friendship of many people, to all of whom I am indebted.

First and foremost, my deepest gratitude to Tom Postlewait, the series editor, for his invaluable advice and enriching intellectual guidance, as well as for his attentive support and encouragement at crucial moments in the course of writing this book. I am grateful, too, to Holly Carver, director of the University of Iowa Press, for her assistance and kindness, and to Charlotte Wright, managing editor, for her invaluable work. I am indebted to Rosemarie Bank for her insights, support, and care throughout. I wish to thank the members of the Theatre Historiography Working Group, International Federation for Theatre Research, who accompanied me through the process of working on this project, in particular Claire Cochrane and Bruce McConachie, for their helpful advice and stimulating commentaries.

My gratitude to my friends in London for their invaluable help and concern: to Frances Rifkin for opening many doors, for stimulating conversations, as well as for her hospitality and companionship; to Irit Rogoff for her immense generosity, enlightening perspectives, and attentive care; to Susanne Greenhalgh for her inspiring commentaries and hospitality; to Susie Gilbert for her information updates and kindness; and to Adrian Rifkin and Denis Echard for their advice and hospitality.

I wish to thank all those who helped with the search for and gathering of information for this book, enabling me to look into the past decades, especially the staff of the Study Room at the Theatre Museum, while still in its former, lovely Covent Garden location, who responded patiently and helpfully to my many inquiries and desperate e-mails. Special thanks are also due to the staff of the British Film Institute, National Library, London, in particular to Sarah Currant and Christophe Dupin, for their kind assistance. I am most grateful to John Arden and Margaretta D'Arcy for their hospitality, kindness, and collaboration during a highly memorable visit.

The Porter Institute, Tel Aviv University, provided financial assistance for this project. For this, as well as for the many other ways she provided crucial support, I am highly indebted to the Institute's director, Ziva Ben-Porat. I owe much to my colleagues and friends from Tel Aviv University: Orly Lubin for inspiring new ways of thinking and for keeping me going; Louise Bethlehem and Sonja Narunsky-Laden for their assistance and encouragement; Eyal Segal for his help; Freddie Rokem, Jeanette Malkin, Shimon Levy, Michael Gluzman, and Anat Zanger for their advice and support. Special thanks to my students at Tel-Aviv University for sharing my passion for the London theatre and for their insightful observations.

I am most grateful to Naomi Paz for her invaluable editorial help and Pnina Zeitz for her indispensable assistance. I heartily thank Miri Gold-wasser for sustaining me through difficult moments, Channa Taub for her long-distance support and Brian McHale, who even when far away was (and is) always an inspiration.

Finally, I am highly indebted to my family for bearing with me through these intensive years, forgiving my frequent absences when I disappeared into the 1960s: to Rivi, Dany, Dudi, Anat, Daniel, and Ruti; to Vera, my London eye, who enabled me to be in two places at once; and to my father, Moshe, who taught me "long-distance running." Last but certainly not least, I am grateful to my son, Guy (himself consumed by questions of evolution), for his intelligent advice and forgiveness of his too often pre-occupied mother, and to my daughter, Michal (although busy working to change evil policies), for being both a highly resourceful problem solver and an insightful companion.

The Making of
Theatrical Reputations

Introduction

IN THE WINGS: MEDIATION IN THE THEATRE

Who is the true producer of the value of the work—the painter or the dealer, the writer or the publisher, the playwright or the theatre manager?
—Pierre Bourdieu, 1980

When I began thinking about the puzzling oscillations in the theatrical reputations of specific events, theatre companies, and individual playwrights reflected in various studies of the modern London theatre, Pierre Bourdieu's intriguing question served as my cue. Who are the figures—individuals or organizations—that authorize theatre companies or playwrights and influence their position on the cultural map? What are the strategies employed by these figures to endow the theatrical work with value and to make it more accessible to audiences? What are the channels they employ to introduce, promote, or evaluate the work? What sorts of patterns of interaction are established among these authorizing figures, and how do they affect the perceived value of the work? What role do the playwrights themselves play in the reception and perception of their works? In sum, how do these authorizing figures and these configurations of interrelated parties, modes, or mechanisms that help organize what I call *the processes of mediation* operate in the theatre and how does mediation influence the status of an event or the position of a company or playwright in the cultural or historical memory?

In setting out to answer these questions, I offer four case studies from the modern London theatre concentrating on the 1950s and 1960s. The first centers on a specific event—the English Stage Company's production of John Osborne's *Look Back in Anger*; the second deals with the trajectory of a specific theatre company—the Theatre Workshop—and in particular with the company's first decade at the Theatre Royal, Stratford East, London; the third and fourth focus on the careers of individual playwrights—John Arden and Harold Pinter, respectively. These four case studies primarily serve to illustrate the various processes of mediation.

Accordingly, in all four cases I present the workings of various individuals or organizations that act as mediators. Mediation in the theatre encompasses theatre reviewers, journalists, interviewers (in the press or on radio or television), funding bodies, censors, publishers, critics and academics—those who describe, comment, judge, assist, reward, restrict, support, promote, evaluate, or assess (or reassess) theatrical works (plays or productions) and theatre creators. Mediation is also practiced by the participants in theatre production, such as producers, managers, and artistic directors of a given theatre company, as well as directors, playwrights, actors, stage designers, and members of a theatre company's council or committees. Among those who partake in one way or another in theatrical production, the role of mediation is ascribed here to those who enhance the value of a work as a result of one or more of the following: their function as decision makers (e.g., artistic directors, producers), their involvement as theatre practitioners (e.g., directors, actors), their prominent standing, or their active promotion of the theatrical enterprise. Promotional mediation is also often carried out directly through participation in theatre festivals, advertisement, press releases, and other media interventions.

Let me clarify at the outset that I do not view the practice of mediation as resulting from arbitrary decisions by powerful individuals or organizations; nor do I perceive it as motivated by a conspiracy of forces operating solely in the name of power or profit. Rather, I perceive those who act as mediators to be driven, more often than not, by their own current conceptions of artistic quality and merit, in addition to their ideological or political orientations, and sometimes possibly also by revised perceptions of the relevant sociocultural issues.

The subject of this book is the making of artistic reputations. In considering the contributing roles of the various participants in theatre production I examine how artistic events, companies, works, and writers are constructed by critics, academics, media, institutions, funding agencies, and governmental decisions. I investigate the methods, aims, assumptions, and modes of description and analysis, as well as the objectives and policies of those who partake in theatre production, and the promotional means employed by them. Drawing upon previous scholarship, I examine how the theatrical works were received; the ways that theatre reviewers, critics, academics, newspapers, journals, and other media, as well as organizations, contributed both separately and collectively to the perception of the theatrical creators and their work. I investigate the role of the theatre creators themselves in shaping the reception and perception of their work and I explore the effect of different configurations of mediating parties on the theatrical standing of the artists (whether an individual playwright or a company) and their work. In the process, in each of the four case studies I focus on a specific topic, each of which serves my primary subject and aims.

Chapter 1 focuses on an artistic event and its participants—the English Stage Company (ESC) production of John Osborne's *Look Back in Anger*. I examine the defining features of the event and its reception—those figures, processes, and developments that contributed not only to the making of the event but also to the narrative that was constructed around it. In other words, I explore the mediation processes that contributed to the emergence and development of the breakthrough narrative surrounding this production: the perception that the first performance of *Look Back in Anger* ushered in a new era in British theatre. I show how and why this narrative—linking company, play, and playwright—came into being, how it was constructed and developed, leaving its indelible imprint on the cultural-historical memory.

Chapter 2 concerns a theatre company and the contributors to its developmental course and reputation—the trajectory of Theatre Workshop, particularly through its first decade at Stratford East. The focus is on the characteristics of the company and its work, as well as on the confused mediation underlying its reception—on those figures and processes that not only had an effect on the company's evolution, oscillating reputation, and eventual demise, but also contributed to the different constructions built around the company and its key production, *Oh What a Lovely War*. I examine the ways in which the reputation of Joan Littlewood—founder-director of Theatre Workshop—was mediated, and her own role in shaping the reception and perception of the company. I have chosen to concentrate on Theatre Workshop's first decade at Stratford East because this period particularly exemplifies the conflicting forces of mediation at play and the consequent twists and turns in the company's reputation: the gradual critical recognition of its theatrical contribution coinciding with the reluctance of governmental authorities to support its work, its rise to prominence accompanied by a series of crises, and its most celebrated production vis-à-vis the culminating factors leading to its demise a decade later. I conclude the chapter with a review of scholarly assessments from the last four decades of the theatrical contribution of the ESC and Theatre Workshop. This review primarily serves to illustrate the shift in scholarly evaluation of Theatre Workshop and its key production while also demonstrating the moderation, change, or rejection of previous narratives constructed around the ESC production of Osborne's play and its significance (the revisionists' challenging of the historical narrative that posits a radical transformation of British theatre because of *Look Back in Anger*). The review, then, serves as a conclusion to both the first and second chapters, showing how the historical explanations and narratives were constructed over the last six decades. These two chapters illustrate contrasting mediatory configurations—convergence versus divergence. The mediating process in the case of the ESC illustrates what happens when the many factors involved in mediation work together, while the mediating process in the case of Theatre Workshop demonstrates what happens when these factors pull in different directions.

Chapter 3 addresses the career of the dramatist John Arden— particularly the troublesome reception, rise to prominence, and eventual break with the London theatre that took place during his first decade as a playwright. The focus is both on the artist—the characteristic features of his drama, aims, and policies—and on the mediating figures and processes that constructed his image, his work, and his reputation. Arden's own responses and contribution to the mediating process form part of this topic. Given that Arden has distanced himself from the London theatre and mediation circles, I also draw upon an interview I conducted with John Arden and his wife, the actress and playwright Margaretta D'Arcy, in 2001 in which they commented on some of the key developments in the first decade of his career.

The more accessible perspective of the playwright Harold Pinter is discussed in chapter 4 which covers the evolving stages of Pinter's image through the different phases of his career. The dual focus here concerns first, the mediating figures and processes (in particular the critical processes) that constructed and eventually modified his image and his work and second, the dramatist's singular conduct, range of assumed roles, and influence as a contributor to the mediating process of his own work. Pinter's effective role, through the later phases of his career, in the modification of his image as dramatist (via his canny use of the many channels of communication) forms part of this topic.

These playwrights' careers illustrate once more the outcome of divergent versus convergent mediating factors. Arden's exemplifies a process in which the many mediating factors pull in different directions, leading to contradictory assessments and oscillations in the artist's reputation. Pinter's illustrates a mediating process that has helped create an aura of attention around the playwright and a desire for more information that has generated yet more mediation, culminating in a Nobel Prize. In both cases the playwrights also played a role: in their responses to the first wave of mediation and in their eventual attitudes or policies.

Having described the specific topics in the four case studies, another clarification is perhaps called for. I am fully aware of the importance of aesthetic issues, but rather than presenting a literary study of specific plays or an analysis of specific productions, I want to look at the *ways* in which the artists and their work are constructed, championed, or judged by those who mediate their drama and, just as important, to look at the course taken by the artists themselves as participants in the mediation endeavor.

Given the aim of this study, my decision to discuss specific events, companies, plays, and playwrights rather than giving a historical survey of the modern London theatre was derived in part from the consideration that each case I chose is perceived as a major contribution to the development of London (and British) theatre in the 1950s and 1960s (notwithstanding the debates over the extent of each one's individual contribution). There are, of course, many other theatrical events and theatre creators that are seen as seminal contributors to the development of the London stage during these two decades. One notable example is the first performance of the Berliner Ensemble in London (with *Mother Courage, The Caucasian Circle*, and *Drums and Trumpets*) from August 27–September 15, 1956 at the Palace Theatre. Yet another example is the first London production of Samuel Beckett's *Waiting for Godot*, directed by Peter Hall and performed at the Arts Theatre in 1955. Both events are widely considered to be major influences and signposts of the new era in theatre. Early London productions of Brecht's plays and of other Beckett plays, as well as of dramas by Eugene Ionesco, Jean-Paul Sartre, and Jean Genet in the mid to late 1950s and early 1960s at the Royal Court (the plays of the latter three European dramatists were initially furiously attacked by London critics), have all come to be seen as influential in the changing of London theatre.[1] The early 1960s are also associated with two key developments: the 1960 opening of the first season of the (newly formed and named) Royal Shakespeare Company at the Aldwych Theatre—the company's London base—under the directorship of Peter Hall; and the 1963 opening of the National Theatre at the Old Vic, under the directorship of Sir Laurence Olivier. These latter developments, as well as the just-noted events and influences and other contributing factors at play in the development of the London theatre in the two decades, have been discussed extensively by many scholars of British theatre and in various cultural and historical studies of the era.[2]

I have undoubtedly benefited from this extensive scholarship and from the vigorous debate among theatre critics and scholars (ongoing over the last three decades), over which plays, companies, and playwrights contributed to the posited transformation of British theatre in the mid to late 1950s. The cases I chose illustrate, separately and together, *distinct mediatory configurations* and *their impact* on the reputations of theatrical works and creators both in their own time and over time. Thus these cases (despite—or because of—being quite specific in their topics) offer four salient instances of the making of theatrical reputations.

The interest in mediating figures, practices, or factors has already been manifested in various critical and historical studies of theatre or related publications. In recent years a number of studies on British theatre, such as those by Stephen Lacey (1995), Dan Rebellato (1999), Dominic Shellard (1999), and Baz Kershaw (2004), reflect a growing interest in the practices of mediation and their effect on theatrical developments. Moreover, key figures in the theatre who have functioned as mediators are themselves attracting increased scholarly attention. Scholars examining the careers and reception of various playwrights (for example, Thomas Postlewait's study on the Ibsen campaign in England or Susan Merritt's study on Pinter's critics and reception)[3] or the histories of theatre companies (for example, Sally Beauman's history of the Royal Shakespeare Company or Philip Roberts's study of the Royal Court)[4] have been acknowledging and discussing the effective powers of a range of individual figures such as critics, directors, and artistic directors. Noteworthy too are essays that center on producers or managers of theatre companies.[5] Eminent critics such as Kenneth Tynan and Harold Hobson, as well as prominent directors (who also often served as the artistic directors of theatre companies) such as George Devine, Peter Brook, and Peter Hall, have become the subjects of individual studies,[6] or biographies[7]; for several such figures there are also autobiographies (for example, Joan Littlewood and Richard Eyre).[8]

During the last three decades there has been a growing interest too in theatre criticism. A number of studies that center on the roles and influence of critics and reviewers have been published, such as those by Engel Lehman (1976), John English (1979), and Wesley Shrum (1996). Lehman assesses the drama critics in major New York daily newspapers, commenting on and evaluating various reviews and reviewers. English looks into various types of popular art criticism (film, dance, books, music, visual art, and television) and devotes a section to theatre criticism. He describes and assesses the standards and influence of each type of criticism, interpreting, evaluating, questioning, and critiquing different critical writings. Shrum sets out to explore the difference between high and popular art as "a function of the discursive practices that mediate the relationship between art and its public."[9] He centers on the role of the critics, offering the Edinburgh Fringe Festival as his case study. The authors of these three studies explore, in varying ways, the differing objectives of drama critics (primarily in the press), the various standards of critical practice, and the critics' use or misuse of their power to influence the careers of playwrights or the fate of new shows.[10] Several books on theatre criticism have been written by the critics themselves (e.g., Irving Wardle and Benedict Nightingale),[11] while a few influential critics, notably Hobson and Tynan, have published collections of their own reviews.[12] Several collections of theatre criticism written between the mid-1950s and the 1980s have also been published.[13]

Drawing upon this valuable body of publications and scholarship, I want to investigate, and especially to integrate, the various practices of mediation and, furthermore, to bring to the fore a range of participating figures, modes, or mechanisms, presenting the four cases—key developments in modern London theatre—through the prism of mediation. In doing so I show how the accumulating processes of mediation have shaped not only the theatrical reputations of specific events, companies, and individual playwrights, but also our historical understanding of their particular role within the overall context of British theatre. In the section that follows I introduce and explain the key terms I use in reference to mediation, as well as a number of the principles that underlie its workings.

MEDIATION PROCESSES:
ESSENTIALS, PRINCIPLES, AND APPLICATION
Public taste is created—never forget that.—John Osborne, 1981

In the four cases presented in this book, the theatre companies, individual plays, individual productions, and individual playwrights (including the poetics of the playwrights) are all subject to and subjects of mediation. The processes of mediation that recur throughout share three essentials: placement, forces, and channels.

The outcome of mediation is the placement of the subject—a company, play, production, or playwright—in relation to other subjects of the same sort. The placement of the subject is a developmental process that entails modifications over time. The placement defines the position—center or periphery, high or low—of the subject, and also locates it within the overall context of the theatre tradition (i.e., influences and innovations) with respect to its distinctive theatrical expression. The theatrical expression is characterized by an aggregation of diverse traits or attributes that differentiate the subject from others of the same sort (i.e., companies, plays, productions, or playwrights). This cluster of characteristics is the unique multidimensional fingerprint associated with the subject. In the case of a company, the cluster of characteristics draws on some, but not necessarily all, of the following: the repertoire (e.g., preference for dramas of specific eras, of particular playwrights, or particular thematic concerns); the specific staging styles; the locale of the theatre or other venues of performance; the target audience; the nature of the cast's training and work methods (such as collaborative teamwork); and the company's ideology, manifestos, or declared agendas (such as a writers' theatre or theatre of the people).

A playwright's poetics or a play will be attached to a cluster of attributes too—such as those pertaining to thematic concerns, devices, setting, dialogue, and characters—that typify the theatrical expression in terms of influences and innovations. The cluster associated with a company will differ from that associated with an individual playwright in terms of scope and potential traits. In this book, I refer to the cluster of attributes associated with a company as its *niche*, and to that associated with a specific dramatist (or the poetics of the dramatist) as the playwright's *construct*. As I shall demonstrate, in particular in the chapters on Arden and Pinter, the placement of individual plays is generally determined with a view toward the playwright's poetics (e.g., the dramatist's masterpiece or atypical works), although in a number of cases a single play or a specific production may achieve independent standing, as have, for example, the plays *Waiting for Godot* and *Serjeant Musgrave's Dance* and the ESC production of *Look Back in Anger* and Peter Brook's production of *A Midsummer Night's Dream*. Factors such as director or company can affect the placement assigned to individual productions.

Changes in entries for dramatists in an encyclopedia over several editions illustrate how a playwright's construct gets presented and modified over time. A few extracts from the entries for Samuel Beckett in the 1967 edition of *The Oxford Companion to the Theatre* and the 2003 edition of *The Oxford Encyclopedia of Theatre and Performance*, which replaced the

Oxford Companion, serve as examples. The entry in the 1967 edition of *The Oxford Companion* centers on the play *Waiting for Godot*: "Beckett abandoned conventional structure and development, in both plot and language, to create a static form which was a perfect dramatic image of his vision of the terrible absurdity of the human situation in a world over which mankind has lost control."[14] On his other plays, the entry reads: "Beckett again expressed his vision of the moral paralysis of mankind, cutting even further on the already minimal action and development . . . and moving on to one of genuine pain at the prospect of man continuing to exist, blithely unaware of the increasing circumscription of his liberty and power of action."[15] The entry in the 2003 edition is more extensive than the earlier one, providing an overview of Beckett's work as well as other relevant information, such as directors with whom he worked and critical commentaries on his plays. An extract from the opening paragraphs reads: "Beckett developed a radically innovative dramaturgy, linked thematically to the theatre of the absurd, and focusing on a formally conceived visual image and a tight, non-linear rhythmic structure. *Waiting for Godot* re-creates on stage the experience of waiting, using comedy, metatheatrical commentary, and popular entertainment references to present theatre and life as passing time, diversionary tactics to keep the void at bay." The entry continues: "The work initially baffled and scandalized audiences but became one of the most critically acclaimed plays of the twentieth century and undoubtedly Beckett's best-known work."[16] The concluding sentence of this entry reads: "Sometimes described as spanning the aesthetics of European modernism and post-modernism, he rigorously revised the materials and structures of both traditional and new media."[17]

Both entries tend to refer to the same typifying elements, though describing them in different ways, and both note influences and innovations, although the 2003 entry is more explicit. Nonetheless, the differences between these two entries are noticeable, even from these few extracts. The 1967 entry offers a description of Beckett's distinctive traits, while in the 2003 entry the emphasis shifts to assessing and locating his drama and poetics within an overall theatrical and cultural context. Noticeable too is this latter entry's comparison of *Waiting for Godot* with other plays of the twentieth century and with Beckett's other dramatic works. The developmental process of the "Beckett" construct exemplified by these two entries reflects, in fact, one option of modification of a playwright construct over time.[18]

As the cases examined in this book will demonstrate, the emergence of a playwright construct indicates that the dramatist has acquired a critical existence, even though other mediators, not just critics, may have their effect on the emergent construct. In the two chapters that center on individual playwrights, I trace the gradual formation and modification of what I call the "Arden" or "Pinter" construct—the outcome of the critical discourse that mediated these dramatists' works.

The views held by different mediators as to the appropriate positions and niches or playwright constructs may of course be incompatible at times. The cases explored in the book demonstrate the struggles that can ensue among the various mediating parties and the range of modes they may employ in their attempts to influence the particular placement to be assigned to a subject. These cases also demonstrate that the placement (either position or niche/construct, and sometimes both) may change not only through the phases of a dramatist's career or of a company's developmental trajectory, but also over history—that is, a shift in scholarly assessments of the subject's artistic contribution evolves over time.

The forces of mediation constitute those individuals and organizations that determine the value of the theatrical works and the standing of the theatre creators. They act to introduce, assist or constrain, support, promote, and evaluate theatrical works and theatre creators. A major distinction can be made between in-house mediators and external ones. In-house mediators are those who partake in one way or another in the production of plays, such as artistic directors (assistants, or associate directors) of theatre companies, members of the councils or boards of theatre companies, directors, and producers. Whether theatre practitioners or administrators, the in-house mediators themselves, or as representatives of the association they serve, are subject to external mediation. External mediators—reviewers, journalists, interviewers, critics, academics, members of various official/cultural committees and of funding bodies—respond to, construct, and assess the work of a company or the dramatic works of individual playwrights. External mediators practice their authority by reporting, commenting, supporting, assisting, and promoting—or alternatively, by refusing to support, in which case they pronounce their critique or dismiss the subject of mediation out of hand.

The forces of mediation or mediators are defined in relation to the role (in-house or external) they fulfill in a given case. Mediatory roles are not inherently tied to specific figures; hence a particular role can be exchanged among different mediators or shared by them, and a single figure can—even simultaneously—fulfill several such roles. In-house mediators often also fulfill external roles, responding to productions other than their own. That is, they may extend their influence by reviewing and assessing productions in which they do not themselves participate, by interviewing theatre creators whose plays they did not stage/direct, or by serving on committees that ultimately leave their mark on the placement of theatre companies or of productions other than those in which they are involved. At times, external mediators—critics, for example—also function as in-house mediators, serving as board members of particular theatrical institutions, or on the councils of companies. Actors or stage designers, especially prominent ones, may also fulfill a mediatory role. Additionally, the playwrights themselves are potential mediators, assuming one role or another either where their own dramatic work or the work of others is concerned. In fact, as the following chapters demonstrate, key roles are frequently interchanged among a limited number of prominent mediators. It should be stressed that figures fulfilling mediatory roles constitute forces to the extent that they exert their power (either as individuals or by joining other mediators) to influence the eventual outcome of mediation, that is, placement of the subject. It is also noteworthy that the relative weight of particular roles, such as those of funding committees,[19] reviewers, producers,[20] directors,[21] or artistic directors, alters in different periods.

When considering the influence of theatrical figures acting either as in-house or external mediators, it is important to note the effect of their own status on the placement assigned to the subject they promote or evaluate. In the case of in-house mediators, especially producers, artistic directors, and directors, the "symbolic goods" (to use Bourdieu's term) they themselves have acquired are necessarily projected onto the play, playwright, or company that they produce, stage, introduce, or manage. If the extent of their prominence may affect the position assigned to the theatrical work or the playwright they introduce or promote, their particular theatrical activities/experience (e.g., classical repertoire; experimental theatre) may, in turn, affect the constituents of the subject's construct or the niche allocation. Artistic directors, for example, who are associated primarily with experimental theatre might accordingly brand a newly founded company in which they serve. Prominent producers, actors, stage designers, and especially directors contribute more often than not to the favorable reception of a theatrical work.

Joe Orton's third performed play, *Loot*, illustrates the effect of a prominent director on the reception of a play and on the career of the playwright. *Loot* was first produced in London in 1966 by Oscar Lewenstein and directed by Charles Marowitz. Marowitz had acquired a reputation as a drama critic, playwright, and director, committed to new and experimental theatre (e.g., his work with Peter Brook on the production of *King Lear* in 1962 and during the Theatre of Cruelty season in 1964).[22] In addition to directing *Loot*, Marowitz published an article in the *Guardian* a week prior to its opening in which he commented on Orton's dramatic innovations. Marowitz's authoritative standing as a director and critic probably contributed not only to the favorable reception of the play—it received the *Evening Standard* Drama Award in 1967 for best play of the year—but also to the positive turn in Orton's career. Through his active promotion and by virtue of his reputation, Marowitz also influenced the eventual critical perception of Orton's poetics as a playwright, that is, the "Orton" construct.

Given that in-house mediators are themselves subject to external mediation, in some cases the critical assessment of the production in which they are involved may affect not only the career of the playwright but also their own careers and reputations as theatre practitioners. The success of the first London production of Beckett's *Waiting for Godot* in 1955, largely due to the enthusiastic reviews of two major critics, Harold Hobson and Kenneth Tynan, undoubtedly contributed to the growing reputation of the director of the play, Peter Hall. In fact, the reception of this production offers a clear example of the influence of prominent critics. The initial critical reception of the London production had on the whole been unfavorable. According to the actors' recollections, during the first week the cast faced tiny, hostile houses. However, the laudatory reviews by Hobson (the *Sunday Times*) and Tynan (the *Observer*), published on Sunday, turned the fortune of the production, eventually filling the houses for the rest of the run.[23] If one prominent critic pronouncing his verdict can influence the fate of a production, then two prominent critics whose verdicts are compatible will certainly double the effect. It is therefore highly likely that when several authoritative critics join forces in promoting a production, play, or playwright and, moreover, when they converge with other prominent external or in-house mediators, their influence on the placement assigned to the work or playwright in question might be extensive indeed. Throughout this book I examine the function, contribution, and influence of individual reviewers or critics as well as their shared roles or strategies as mediators.

The third shared essential of the processes of mediation is that of the channels through which mediation is practiced, which are bound to institutional frames or regulations. Mediators exploit a wide range of channels to disseminate their commentary; introduce, publicize, or mark an artistic merit; or promote theatrical activities, individuals, and works. Mediatory channels include the various media (press, radio, television, film, newspapers, magazines, journals, textbooks) that convey the description, analysis, and evaluation of the plays, productions, companies, playwrights, directors, actors, or other theatrical practitioners and activities. Other channels of mediation include program notes accompanying productions, advertisements publicizing theatre productions (such as posters), and theatre company brochures and manifestos. Theatre competitions for awards or grants also constitute mediatory channels by virtue of their function of and potential for advancing theatrical enterprises. Awards and grants are markers of artistic merit or contribution and thereby serve to enhance the value of the winning theatrical works, companies, and individual theatre creators. Yet another channel is the theatre festival—whether academic or performance oriented, national or international. Theatre festivals provide public exposure of works and practitioners, but they are often also markers of status, which in turn further cultivates the reputation of theatrical individuals, plays, productions, or companies.

These many and diverse channels at the mediators' disposal provide numerous opportunities. The press as a mediating channel, for example, is employed by in-house and external mediators alike: the former use it to announce a forthcoming production or to introduce a new playwright; theatre critics use it to review new productions; journalists or critics (at times also theatre practitioners) use it to publish articles on or interviews with theatrical figures and to cover or comment on theatrical festivals; and gossip columnists use it to titillate their readers with exposés relating to the social life, marriages, and affairs of theatrical figures. Television can also be exploited in a variety of ways. A broadcast of an excerpt or of an entire production as well as interviews with the involved individuals can publicize or further cultivate the fame of a play, playwright, theatrical activities, or practitioners. In a similar vein, television panel shows that present theatre critics or scholars provide wide publicity for external mediators, enabling them to exert their influence, and simultaneously serve to cultivate further their authoritative stance.

The various publishing practices of mediators also disseminate their evaluations, critiques, and analyses or cultivate the reputation of theatrical works, activities, or individual careers, for example, through the biographies and autobiographies of theatrical figures such as playwrights, directors, or critics. In some cases, biographies or studies of theatre creators written by critics or scholars enhance both the fame of the subjects and the authoritative stance of the writers. Studies dealing with individual playwrights or works are often a result of the collaborative effort of practitioners and critics or scholars. Yet another form of collaboration is a print edition of plays, either individually or as a collection, with an introduction by a critic, again enabling external mediators (critics and publishers) to promote these dramas, as well as their own authority. Scholars of theatre often exploit professional journals, courses and syllabuses, academic presses, or conferences to convey their assessments, explanations, or criticism of theatrical works, practices, and individual careers.

It is obvious that when a variety of mediating channels are exploited in promoting a particular play, production, company, or playwright, the influence of such mediation increases. The power of mediation can be seen to reside not only in the authoritative or prominent stance of the operating mediators but also in the number of mediating parties involved and the extent of the repertoire of channels exploited. Given these essential factors at play in the making of theatrical reputations, it is equally essential to recall that the effect of mediation on the standing of theatre creators or works is also an outcome of the configurations that emerge from the relations between the various mediating parties (collaborating, competing, diverging, or converging). As the four cases examined in this book illustrate, the theatrical reputations of specific events, companies, or individual playwrights, largely conditioned by the sometimes changing mediatory configurations, may indeed oscillate not only during their own era but also throughout history.

In the four chapters that follow, I present the case studies. The concluding chapter provides an overview of the major issues pertaining to mediation that emerge from this inquiry.

1 Convergent Forces

The English Stage Company and
Look Back in Anger

*In April 1956, the English Stage Company began its first season at the
Royal Court and had an immediate impact upon the course of British
theatre. The success of the first season was the premiere of John
Osborne's* Look Back in Anger, *an unknown play by a then unknown
writer, which lent the tone of crusading radicalism, often bitter and
angry but never lazy or complacent, to the Royal Court's programmes.
—Cambridge Paperback Guide to Theatre, 1996*

*The company changed the course of British theatre almost overnight
when it staged John Osborne's* Look Back in Anger.*—Philip Barnes, 1986*

*With extreme precariousness, through one touch-and-go crisis after
another, the Royal Court has survived uniquely as a writers' theatre
ever since the ESC's first discovery, John Osborne, changed the course of
theatrical history with* Look Back in Anger, *staged five weeks after the
opening production in 1956.—Richard Findlater, 1981*

LAYING OUT THE QUESTIONS

One thing emerges consistently in any study of British theatre in the
1950s: the English Stage Company's unique role in inaugurating a new
era in British theatre. This perception is closely bound up with the claim
that the third play performed by this company, John Osborne's *Look Back
in Anger*, marked a turning point in the evolution of British theatre, a
judgment which explains the metaphors that are so frequently invoked
to describe the event: watershed, landmark, ground-breaking intervention, turnabout or turning point, renaissance, key-date. But despite this
apparent critical consensus regarding the singular role of the play, many
critics also agree that it is rather conventional in nature. The discrepancy
between critical assessments of *Look Back in Anger* as a formally conventional play, and its remarkable historical reception and impact, presents

itself as something of a conundrum. Equally puzzling is the centrality that Osborne's play has been given in the historical assessment of the company that performed it—the link established between company and play, manifested in the breakthrough narrative that has come to be associated with this production, a link which provokes still more questions.

The assessment of a theatre company draws, more often than not, on its repertoire of plays, or the playwrights associated with it, as well as on factors such as ideology, policy, actors, and work methods. The English Stage Company (ESC) came to fame as a writers' theatre, and its reputation was based on its policy of presenting new and innovative plays. The repertoire of the ESC included several works by new playwrights widely conceded five decades later to have surpassed Osborne's play in their innovation. *Look Back in Anger* was neither the first play performed by the ESC nor the one seen over time as the most innovative of the company's productions, yet it is Osborne's play that is prominently held to account for the company's revolutionary role. The influential position of the English Stage Company during the postwar era in Britain and the role attributed to this company in contemporary British theatre have retained a legendary status into the twenty-first century.

In recent years, however, revisionist histories query the revolutionary role ascribed to this company. Studies by Lacey (1995), Rebellato (1999), and Shellard (1999 and 2006), and essays by Baz Kershaw and Derek Paget in *The Cambridge History of British Theatre* (2004), question either the overnight transformation associated with the ESC production of *Look Back in Anger* or the uniquely radical nature of this company compared with other companies during the postwar era. These studies and essays suggest other agents that contributed to the changes in the British theatre and also argue that various plays performed by other companies, before or during the same years as the ESC's appearance on the theatrical map, were at least as radical as those performed by the ESC. The question of the significance attributed to Osborne's play is thus further entangled with the question of the revolutionary contribution ascribed to the ESC. In view of these concerns, one might ask what accounts for the emergence and robustness of the historical judgments surrounding Osborne's play and the ESC, judgments that have left such an indelible imprint on cultural-historical memory.

My primary aim here is to reveal the major role of the mediating processes both in making the ESC production of *Look Back in Anger* a celebrated event and in the emergence and development of the breakthrough narrative constructed around it, a narrative that had a formative effect not only on the reputations of the play, company, and playwright but also on the scholarly assessments of modern British theatre in the following decades.

EARLY CONSTELLATIONS AND SCHEMES

A commonly held assumption, especially prevalent in guides and dictionaries of theatre, views the founding and establishment of the ESC at the Royal Court Theatre primarily as the achievement of a single leading figure, George Devine, the first artistic director of this company.[1] But it is more accurate to consider the primacy of Devine to be the end result of a number of contingent processes recounted in various histories of the ESC, such as those by Irving Wardle (1978a), Oscar Lewenstein (1994), and Philip Roberts (1999). Significantly, these three major accounts, from different perspectives, describe the sequence of events leading to Devine's formative intervention in the creation of the English Stage Company. Whereas the hero of Wardle's account is explicitly George Devine (the title of his book is, in fact, *The Theatres of George Devine*), Roberts takes the Royal Court as the stated subject matter of a thoroughly documented account which nevertheless retains Devine as its implicit hero, detailing his role not only as the founder of the ESC but also as "the father of modern British theatre."[2] Lewenstein, whose essential mediating role in the company's founding phase is apparent from all accounts of the ESC, presents us with a volume of memoirs and is thus himself the hero of his account.

All historical accounts concur, however, that the founding of the company involved two groups. The first one, originally containing six figures, centered on Ronald Duncan, while the second centered on the partnership between George Devine and Tony Richardson. In fact, the emergence of the ESC was the consequence of the joint efforts of various leading figures, only some of whom were directly involved with theatre production. These figures shared certain common goals: primarily, to found a new theatre company, and secondarily, to promote a new form of theatre. They can be distinguished, however, on the basis of the kinds of plays they wanted to seek out and produce. More specifically, they were motivated by diverse and, at times, conflicting interests. As early as the founding phase of the company and during its first years of operation, the struggle between Devine and several members of the ESC council could be discerned as a major undercurrent in their interactions. In essence, the conflict often revolved around the two competing theatrical agendas of the lead figures of each group, Duncan and Devine.

It is hardly surprising that Roberts's historical account of the Royal Court, which presents Devine as a leading figure in the founding of this enterprise, begins with the collapse of the Old Vic Theatre Centre in 1952. It was upon the break-up of the Centre that Devine, one of the "three boys" running it (the other two being Michel Saint-Denis and Glen Byam Shaw), started on the long road toward realizing his theatrical vision. Another crucial reason to trace the ESC's founding to the closing of the Old Vic Centre arises out of the institutional context of the theatrical field itself.

In his account of the sponsorship of drama up to 1953, Charles Landstone, associate drama director in the Arts Council,[3] attributes the break-up of the Centre to "the demon of the National Theatre itself."[4] Although it would be another decade before the National Theatre became a reality, the anticipated founding of this institution (which was perceived as a threat to various forces in the theatrical field) clearly affected the developments of the 1950s. Following the break-up of the Old Vic Centre, major theatrical figures who had previously been involved with its activities—including the three past directors Laurence Olivier, Ralph Richardson, and John Burrel, and the three boys, Michel Saint-Denis, Glen Byam Shaw, and Devine—sought to relocate themselves.[5] The period was also one of rearrangement on a grand scale in terms of the theatrical/institutional map. The Old Vic Theatre Centre, founded in 1946, had originally been perceived as the successor of another relatively short-lived enterprise run by Saint-Denis and Devine, the London Theatre Studio (1936–1939), which closed after only four years. Established under the direction of Michel Saint-Denis, the Old Vic Centre consisted of a school and a children's theatre—the Young Vic—although it was originally planned to include an experimental stage and two major acting companies as well. An influential presence at the time among the theatre institutions in London, the Old Vic Centre (1946–1952) is often considered the most important theatre experiment of the immediate postwar era. Upon its closing, other institutions sought to fill the functions and roles associated with this institution.

Attempting to seize the opportunities that emerged, Anthony Quayle, then the artistic director of the Shakespeare Memorial Theatre at Stratford-upon-Avon, sought to fortify this theatre's position in the theatrical field, embarking on a plan to expand the organization. In fact, under the directorship of Quayle, although the Memorial Theatre attracted increasing audiences and publicity, competing with the Old Vic's prestige, it too was inevitably threatened by the anticipated founding of the National Theatre. Quayle feared that the National Theatre, backed by state subsidy, would attract star actors, thereby becoming a rival to Stratford. It was Quayle's intention to expand the Memorial Theatre's operations to London—by leasing a theatre—before the National came into existence.[6] An eight-year course of twists and turns, closely interwoven with the founding of the National Theatre, would stand between this plan and its realization. By the beginning of the 1960s, moreover, the ESC, clearly an effective presence, would already be acquiring its reputation in the field as a writers' theatre.

According to Wardle, Devine learned his lessons well from his involvement in the Old Vic project and applied them extremely effectively to his next enterprise, the ESC.[7] The Old Vic Centre had dominated Devine's life for six years, and although his role was minor in comparison to the major figure, Saint-Denis, it was an important episode in his career, second only to the Royal Court. During the years that elapsed between these two enterprises, several significant events took place which clearly affected Devine's new quest. These events require a closer look if their full significance is to be appreciated.

Between 1952 and 1955, Devine worked as a freelance actor and director. In addition to his freelance productions, he directed five plays for the Shakespeare Memorial Theatre during the period 1953–1955. In 1952 he met Tony Richardson, then a television director at the BBC. Richardson had asked him to play in an adaptation of a Chekhov story and although Devine refused at first, it was the beginning of a close friendship and professional collaboration. According to Sally Beauman,[8] Richardson's conception of a new theatre company which would focus on the work of new writers, whether British or foreign, was positively aligned with Devine's quest, on Quayle's behalf, to acquire a London theatre which would expand the Memorial Theatre's operations, and the two projects were combined. Given Beauman's overall narrative concerning Devine's role in Quayle's scheme, her presentation of Richardson's influence on Devine is somewhat surprising. Her perception of Richardson as the figure "who was to lead [Devine] away from the Stratford involvement," can nonetheless be explained within the context of her study, which focuses on the history of the Royal Shakespeare Company.[9] Stage designer Jocelyn Herbert, who had a close personal and professional relationship with

Devine, presents a somewhat different account. She attributes Devine's alliance with Richardson, which coincided with Devine's shift of priorities regarding the Memorial Theatre, to what she calls "his only interest," that is, "to have a theatre to encourage new writers. . . . That was the basis for it."[10] Both versions, however, appear to confirm that the coalition established between Devine and Richardson was based on their shared vision (despite the fact of their differing beliefs) of another sort of theatre which would present new works, not functioning as an elitist theatre club but rather targeting the general public. It is also important to note how much these two figures had in common in terms of their background.[11] Both Devine and Richardson were Oxford graduates, as well as members and former presidents of the Oxford Dramatic Society.[12]

Initially, Devine and Richardson started exploring theatres such as the Royalty, the Kingsway, and the Royal Court, and prepared a nine-page memorandum of their scheme. In their search for funding Richardson suggested that they approach Elaine Brunner, a wealthy patroness who had expressed an interest in his idea for a new theatre, but their attempt to elicit her support ended in failure.[13] Throughout 1953, Devine and Richardson continued to look for funding sources. They were also simultaneously negotiating a three-year tenancy at the Royal Court, which had been leased by the Cadogan Estate to Alfred Esdaile, a retired music-hall comedian. Devine and Richardson met with Esdaile and Oscar Lewenstein, the general manager of the Royal Court at the time (1952–1954). Lewenstein was one of the major figures in the left wing Unity Theatre movement, general manager of the Glasgow Unity Theatre (1946–50), former manager of the Embassy Theatre in Hampstead, and an editor of Unity's *New Theatre* magazine to which Devine was an occasional contributor. Lewenstein was interested in creating an outlet for new drama. Esdaile, despite supporting the cause of advancing new drama, seems to have been interested primarily in subletting the building for a high rent. On April 22, the production of *Airs on Shoestring*, which Lewenstein had arranged, opened at the Royal Court.[14] In fact, the success of this production (which ran for nearly two years) may have contributed to the difficulties in the forthcoming negotiations with Esdaile regarding the lease of the theatre. Although the Arts Council was supportive of Devine's scheme, he still lacked sufficient means to lease the Royal Court and subsequently approached Anthony Quayle as a possible collaborator.

At this point the narrative diverges, depending on whom one considers to be its chief protagonist. Roberts recounts two versions, Devine's and

Quayle's, regarding the plan to lease the theatre.[15] Whereas, according to Devine, he and Richardson had convinced Quayle of the necessity and benefits of establishing a London-based theatre for the Memorial Theatre, Quayle's version presents the collaboration with Devine differently, casting it as the result of an earlier plan. According to Quayle, the prediction of the Stratford theatre was that the Old Vic was destined to become the National Theatre, lending impetus to the organization's proposed plan to establish a London-based theatre. Devine's endorsement of the Royal Court suggestion thus appears to have been the realization of his goal to find a London base for Stratford, and subsequently to run it. In any case Quayle supported Devine's proposal and attempted a negotiation with Esdaile, which proved unsuccessful, followed by an intervention by the Arts Council supporting the scheme. But Esdaile's insistence on a very high rent brought the negotiations to a dead end. Devine's disappointment regarding the outcome is indeed reflected in the letter he wrote to Saint-Denis; yet his conclusion—"I still think the scheme is good and right for me but maybe I shall approach it in a different way"[16]—can be seen retrospectively to have shaped his conduct in the events to follow. Moreover, Roberts's claim that Devine's (abortive) scheme complied with the Arts Council's emerging policy at the time is significant.[17] Although the Arts Council was unable to save the plan at this stage, its favorable attitude would serve Devine well in the years to come.

Despite the failure of Devine's scheme, the principal forces and factors involved—the Arts Council's and Stratford's planned new policies, the closure of the Old Vic Centre, and the imminent foundation of the National Theatre—would all go on to play a dominant part in the shaping of London's theatrical map. By the time the historical coil eventually unwound in the 1960s, two rival companies, the National Theatre and the Royal Shakespeare Company, would have established themselves in London; while two other companies, the ESC at the Royal Court Theatre and the Theatre Workshop at Stratford East, established themselves as the premier sites for the staging of new dramatic and theatrical works.

GATHERING FORCES: FOUNDING OF THE ESC

The eventual founding of the ESC during the mid-1950s resulted from Devine's collaboration with a different group of partners. The key figure in this group was Ronald Duncan, a journalist, librettist, and playwright with two long-running West End plays to his credit. Lewenstein, who traces in his memoirs the forming of the group centering on Duncan, describes him as a man who "seemed to know everyone."[18] In 1953 Duncan, together with a number of very illustrious partners, launched the Taw and Torridge Festival in Devon. These included the composer Benjamin Britten; Edward Blacksell, the headmaster of a Devon school and a friend of Duncan; and Lord George Harewood, Princess Mary's son and the eventual director of the Royal Opera House.

Most commentators agree that Duncan's primary objective was to stage his own plays.[19] Together with Lord Harewood and Blacksell, Duncan pursued his idea of establishing a managing body for the performance of noncommercial plays, an effort that led him to recruit his friend from Cambridge, Greville Poke, an amateur actor and editor of *Everybody's Magazine,* and to draft an appeal to the Arts Council. According to Philip Roberts's study of the Royal Court, Duncan "began a process which eventually turned into the ESC," but "it is not true that he founded the ESC."[20] Whether the true founder was Devine or Duncan, it is clear retrospectively that their timely agreement to collaborate in the cause of noncommercial theatre was essential in the forming of the ESC, an agreement that Duncan would later claim came about because Devine had deceived him.[21]

According to some accounts Duncan approached Lewenstein with his idea of forming a company, but Lewenstein states in his memoirs that the idea was actually a consequence of the encounter between the two of them. There is no doubt, however, that Lewenstein was involved in the formation of the new company from the very start. He notes that he had very little in common with Duncan in terms of background and political orientation and that their collaboration relied almost exclusively on their shared perception of the need to intervene in what they saw as the terrible state of British theatre at the time. Most of the prospective members of the new company were Duncan's friends or acquaintances, with the exception of Alfred Esdaile, owner of the Royal Court, whom Lewenstein claims to have recruited. This is further evidence of Lewenstein's crucial mediating role. He clearly used his previous professional experience and connections, such as his link to the Royal Court, in order to advance the new enterprise. Lewenstein's function as a connecting link in the next crucial phase of the company's founding would indeed prove significant for the company's future trajectory.

When it was time to choose a name for the new company, after considering several different titles, the founders decided upon the English Stage Company.[22] Next came the question of a chairman. The first choice for the post was Lord Harewood, who rejected the offer. Consequently, at Edward Blacksell's suggestion, the post was offered to Neville Blond, a businessman from Manchester and a chief government adviser on trans-Atlantic trade, who had just retired. In the wake of a lunch meeting with Greville Poke and Duncan, Blond consented to accept the post on condition that the company would lease a theatre in London. At this point, the theatre in question was the Kingsway, another of Esdaile's buildings, and Blond soon reached an agreement with him to acquire the property. In November 1954, Blond became the official chairman of the ESC.

A crucial step for the company's future was the appointment of an artistic director. Significantly, most of the council members (an "unlikely combination of personalities," in Lewenstein's words)[23] were not practical men of the theatre. Lewenstein, it should be remembered, had already been exposed to Devine's and Richardson's plan, and was thus the only council member who had been directly involved in the plans of both groups. This was to prove crucial. Lewenstein, who suggested George Devine as a candidate for artistic director of the new company, recalls: "Looking back, it seems strange that no one had a convincing suggestion for this very important, all important role. But then, apart from Ronnie [Duncan] and to a very limited extent myself, no one on the council had much experience of the London straight theatre."[24] Lewenstein's recollection, reported in his memoirs, offers at least a partial explanation for the council's decision to appoint Devine as artistic director. Lewenstein also notes that Devine had served as president of the Oxford University Dramatic Society (OUDS). This experience, along with his growing reputation in the theatre community, distinguished him as an insider, unlike the other members of the council, whom Lewenstein presents as outsiders. "George Devine," Lewenstein asserts, "belonged to the central magic circle, we did not."[25]

Following a meeting with Lewenstein, Devine met with the other members of the council. These meetings convinced Duncan that Devine shared his desire to create a playwright's theatre. According to Lewenstein: "A Playwright's theatre, a theatre in which the play came first and everything else, director, designer and actors served the play, . . . went right against the current prevailing style of West End, where Tennents, the most powerful producers of the day, dominated the scene and, under the direction of 'Binkie' Beaumont,[26] produced plays which were vehicles for their stars in elaborate décor."[27] In the early 1950s the London stage was, in Findlater's words, "dominated by the long-run system." It "had to be an instant box office success or it would be an instant casualty, probably never to be seen again."[28]

Devine's suitability for the post of artistic director in the eyes of the other council members was apparently grounded on the premise that he shared the same underlying conception for the newly formed company and that, as a professional and an insider, he would implement the decisions for which he was responsible. Devine's condition for joining the newly formed company was to appoint Richardson as his associate director. His condition was accepted, and on March 1955, Devine became the first artistic director of the ESC. The agreement with Devine was that the plays produced would have to be approved by him and by the artistic subcommittee, which was comprised of Lord Harewood as chairman, Duncan, Lewenstein, Devine, and Richardson (the latter two ex officio without voting rights). The intent was to seek out a reservoir of potential contributors: novelists who would be encouraged to write plays, neglected British playwrights, new playwrights, and contemporary foreign playwrights. Although it is apparent from all accounts that Duncan and Devine differed as to the nature of the plays to be sought, there are no indications that the criteria for selecting the plays were fully articulated in this initial phase.

Lewenstein describes the early days of the ESC as harmonious.[29] Yet Roberts mentions Devine's initial suspicion toward the Devon group—the members recruited by Duncan. Devine apparently felt that these participants "carried in many ways the marks of the theatre attitudes he most resented and from which he wished to free the English theatre."[30] In particular, the appointment of the press officer, George Fearon, who had served as press officer for the Taw and Torridge Festival, perpetuated the kind of attitude that Devine mistrusted. Fearon's approach to Devine, whom he treated "as an employee much like himself," according to Roberts, led to a very troublesome set of interactions between these two.

Lewenstein's recollections reveal that the council members were somewhat ignorant of the role, duties, and importance of the artistic director, but Devine's major standing in the field soon gave him the central place in the ESC. This inevitably led to some disagreements between Devine and various members of the council, in particular Esdaile and Blond.[31] Even more significantly, Devine and Duncan were soon at odds, with Duncan at a disadvantage. From the perspective of reviewers and journalists, the initial external mediators of the reputation of the ESC, Devine was the guiding force. The fame he had acquired as an actor and director and his association with innovative theatre styles and projects were dominant factors in determining the image of the newly formed company. Devine, not Duncan, had the "symbolic goods" of innovative leadership to carry forward the development and accomplishments of the company. He was soon able to exploit the benefits that came with his growing reputation.

Although Esdaile initially offered the group the Kingsway Theatre, a complication in obtaining the building permits led him to offer the lease of the Royal Court Theatre instead. According to Wardle, Devine recalled that when the news reached him he "flipped, naturally, with the history of that theatre, and said, Sure."[32] Seizing the opportunity to realize his long-standing intentions vis-à-vis the Royal Court, Devine convinced Blond to accept the offer but did not disclose the cost of the repairs needed to make the theatre functional. The theatre's location in Chelsea, miles from the West End, was a factor in shaping the company's initial radical image. Another factor was the first group of actors to be employed.

Richardson did the preliminary screening of actors in line with the company's stated policy. Plays, not actors, were first priority, and Richardson rejected actors who had trained at or worked for the Stratford Memorial Theatre on the grounds of their unsuitability to act in the Royal Court's realistic repertoire. Among the actors selected—including Joan Plowright, Robert Stephens, Alan Bates, Mary Ure, and Kenneth Haigh—there were very few who had studied at the Old Vic, while most of the others were new and still unknown performers. According to Terry Browne, in addition to the eleven actors selected for the permanent company, five others agreed to contract for limited periods.[33] It was decided that this core group of young actors would be supplemented by bigger names for individual productions. Indeed, in their responses to the new company the critics presented the selected group of actors as one of the hallmarks of the ESC's radical nature. Wardle explains that "if the acting company represented a break with Devine's past, there was no such break on the technical side. Virtually everyone in the production team came out of the L.T.S. [London Theatre Studio] or the Vic School."[34]

For financial support, the company relied on private donations and a relatively small sum from the Arts Council, a preproduction grant of 2,500 pounds and a subsidy of 7,000 pounds, including guarantees against loss.[35] When considering the state of the newly formed company, one should also bear in mind the social standing of several of the members of the ESC council as well as the posts held by a number of in-house mediators and by patrons of the company. Among the people serving on the Drama Panel of the Arts Council in 1955–1956 was Dame Peggy Ashcroft, whose professional collaboration with Devine had begun in the early 1930s and who had been involved with the ESC from its very first season.[36] Two other distinctive supporters of the ESC, Richard Findlater, critic and writer, and Glen Byam Shaw (CBE), were also serving at the time on the Drama Panel of the Arts Council.[37]

ENTER THE CRITICS: THE FIRST SEASON REVIEWED

In early 1956, prior to the ESC's opening season, Oscar Lewenstein's coproduction of Bertolt Brecht's *The Threepenny Opera* was performed at the Royal Court as a sort of preseason run.[38] This production was well received by the critics, enhancing Lewenstein's position as a producer particularly associated with innovative theatrical styles.[39] Some months later, on April 2, 1956, the ESC inaugurated its first season, which was originally to have included six productions: *The Mulberry Bush* by Angus Wilson, *The Crucible* by Arthur Miller, *Look Back in Anger* by John Osborne, *Don Juan* and *The Death of Satan* by Ronald Duncan, *Cards of Identity* by Nigel Dennis, and *The Good Woman of Setzuan* by Bertolt Brecht. The first brochure of the ESC, prepared on December 3, 1954, contained the company's "Aims and Objects." Slightly altered in subsequent versions, this brochure stated the ESC policy: "London has no theatre with a consistent policy toward contemporary drama. The English Stage Company, which was formed in the interests of the modern playwright of poetic imagination, has acquired the Kingsway Theatre for the production of plays by such dramatists."[40]

Not surprisingly, given the several agendas of the ESC founders, the repertoire for the first season reflected a series of compromises. Devine had initially sought to commence the season with a foreign play. In face of objections from several council members, however, he selected a play written by the British novelist Angus Wilson. Duncan had proffered two plays, but Devine, less than enthralled, convinced him to shorten them in order to make one evening out of the two rather staid pieces. The choice of Arthur Miller and Brecht signaled the commitment to contemporary social drama. The selection of two foreign playwrights and of two novelists, the other being Nigel Denis, also signaled the lack of viable new plays by British playwrights who could fulfill that commitment. Yet at least one new playwright, John Osborne, came forward with a social drama.

Overall, the initial response of critics and journalists to the ESC was highly favorable. Serving as external mediators, they used their reviews and articles to reiterate the founders' primary aims and to endorse the projected agenda of the company. Proclaiming that the aims of the ESC corresponded to the needs of the times, they bestowed legitimation on the new enterprise. "At last," announced *Plays and Players*, "with the formation of the ESC, there are glimmerings of hope. This company . . . has as its chief aim the fostering of new dramatists."[41] According to the *Sunday Times*: "Modern English plays which concern themselves with current problems, political or social, are rare. It is for this reason that the debut tomorrow week of the English Stage Company has become one of the most eagerly awaited events of the present season."[42] With regard to Devine, the reviewer stressed: "It is his specific aim to encourage the rise of a new school of native dramatists."[43] Setting the tone for the reception of the company's first season, another notice declared: "What promises to be one of the most exciting and important events in the English Theatre for a great many years, takes place in Easter week. This is the opening on Easter Monday of the newly founded English Stage Company's season under the direction of Mr. George Devine, at the Royal Court Theatre Sloane Square."[44]

The positive attitude of the press and the critics to the company's founding manifested itself in the description of the company's opening as "a great event." Endorsing the aims of the new company, the critics stressed in particular its intention to become a writers' theatre and expressed their expectation that the ESC would provide a stage for new British dramatists. Clearly, several reviewers felt a need to make a case for the importance of the ESC, even though it had hardly begun its first season. Responding to the company's declared mission, these external mediators assigned the ESC a special niche in the London theatre community, which accorded with their perceptions of the needs of the time. In their enthusiasm for the potential of the ESC, the critics effectively fleshed out the somewhat vague agenda of the "Aims and Objects" brochure. By doing so, they were not simply reporting on the formation of a new company and its initial productions; they were taking on an active role as advocates for a new idea of British drama and theatre. It was almost as if they were infecting one another with their vision for a new theatre. In the process, they proceeded to turn their own expectations and hopes into a cultural program for both the ESC and the London theatre. In other words, they were not only voicing their support for the new venture, but they were also providing justification for this development. They thereby set the grounds for the historical narrative that served to launch the ESC, the plays and careers of new playwrights, and a new group of actors for their natural style of acting. The critics' reception of the ESC is a prime example of a key moment in the process of mediation. Their campaigns in support of the ESC demonstrate both their attempt to influence the perception of the new company in terms of its designated placement and their own function as active participants in dictating new agendas and developments.

The critics' role as assessors of and participants in theatrical developments is most apparent in their celebration of Devine. On the one hand, they evaluated the new company's position in light of the reputation of its lead figures, notably George Devine; on the other, they anointed Devine as a representative artistic director for what was transpiring—according to their own terms of assessment. This campaign is especially noticeable in magazines devoted to theatrical issues. In the March 1956 issue of *Plays and Players*, for example, Devine starred as "Personality of the Month." The opening statement that "George Devine should prove an ideal artistic director of the English Stage Company" is further justified by a description of Devine's versatile career—his "enviable reputation as a player of leading roles," his productions at Stratford and the Old Vic "distinguished by a personal imaginative approach," his successes at the Opera, "his passion for experiment in broadening the general present-day conception of theatre" displayed in his work with Saint-Denis and Glen Byam Shaw at the Young Vic and the Old Vic School, and his expertise in stage lighting and stage design. A similar belief in Devine's suitability for the post of artistic director of the ESC was expressed in another report published in the *Stage*: "He certainly appears to be the right man to lead the way in tackling such a scheme."[45]

The favorable reception of the new theatre company, manifested in the reactions of the press and theatre periodicals alike, is especially striking in light of the poor notices received by the first play performed by the ESC, *The Mulberry Bush* by Angus Wilson, on April 2, 1956. Wilson's play was initiated by Devine and Richardson, who specifically commissioned the novelist to write a play for the company. *The Mulberry Bush* examines the ideologies of three generations of a benevolent and distinguished university family. Centering on a crisis in the lives of the family members, it features a series of revelations that point to the shifting values between the generations. The majority of the notices were reserved, reflecting the reviewers' disappointment. A typical assessment, for example, stated that "Mr. Wilson's good intentions . . . do not always lead to happy results."[46]

But even the most unfavorable reviews did not fail to express a belief in the newly formed company and in its artistic director. The reviewers uniformly praised the artistic conception that guided the ESC and reiterated their pledge to encourage new British playwrights. A characteristic example of this mixture of praise and critique is manifested in the review in the *Stage*, which referred to the ESC as "a courageous enterprise, full of promise. All the more pity, therefore, that the first play . . . in spite of its basic distinction is so disappointing."[47]

Arthur Miller's *The Crucible*, for which Lewenstein had the rights, followed Wilson's tepid play. From the perspective of both Irving Wardle and Philip Roberts, this production came closer to fulfilling Devine's promise for a new staging style than any other of the season's plays.[48] Most of the reviews, which were favorable, pointed out the obvious: though the play was set in seventeenth-century Salem at the time of the witch trials, its meaning applied to the recent anticommunist frenzy in the United States. Whereas *The Mulberry Bush* won neither a large attendance nor very favorable reviews, *The Crucible*, which opened on April 9, 1956, attracted a good turnout and aroused a certain amount of critical enthusiasm. Pointing out that "the English Stage Company promises well," one review described *The Crucible* as "more gripping" than the ESC's first production[49] but at the same time it stressed the remote setting of the play in time and place. An essentially rave review by Paul Graham nevertheless complained that "British playwrights are playing little or no part in the boom."[50] While there was praise for the overall production of Miller's play, most reviews chose to highlight the effective performances of Mary Ure as Abigail and George Devine as the judge. Several reviewers, in addition to offering commentary on the play and production, also praised the governing aims of the newly formed company. Graham noted, for example, that "this company has embarked on a notable experiment. It seeks to re-establish the writer's theatre."[51] He concluded that "to hear the writer's voice rather than merely star gaze" was the new mission of the ESC. The critics' reception of the productions of Wilson's and Miller's plays reveals that their criteria for assessing the plays were largely circumscribed by the perceived correlation between the individual play and the niche they, the critics, ascribed to the ESC.

Before a discussion of the third production of the season, John Osborne's *Look Back in Anger*, there appears a brief summary of what happened with the other productions of the ESC's first season in order to clarify not only the basic picture of the emergence of the ESC in 1956 but also the decisions made by the company and the developing narratives which critics and others presented at the time. The initial reception of the whole season, as well as other mediating processes involved in launching the company, helped lay the groundwork for subsequent narratives of the arrival of the ESC.

The three productions that followed Osborne's were the two Duncan plays, *Don Juan* and *The Death of Satan*, Nigel Dennis's *Cards of Identity*, and Bertolt Brecht's *The Good Woman of Setzuan*. On the ESC's production of Duncan's plays—a double bill about Don Juan—Kenneth Tynan wrote that "the first, restatement in verse of the familiar legend, belonged more in the library than on the stage: 'Juan for the Books' might have served as an alternative title. In the second half of the evening Duncan brings the Don back from hell to contemporary Seville, a device which leads into some angry Puritan satire on modern decadence. I found it all shrill and abrasive."[52] All accounts agree (and the reviews verify) that the two Duncan plays, which opened May 15, 1956, and were directed by Devine, were perceived as a disaster. They also agree that Devine's attitude toward Duncan had been ambivalent from the start. Although he treated Duncan with respect, Devine opposed the literary tradition that Duncan promoted and had no belief in his plays. The accounts vary as to whether the tension between these two figures had been evident before the Don Juan productions, but there is no dispute as to the public breakdown in their relationship following the failure of Duncan's plays. Moreover, Duncan's hostility toward Devine led to a division among the members of the artistic subcommittee and thus contributed to the struggle over the Royal Court's policy. From the perspective of Irving Wardle, Devine's production of Duncan's plays dealt the poetic drama its deathblow.[53]

The next ESC production commissioned by the company was Nigel Dennis's *Cards of Identity*, based upon the author's successful novel. The play, which opened June 26, 1956, is a melodramatic satire of an individual's recourse to experts in order to establish a sense of identity. Both Devine and Richardson perceived Dennis's play as embodying the Royal Court's vision, and both believed that it would become the success of the season. Although the play indeed received some good reviews, many critics found it confusing and difficult to follow, and it was not a great success at the box office. *The Good Woman of Setzuan* by Bertolt Brecht, the next ESC production, opened on October 31, 1956. This production, in which much work had been invested, was also not well received.[54] Neville Blond, alarmed by the lack of financial success of the ESC's early productions, next opted for a revival of the classics in the hope of attracting a larger audience. *The Country Wife*, a Restoration comedy by William Wycherley, proposed in early June, complied with the company's policy to revive neglected classics. It opened on December 12, 1956, and was the last ESC production of the year. It received mixed reviews but attracted large audiences.[55] Overall, none of the plays performed by the ESC during its first year came close to the success of John Osborne's *Look Back in Anger*. As Findlater explains, "Although it [the ESC] had set out to attract novelists to the stage (and did so, from time to time) its first new major author came from *inside* the theatre. John Osborne's success, and persistent fertility, helped to ensure (as Irving Wardle says) that although the Court might be a writers' theatre it was certainly not going to be a *literary* theatre."[56]

Look Back in Anger was one of 750 texts submitted to the Royal Court in response to the company's advertisement for new plays.[57] Of all the plays submitted, Osborne's was the only one to be accepted by both directors, Devine and Richardson. Before writing *Look Back in Anger*,[58] Osborne had collaborated in the writing of two other plays and had acted in a touring group and in various repertory companies. As Wardle writes: "The story of the rejection of *Look Back in Anger* by the agents, its discovery by Devine and Richardson, their first trip to meet the penniless author on his Chiswick houseboat, and the play's decisive effect on the Royal Court's fortunes and the direction of the theatre at large, no more needs retelling than the fable of David and Goliath."[59] Wardle recounts that, in the meeting between the playwright and the two ESC directors, Osborne was also engaged as a member of the cast, an understudy, and a playreader.[60] Indeed, the place Wardle allots Osborne's play in his narrative cultivates the singular significance of *Look Back in Anger* from the start.

The members of the artistic subcommittee—Lord Harewood, Duncan, and Lewenstein—immediately saw promise in Osborne's play, but they also warned that its provocative traits might have a disturbing effect on the audience.[61] As for Devine's take on the play, subsequent accounts present him as the catalyst for the meteoric trajectory of the play, production, and career of Osborne, but he has also been represented as someone who recognized the play's flaws. As the history of the event developed, then changed, so too has Devine's role in it been modified. Roberts states that Devine's promotion of the play was "a shot in the dark"[62] by a man primarily interested in European art theatre, but who thought that *Look*

Back in Anger introduced "a completely new dramatist and a powerful play."[63] Wardle claims that "no one would have championed *Look Back in Anger* for its formal qualities," that "it was the content of the tirades that mattered," and that "for Devine, the piece was a stylistic watershed." Still, Wardle insists that Devine was completely convinced of the play's importance and reports him as saying, some six years later: "I knew that this was the play we must do even if it sank the enterprise."[64] Whatever the case, in 1956 Devine promoted the play and production, which Tony Richardson staged with Kenneth Haigh as Jimmy Porter, Mary Ure as Alison, Alan Bates as Cliff, and Helena Hughes as Helena.

PRESENTING *LOOK BACK IN ANGER*:
FIRST AND SECOND ROUNDS

The first performance of *Look Back in Anger* took place on May 8, 1956. Despite subsequent versions of this event, the first evening gave no hint of the meteoric success of the play and production that was to follow. Most accounts of the initial reception agree that the critical response was mixed at best. Although there were a few favorable notices,[65] most reviews reflected to varying degrees their authors' critical reservations and some reviews were clearly unenthusiastic. Several reviewers perceived the play as an attempt to comment on the younger postwar generation and contemporary life and pronounced the attempt unsuccessful. In his autobiography, Osborne describes the "protective" attitude of the two directors (Devine and Richardson) toward him following the play's unenthusiastic reception.[66] If the production had run for only three or four days, it would almost certainly have disappeared into the historical dustbin. But on Sunday, May 13, 1956, favorable reviews by two influential critics appeared. The First, by Harold Hobson, the prominent theatre critic for the *Sunday Times*, referred to Osborne as "a writer of outstanding promise" and congratulated the ESC on "discovering him."[67] The second, by Kenneth Tynan, has become one of the most famous reviews in British theatre history. Writing in the *Observer*, he proclaimed:

> *Look Back in Anger* presents post-war youth as it really is. . . . To have done this at all would be a signal achievement; to have done it in a first play is a minor miracle. All the qualities are there, qualities one had despaired of ever seeing on stage—the drift towards anarchy, the instinctive leftishness, the automatic rejection of "official" attitudes. . . . The Porters of our time deplore the tyranny of "good taste" and refuse

to accept "emotional" as a term of abuse; they are classless, and they are also leaderless. Mr. Osborne is their first spokesman in the London theatre. . . . I doubt if I could love anyone who did not wish to see *Look Back in Anger*. It is the best young play of its decade.[68]

Tynan attributed the play's originality to its radical and antiestablishment attitudes, presenting it as the distillation of the voice of the masses. He specifically positioned the playwright as the first spokesman in the London theatre of a large sector of the population: postwar youth. Using his emerging authority as a major theatre critic (notably manifested, for example, in his campaign in 1955 for Beckett's *Waiting for Godot*),[69] he energetically promoted the play and the new, then unknown, playwright.

Following Tynan's ecstatic review and the failure of Duncan's plays, which lasted only eight performances, the ESC council added three more performances of *Look Back in Anger* in May. Devine also added a two-week run in June, even though the fortunes of the play had not yet changed significantly. In his autobiography, Osborne describes meeting with Tynan at the end of May when Tynan rather unexpectedly raised the possibility of making a film of the play. In another meeting, Osborne spoke with Harry Salzman, the U.S. producer, who suggested that the play would be a great success in New York.[70] In early July the council had to decide which play, *Cards of Identity* or *Look Back in Anger*, to put on until the scheduled opening of Brecht's play on October 31. (*The Crucible*, *The Mulberry Bush*, and Duncan's play had been withdrawn.) The council opted for *Look Back in Anger*, which ran for an additional eleven weeks.

By the second week of July ticket sales had risen significantly. The play's growing popularity at this point is generally attributed to a remark made by George Fearon, the company's press officer and hence an in-house mediator by virtue of his post, who described Osborne as "a very angry young man." This description, later a staple component of the media campaign associated with the play, set in motion a sequence of events that would enhance Osborne's enthusiastic reception. Subsequent accounts vary regarding, first, the origins of what would eventually become a catchphrase and second, Fearon's intent in using the phrase. Terry Browne recounts that during a meeting over the fate of the play Fearon suggested promoting it by using the "'angry young man' theme," a suggestion he followed up with several press releases.[71] Roberts, who attributes to Fearon an "inspired use of the term 'angry young man'," agrees with several other commentators who claim that the phrase was

Program cover of Look Back in Anger, Royal Court. © V&A Images/Theatre Museum.

not original. He cites as the source Leslie Paul's 1951 autobiography, *Angry Young Man*.[72] Harry Ritchie, however, disputes the "conventional account" that the catchphrase was somehow inspired by Leslie Paul's title, describing the phrase as "an intended masterstroke of arts publicity," and argues that it was "invented" by Fearon when he was asked by a journalist for his opinion of the playwright.[73] Fearon, Ritchie maintains, "was having great difficulty in publicizing *Look Back in Anger*, a play he loathed." Osborne, in his autobiography, recalls that before the play's first production, Fearon confessed to him with great pleasure his dislike of the play and then remarked: "I suppose you're really—an angry young man."[74]

Most commentators agree that Fearon disliked the playwright and had little faith in his play, a negativity compounded by his hostile attitude to Devine, whose belief in the play and in the playwright are matters of record. Fearon's catchy remark might have been a tactic deployed to resolve the contradiction between his dislike of the play and his duty, as the company's press officer, to promote it.

Osborne himself publicized the catchphrase in an interview with Malcolm Muggeridge on BBC's *Panorama* on July 9, 1956, where he appeared with George Scott, who had just published his autobiography, *Time and Place*.[75] In the course of the interview Muggeridge asked the two to clarify their views on the subject of class and culture in the welfare state. Scott denied that these issues made him in any way angry, but Osborne justified both the need for anger and the need to give it expression. "You see," he said, "if one recognizes problems and one states them, immediately people say—oh this is an angry young man." Harry Ritchie, in his account of the interview, argues for its importance to Osborne's reception, claiming that it "brought him and the new catchphrase to the attention of a wide public—and more journalists.[76]

By mid-September the play was not covering its expenses and the council considered bringing it off three weeks earlier than planned. Further, a twenty-five-minute excerpt of the production—a version of act 2, especially adapted for television—had been sold to the BBC, to be aired on October 16. ESC directors Devine and Richardson feared that the broadcast would reduce audience attendance even more. Neville Blond, who had initiated the deal with the BBC, persuaded them to keep the play running.[77] Insisting that the broadcast would arouse public interest in the play, he guaranteed the company against any loss of revenue after October 16. The critics announced and promoted the televised event days before the broadcast,[78] and Lord Harewood also pitched in and agreed to introduce the broadcast personally.[79] The fate of the play—and everyone connected with it—changed after October 16, 1956. Within several days of the broadcast, by most accounts, the play had become a box-office hit.[80] Roberts explains that the extract on television brought the play to the attention of young people who had until then regarded theatre as irrelevant to their lives. Roberts's claim is especially significant considering the evolution of the narratives surrounding the play, but what is confirmed by all accounts—and what is hardly surprising, considering the effectiveness of a TV broadcast as a means of promotion—is the result at the box office.[81] The state of British television in 1956 is a factor here. There were only two television channels: the BBC and Independent Television (ITV), the commercial channel that had started broadcasting on September 22, 1955. There were also very few original television dramas. This lack of competition meant that a televised excerpt from a play could reach a massive audience and make a far greater public impact than it might today.

Though it took the broadcast more than a few days to prove its effectiveness, Osborne seized the momentum at once. On October 18, his article "The Things I Wish I Could Do . . . by the Theatre's Bright Boy,"[82] appeared in the *Daily Express*. This early press exposure is further evidence of Osborne's attempt to become directly involved with the promotion of his play and career. *Look Back in Anger* was transferred to the Lyric Theatre on November 5, three weeks after the broadcast, when Brecht's play opened at the Royal Court. It continued to play to full houses for another three weeks, closing only because of the Lyric's prior commitments.

On November 28, 1956 *Look Back in Anger* was aired as ITV's *Play of the Week*.[83] Announcing the forthcoming broadcast, the *TV Times* claimed that *Look Back in Anger* was "the most controversial play of the day," one that had "already provoked an amazing reaction from audiences and critics." The *TV Times* article also quoted Tynan's judgment that it was "the best young play of its decade," along with the *Daily Express* comment proclaiming it the "first play by an exciting new English writer."[84]

The televised performance took place at Didsbury Studios, Manchester, with the London cast. Richard Pasco played Jimmy Porter, Doreen Aris played Alison Porter, Alan Bates played Cliff, and Vivienne Drummond played Helena. A viewing audience of 1,718,000 ranked the broadcast high compared to other programs shown during November,[85] and the critics praised both the play and its brilliant cast. Cyril Aynsley, in the *Daily Express*, wrote that Osborne's play "arrested the attention from the moment it opened. . . . Rough language, brutish humour, and outrageously callous remarks poured in a torrent from the TV screen into millions of homes. . . . All played out at breathtaking pace and all compressed almost to exploding point in the tight-knit medium of television."[86]

At the end of 1956, John Osborne won the *Evening Standard* Drama Award for the Most Promising Playwright of the Year. *Look Back in Anger* returned to the Royal Court, after some changes in the cast, on March 11, 1957. A production of the play opened in New York on October 1, 1957, where following a successful run it received the New York Drama Critics' Circle Award for Best Foreign Play of 1957.

The events that followed the opening of the play on May 8, 1956, were full of unexpected twists and turns, charged with decisions taken and then reconsidered by the ESC, and abounding with sundry actions on the part of individuals motivated by diverse—and at times incompatible— agendas. This sequence of events also reflects the different operational modes various in-house mediators employed to promote the play and their oblique and unpredictable effects on its reception.

The discrepancy between Fearon's opinion of the play and the unforeseen turn that resulted from his unwitting creation of a highly effective catchphrase, in a sense resembles the chance effect of the TV broadcast, a mediating tactic pursued in spite of the hesitation of Devine and Richardson. Osborne himself played a significant part in turning the production into a media event. Osborne's willingness to collaborate with his various mediators such as the directors of the ESC and agents of the media, as well as his aptitude for doing so, already manifest at this early stage, clearly contributed to the development of his career. His role in the promotion of his career, however, should be seen as complementary to the opportunities with which he was presented. Apart from the crucial opportunity afforded by the ESC's decision to stage his play, the critical context established through the 1950s, which revolved around the Movement, paved the way for its favorable reception.

CRITICAL CONTEXT: MEDIA AT PLAY

"The Movement" refers to a number of novelists and poets (some were both) whose works were published in the early 1950s, including Kingsley Amis, John Wain, Philip Larkin, Donald Davie, D. J. Enright, Elizabeth Jennings, and Tom Gunn. The Movement had, according to Stephen Lacey, a "well-publicized presence in the 1950s" that "generated a series of stereotypes that were simultaneously literary and social, that were closely related to emerging explanations about post-war social change, and around which a critical context appeared that was to have considerable consequences for the way that *Look Back in Anger* was read."[87] According to Harry Ritchie's illuminating study of the role of the media in shaping literary developments during the 1950s, however, the "well-publicized presence" of the Movement is something of a retroactive consolidation of a process that needs to be seen as far more gradual and cumulative.[88] Ritchie's narrative can in fact be read as an illustration of yet another distinctive case of mediation. It exemplifies the role filled by various agents, employing different channels (such as the radio, professional journals, the press, and scholarly studies), in the formation of literary or theatrical trends or schools.[89]

Tracing the critics' and the media's reactions to the Movement step by step, Ritchie reconstructs its emergence within a larger critical context. He refers to John Wain's introduction of Kingsley Amis's *Lucky Jim* in the BBC radio series *First Reading* on April 26, 1953, and to the third program of the series on July 1, in which Wain, promoting several other writers, announced the emergence of a new literary generation—in effect, the first signs of what would eventually be perceived as the Movement. The critical buildup continued, in Ritchie's account, through Walter Allen's key review of *Lucky Jim* (published in the *New Statesman and Nation* on January 30, 1954) and J. D. Scott's influential essay "In the Movement," appearing in the *Spectator* on October 1, 1954, which gave the new trend its lasting title.

Ritchie charts a continuous stream of critical discourse appearing in magazines, periodicals, and literary supplements and on the radio. Gradually the Movement filtered down to the daily press. At first, discussion was limited to a few critics who were acquainted with each other from Oxford, or by virtue of professional collaborations. A series of topics emerged: the writers who were qualified to be members of the new literary group, its defining attributes, and its importance in the contemporary scene. However significant this discussion was in its own right, its impact came with the breakthrough that is said to have occurred in May 1956.

"The debuts of John Osborne and Colin Wilson," recounts Ritchie, "sparked off extraordinary media interest which placed young writers in the forefront of public life. The hype involved controversies, scandals, and the creation of a definitive literary image for the decade—the Angry Young Man."[90] Ritchie's claim that it was Colin Wilson's work—*The Outsider*, published May 28, 1956—that won overnight critical acclaim rather than John Osborne's further confirms the effect of narratives built around *Look Back in Anger.*[91] The media's interest in the Angry Young Men as a group can be traced to two features by Daniel Farson that ran in the *Daily Mail* on July 12 and 13, 1956, which announced the emergence of a "Post-War Generation" in literature and held Osborne, Wilson, Michael Hastings, and Kingsley Amis to be the representatives of a new literary movement.[92] Farson's articles elicited a chain of critical reactions, beginning with John Barber's response on July 26, 1956, in the *Daily Express*, which referred to the four writers as the Angry Young Men. Considering that Ritchie dates the earliest use in the press of Fearon's famous remark about Osborne as "a very angry young man" to July 7, and that Osborne's interview in *Panorama*, where the playwright elaborated on his anger, was broadcast on July 9, the reference to the phenomenon of anger was being reiterated within a very short span of time and through various mediatory channels. This cumulative effect was possibly enhanced by the Royal Court's participation in the International Youth Festival in Moscow in July 1956, with the featured production of *Look Back in Anger.*

Largely as a result of these activities, the popular press now began to find the Angries a worthy topic. They allowed journalists to present themselves as involved in timely cultural developments, and to investigate a topic that appealed to various sectors of the population. John Hill remarks about the Angries that, "more than their 'youth,' it was their status as both products and bearers of a new 'welfare' culture which commanded attention."[93] Ritchie comments that, "middlebrow newspapers had discovered that these 'Angry' writers carried definite news value as indefinite representatives of a new Welfare State generation."[94] As a cultural label, therefore, the term "Angry Young Men" was vague enough to lend itself to a large variety of contemporary uses. In fact, the British interest in the Angries exactly paralleled the extensive coverage of the beat generation in the United States.[95]

There was a significant overlap between the critical discourse on the Movement and the media's treatment of the Angry Young Men (hereafter, AYM). For example, the dates of publication of two collections— D. J. Enright's *Poets of the 1950s* in 1955 and Robert Conquest's anthology of Movement poems *New Lines* at the end of July, 1956—closely paralleled the media's growing interest in the AYM. Consequently, commentators argue as to whether the Angry Young Men should be seen as a continuation of the Movement or considered a new development. Whatever the case, the critical context established by the critics' discourse around the Movement and the media's growing interest in the AYM are closely interrelated and appear to constitute a major factor in accounting for the reception of Osborne's play.

The popular perception of the Angry Young Men, Hill claims, was as the "Sons of Labour's post-war Brave New World and the 1944 Education Act. . . . [As] harbingers of the new 'classless' culture, their voice spoke the 'anger' of a generation for whom in the end nothing really seemed to have changed."[96] Osborne's play certainly fit the bill. Conventional in form and with a plot replete with speeches, it centers on the unfocused rage of the protagonist, Jimmy Porter, a university graduate who feels socially alienated in a class-structured society. Although dissatisfied, he does not attempt to change the society in which he finds himself and suggests no alternative to his sense of frustration and anger. Clearly Osborne's Jimmy Porter, a young man discontented and angry, was a perfect match for the profile of broad dissatisfaction that had come to characterize the Angry Young Men. The play's familiar form in the tradition of the well-made-play called attention to its content and perfectly suited its ascribed function as a banner and lending itself to diverse interpretations. If the growing publicity of the AYM (1956 and into 1957) coincided with the en-thusiastic reception of *Look Back in Anger*, the fame acquired by the play in turn enhanced the promotion of the AYM cult, consequently turning the playwright, John Osborne, into a media celebrity. It is no coincidence that Osborne starred in the *Evening Standard* as the most controversial "personality" of the year 1956.[97] John Osborne was collapsed into the figure of his hero, Jimmy Porter, as the paradigmatic representative of the AYM. Indeed, Osborne himself was a major contributor to this con-structed image: he wrote provocative press articles, gave raging speeches, and in interviews tended to elaborate upon his anger.[98] He particularly seemed to cultivate his image as an Angry Young Man toward the end of 1956. And although, in an article in the *News Chronicle* at the beginning of 1957, he dismissed the Angry Young Man label as "cheap journalistic fic-tion,"[99] his public appearances and provocative responses to journalists' questions further validated his press reputation. He gradually became known as "the angriest young man of them all."[100]

The press's and critics' handling of Osborne exemplify the way in which the media treated the AYM. Writers and their works were reduc-tively packaged under the same label; authors became synonymous with the heroes of their works, and cultural and social issues were seen as the target of the writers' anger. Furthermore, the media co-opted the AYM, playing on the titles of their works for slogans and headlines.[101] Osborne's play, for example, proved especially useful for the end-of-year surveys of 1956, such as the *Observer*'s "Look Back in Sorrow."[102]

Many studies suggest a link between political protest in Britain and the growing popularity of the Angry Young Men. The year 1956 was one of political crisis in Britain, with the Suez crisis paramount, closely followed by attention to the Hungarian revolution and the arrival of the Soviet tanks on the streets of Budapest. Protests by the Campaign for Nuclear Disarmament (CND) made front-page news. Liberals and intellectuals were increasingly angered by the imperialist policies and failures of the government. Both Ritchie and Hill, however, claim that the only link between the AYM and the Suez crisis was simultaneity.[103] As a group, the Angry Young Men were concerned with a variety of issues, but they neither focused on British foreign policy nor voiced a particular political position (although Osborne was relatively more involved politically, especially with the CND).[104] As Ritchie shows, the Angry Young Men were not portrayed in the pre ss as political writers at the time of their first emergence, and the very newspapers that promoted them also supported the government's policy in the Suez crisis. It is reasonable to concur with Hill and Ritchie that the association between the AYM and radical political protest, which has indeed become a recurrent component in narratives built around *Look Back in Anger*, seems to have been retroactively imposed. In other words, subsequent histories have overinflated the political aspects of the Angry Young Men.

Arnold Wesker, another major and successful playwright associated with the Royal Court during the late 1950s and 1960s,[105] also seen as one of the Angries, raises doubts about the AYM movement. Four decades after the fact, he proclaimed: "There never was an 'Angry Young Man' nor any such group as 'The Angry Young Men.' Neither John nor we, his peers, were angry; on the contrary, we were happy. . . . But there we were, lumped together, boxed away with a label under which we were read, studied in schools and universities around the world, and written about in countless books on British drama. The plays were not allowed to describe themselves; they were described before they were read *and were read that way*."[106] Predictably, Wesker, like other writers, wants to free himself and his work from the limiting category. But by denouncing the label under which he and other diverse writers were grouped, he inadvertently confirms the effect of this mediation strategy. While certainly restrictive, the AYM tag made the works associated with it much more accessible and thereby enhanced their popularity.

The Angry Young Men designation cannot be codified as a single movement. Nor did its advocates in the 1950s articulate a coherent aesthetic movement. Nonetheless, the idea itself proved to be a touchstone for certain feelings, attitudes, and values among various artists and intellectuals, including Osborne. And the tag surely served the media, which used it to unify many and diverse contemporary concerns, whether economic, educational, social, or cultural.

The end of the AYM craze was marked by the publication of *Declaration* in 1957, a collection of essays by several of the figures associated with the AYM trend, including Osborne, Wilson, Wain, Tynan, Doris Lessing, and the director Lindsay Anderson. Kingsley Amis, certainly a famous angry man, refused to contribute an essay to the collection, perhaps in keeping with his noncollaborative position vis-à-vis the media. In his introduction to the anthology, the editor Tom Maschler explains that although "most of the contributors to this volume have at some time or other been termed Angry Young Men they do not belong to a united movement. Far from it; they attack one another directly or indirectly in these pages."[107] Despite this disclaimer and the feisty infighting among some of the contributors, *Declaration* was widely received as evidence of an Angry Young Men movement even though most reviewers found it a confused collection of unformulated attempts at social analysis. It received wide coverage, however, and was a commercial success.

Ritchie points to the "dramatic decline in the literary prestige" of the Angry Young Men after the publication of *Declaration*, noting that "it had taken only seven or eight months for the press to turn from hailing the Angries as an exciting new band of literary rebels to holding them up as targets for ridicule and condemnation. By October 1957 the reaction was complete."[108] The popular press coverage became more sporadic and dismissive. Rather than extolling the phenomenon, many critics began rationalizing the extraordinary success of the AYM and exposing the reasons behind their supposed anger. In reassessing the phenomenon, several critics began to question these writers' credentials as rebels and found their success undeserved; some considered that the Angry Young Men owed their success to the press.[109] Anger, suggested one critic, was an advertising gimmick which the press provided free of charge.[110] Certainly anger, whether as tag or as catchphrase, proved most effective in promoting the standing of *Look Back in Anger* and of its author.[111] The changed fortunes of the AYM indeed barely affected the reputation of Osborne's play, which seems to have exceeded the particular circumstances of its initial reception.

JOINING FORCES WITH THE BIG SCREEN

The emergence of the Movement as a literary phenomenon, rooted in its critical context, laid the necessary grounds for the emergence of the cult of the Angry Young Men, whose impact can be seen most clearly in the reception of *Look Back in Anger*. In turn, the success of this play ties in with the developments taking place in British cinema. The commercial film is yet another medium that contributed not only to making *Look Back in Anger* a highly significant cultural event, but also to extending the set of narratives constructed around it.

In 1959 the film version of *Look Back in Anger* was released as the first film produced by the Woodfall Company, which was formed by Tony Richardson, John Osborne, and the Quebec-born American producer, Harry Salzman.[112] The script of the film was the joint work of Osborne and Nigel Kneale, who had worked with Richardson at the BBC and was recommended by Kenneth Tynan.[113] The film differs from the original play to the extent that it explicitly foregrounds the sociocultural inter-pretation of the text. It omits a large number of Jimmy Porter's mono-logues and adds a number of other characters. Richardson directed the film and the casting drew substantially on the theatre community. Be-sides Richard Burton in the role of Jimmy Porter and Claire Bloom in the role of Helena Charles, Mary Ure played Allison Porter and Glen Byam Shaw took the role of Allison's father, Colonel Redfern. The character of Ma Turner, Hugh's mother—who is mentioned only in passing in the play—was played by the renowned Edith Evans. George Devine appears briefly as a physician, a character added to the film, as is the character of an Indian trader, Kapoor, who is in search of a new life in Britain, and the policeman who harasses him, played by Donald Pleasance.

The accounts vary as to whether it was initially Osborne's or Richard-son's idea to turn *Look Back in Anger* into a film, but there is no doubt that its production relied in many respects on the success of the play. In fact, the Woodfall Company was founded on the basis of Osborne's theatre royalties. The third collaborator in Woodfall, the producer Harry Salzman, obtained the financing for the film from Warner Brothers, whose participation was in large part due to Richard Burton's interest in the production. Perceiving Richardson as an inexperienced film director,

Warner was reluctant to finance the production, yet since they had a deal with Burton, to either pay him or cast him, they consequently agreed to finance the production without a fee for either Richardson or Osborne.

In his study of British cinema, John Hill claims: "It has become something of a commonplace to view the British cinema of the late 1950s and early 1960s in terms of a breakthrough, surfacing, first, as a series of documentaries screened at the National Film Theatre under the banner of 'Free Cinema' and bursting into full bloom with the appearance in commercial cinemas of *Room at the Top* and *Look Back in Anger* in 1959."[114] The Free Cinema, one of many collaborations between Lindsay Anderson, Tony Richardson, and Karel Reisz, was launched in February 1956. The three had worked together in the past. In 1946 Anderson had cofounded (with Peter Ericsson), the provocative film journal *Sequence* at Oxford,[115] to which Reisz contributed, joining as coeditor for the last issues of 1952, when *Sequence* was discontinued. Anderson, Reisz, and Richardson then became involved with the journal *Sight and Sound*, edited by Gavin Lambert, in which they published hard-hitting attacks on the cinema establishment of the time—notably, Anderson's famous essay "Stand Up! Stand Up!" in 1956.[116] The Free Cinema itself centered primarily on documentaries with an underlying commitment to poetic realism. Poetry, according to Hill, "completed the Free Cinema equation: independence from commercial constraint and personal freedom of expression equals 'poetic' cinema."[117]

In interviews conducted with Anderson between 1982 and 1994, he stressed: "It is important to realise what people get wrong: they think of Free Cinema as being a deliberate conscious movement." In fact, as Anderson recalled, the Free Cinema enterprise was an outcome of the talks taking place between him, Reisz, Lorenza Mazzetti, and Richardson about the films they were making at the time. "We came to the conclusion that we really should start a movement purely to attract critics and journalists, to get the films reviewed and if we did invent a movement we should try to get booking for a season into the National Film Theatre. Karel was programme manager of the NFT and we managed to do that. Our aim was to get press coverage, and of course we had to concoct a manifesto—which we did; although not entirely cynically, we *did* all feel the same, that mainstream British cinema was unadventurous, classbound and uninteresting."[118]

Indeed, the Free Cinema's manifesto, the articles published by members of the group, and the six programs of films screened under the Free

These films were not made together; nor with the
idea of showing them together. But when they came
together, we felt they had an attitude in common.
Implicit in this attitude is a belief in freedom,
in the importance of people and in the significance
of the everyday.

As film-makers we believe that

No film can be too personal.

The image speaks. Sound amplifies and comments.
Size is irrelevant. Perfection is not an aim.

An attitude means a style. A style means an attitude.

Lorenza Mazzetti
Lindsay Anderson
Karel Reisz
Tony Richardson.

Free Cinema Manifesto. © British Film Institute, National Library, Special Collections.

Cinema banner at the National Film Theatre between 1956 and 1959 (all the British films, excluding Lorenza Mazzetti's *Together*,[119] were documentaries), all generated considerable media interest in the enterprise. The Free Cinema filmmakers made little headway in the commercial film industry, however.[120] The breakthrough into a new kind of cinema occurred with the appearance of the films *Room at the Top* and *Look Back in Anger*.[121] These films, in hard-edged black and white, had a documentary quality to them that expressed a critique of the British social class system. Both films were released with an X certificate, due to the conservative policy of the Censorship Board in England at the time.[122] Although the X rating could have been a potential financial disaster for their makers, both films did well at the box office. *Room at the Top*, produced by the brothers John and James Woolf and directed by Jack Clyton in April 1959, was based on John Braine's 1957 novel, which had been a best seller. Unlike Clyton, Richardson, who directed the film *Look Back in Anger* in June 1959, had little experience in the film industry.

Prior to his arrival in Oxford from Bradford in 1948, Richardson had already formed a local amateur theatre company, the Shipley Young Theatre Group.[123] During his years at Oxford he directed several theatre productions, served as president of the Oxford University Dramatic Society, and acted as a university theatre critic, publishing several articles in *Sequence*. His most notable production was *The Duchess of Malfi* in 1951. In the early 1950s he worked at the BBC as a television director, and in 1955 he made the film *Mama Don't Allow* together with Reisz, later joining Devine at the newly formed ESC.

Richardson used the success of *Look Back in Anger* to enter the film industry. His cinematic vision and the techniques he employed in the film were partly based on the objectives elaborated by Richardson, Anderson, and Reisz in their Free Cinema collaboration. Richardson explicitly stated his intention: "It is absolutely vital to get into British films the same sort of impact and sense of life that what you can loosely call the Angry Young Man cult has had in the theatre and literary worlds."[124]

The change of emphasis in the film version, and especially its additions, appear to derive from the makers' intention to accommodate the new version to the sociocultural reading of the play that was then current. Richardson's statement seems to indicate that the prevailing view of the play was incorporated directly into the film version. Given the play's success, the filmmakers clearly attempted to expand the range of figures representing the "oppressed" as an oblique commentary on the demise

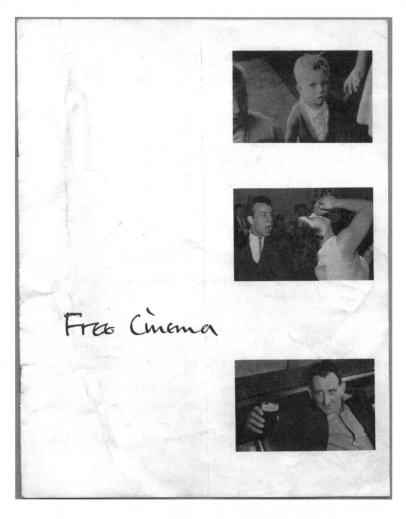

Cover of the program note to Free Cinema 1, February 5–8, 1956, National Film Theatre,
Southbank. © British Film Institute, National Library, Special Collections.

FREE CINEMA

FREE CINEMA is the comprehensive title that has been chosen for a special programme of new films which will be shown at the National Film Theatre for four days from February 5th to 8th.

NONE OF THESE FILMS has been produced within the framework of the commercial cinema. *Momma Don't Allow* and *Together* were made with the support of the British Film Institute's Experimental Production Fund; *O Dreamland* was completely unsolicited.

THE MAKERS of the films prefer to call their work "free" rather than "experimental". It is neither introverted nor esoteric. Nor is its concern primarily with technique.

THESE FILMS ARE FREE in the sense that their statements are entirely personal. Though their moods and subjects differ, the concern of each of them is with some aspect of life as it is lived in this country, to-day. A jazz club in a North London pub ; the mean streets of London's East End dockland; an amusement park in a south coast resort . . . these locations may have figured in British films before. But here is an effort to see and to feel them freshly, with love or with anger—only not coldly, hygienically or conventionally.

IN EFFECT, the makers of these films offer them as a challenge to orthodoxy.

NATIONAL FILM THEATRE · SOUTHBANK

The leaflet distributed in February 1956 for Free Cinema 1.

of the British Empire. To this extent, the film version may have led to the impression, cultivated by later studies, that British foreign policy was one of the targets of the AYM protest. Jimmy Porter's rage, in the film version, is directed toward concrete social matters. He attempts to correct Kapoor's notions of an enlightened England and tries to defend him against the mob controlling the market, headed by the policeman. Typical of film, the single location of the stage play is opened up to several settings—some of working-class significance, including a market, the hospital, a pub, a train station, and a jazz club.[125] Jimmy's jazz trumpet solo, which opens the film, attempted to capture the spirit of jazz music in the 1950s. Understood to be "music of the people," jazz thus reflected the play's rejection of upper-class norms and values.[126] In this way, the film attempted to emphasize the anti-establishment attitude and social critique of the play.

Most film critics responded favorably to the changes made in the film version. Gavin Lambert, for example, wrote that the film's major advance on the play derives from its ability to take Jimmy's "anger out of the vacuum of the bed-sitting room, and shows it in relation to what he finds outside."[127] Another critic, Henry Hart, felt that although the film "is faulty as a motion picture, it is unusually powerful as a social document, and it is very much worth seeing. Not as an entertainment—it is a depressing experience—but as exposition of some of the intellectual attitudes and beliefs currently contributing to social disintegration in England."[128] The decision of the filmmakers to transform *Look Back in Anger* into an explicit, up-to-date, sociocultural manifesto, flavored with a touch of romance, may also have been motivated by their marketing aspirations. Whatever the case, this decision seems to confirm their awareness of the play's emergent social trademark, bolstering the historical significance of Osborne's play as a transformative work in British culture.

Woodfall's next film, based on Osborne's next play, *The Entertainer*, which was produced April 10, 1957 by the English Stage Company, with Sir Laurence Olivier playing the lead, again reiterated the link between the theatrical and cinematic domains and, in particular, between the ESC and Woodfall. The dictum of the ESC "Right to Fail" policy clearly resembles the Free Cinema motto declared in its manifesto, "Perfection Is Not an Aim."[129] Unlike the critics' favorable reception of the film version of *Look Back in Anger*, notices of the 1960 film version of *The Entertainer* were at best reserved. Richardson, who directed the film, subsequently left for Hollywood to direct the film *Sanctuary*. Woodfall's next production,

Saturday Night and Sunday Morning (1961), based on Alan Sillitoe's novel and directed by Karel Reisz, proved both a critical and financial success. Critics hailed the film as a landmark in British cinema, while the box office returns were sufficient to secure Woodfall financially. With the company finally on a firm financial footing, Richardson was able to bring his cinematic ideas to fruition in directing the film *A Taste of Honey* in 1961. Based on Shelagh Delaney's play produced by the Theatre Workshop, Richardson's film version drew largely on the conceptions of the Free Cinema. The film was a great commercial success and is considered one of Richardson's best.

Richardson, whose prestige as a film director was steadily enhanced throughout the 1960s, continued to direct for the stage in spite of prolonged absences due to his film career, enabling him to operate as a mediator in more than one cultural domain. In his two professional roles he contributed to a growing cultural aura around not just Osborne and his plays but also around the social movement in the arts, from novels to films, that presented a critique of the British class system. He also helped to put the voice and talent of the British working class on the stage.

Richardson continued to pursue his collaboration with the two other founders of the Free Cinema. He was the producer of Reisz's first feature, *Saturday Night and Sunday Morning*, and was joined by Lindsay Anderson as assistant director at the Royal Court in 1957. It was at the Royal Court that Anderson directed several renowned plays, such as Willis Hall's 1959 *The Long and the Short and the Tall* and John Arden's 1959 *Sergeant Musgrave's Dance*. Anderson's first feature film, *This Sporting Life*, produced by Reisz in 1963, is highly regarded among British films of the 1960s. Anderson also served as artistic director of the ESC with William Gaskill and Anthony Page between the years 1969 and 1972. The careers of both Anderson and Richardson show the confluence that emerged between key mediators in the theatre and in the cinema over the course of the 1960s.

By virtue of the diversity of its mediators, the trajectory of *Look Back in Anger* interlinks the two cultural domains: theatre and cinema. The success of the ESC production of the play led to the forming of the Woodfall Company and the making of its film version, thereby contributing to new developments in the cinematic domain. In turn, the film version further established the reputation of this play, its playwright, and its director. Significantly, the film version also proved beneficial to the ESC, which profited from the sale of the film's rights and from the leasing of its stage rights.[130] The subsidy from the Arts Council remained relatively small during the ESC's early years, and therefore its survival at this time depended primarily on the profits made from Osborne's plays, their successful transfers to the West End, and a cut of their run on Broadway, in addition to the income generated from the film rights.[131]

A GRADUAL CONVERGENCE

May 8th is the one unforgettable feast in my calendar. My father, Thomas Godfrey Osborne, was born in Newport, Monmouthshire, on May 8th. Had he lived he would now be the age of the century. The Second World War ended on 8 May 1945, a date which now passes as unremembered as 4 August 1914. On 8 May 1956, my first play to be produced in London, Look Back in Anger, *had its opening at the Royal Court Theatre. This last date seems to have become fixed in the memories of theatrical historians.—John Osborne, 1981*

In his memoirs Tony Richardson, who died in 1991, recalls the reception of *Look Back in Anger*, his first show at the Royal Court.[132] While the next day's notices, he recounts, "were almost universally disastrous," Sunday saw the publication of key British notices, by Harold Hobson and Kenneth Tynan. Yet even these rave reviews by two prominent theatre critics failed to have an instantaneous effect on the production's fortunes—a version of events that complies with most other accounts of the play's reception. At this point, however, Richardson's account diverges somewhat from the rest, claiming that "in England, *Look Back in Anger* was never a commercial success (another myth that needs dispelling): it didn't ever sell out at the Court."

Richardson goes on to say that the television broadcast on October 16, 1956, "created enough interest to sell out" the three-week revival at the Lyric, though he comments that "on later revivals we did okay but not sensational business." His verdict is somewhat surprising, given that most other accounts emphasize the play's transformation into a commercial success following the television broadcast. More significant than this odd discrepancy is Richardson's take on the impact Hobson's and Tynan's reviews had on the play's subsequent fate. It was these two notices, Richardson claims, that "made us the theatre of the moment, the place where it was happening, take it or leave it, love it or hate it." Tynan's review, Richardson explains, had influenced "the theatre people" who came to see the play and, although "most of them didn't like what they saw, they slunk back and took another look, thinking maybe this was what they'd better be part of. That, over a year, was to have many consequences."[133] Richardson views these consequences in the context of the overall reception of the ESC's first season, pointing out that expectations often turn out to be mistaken. "Though *Look Back in Anger* was our favorite," he acknowledges, "George [Devine] and I had thought it our worst bet."[134] It thus appears that Richardson's judgment regarding the two reviews' effect on the play's fortunes was an attempt on his part to explain, retrospectively, its eventual triumph. But while it is probable that Hobson's review, and certainly Tynan's, greatly magnified the cultural significance of *Look Back in Anger*, this production became a key cultural event largely as a result of the gradual convergence of many and varied mediating factors.

While the media's treatment of the Angry Young Men can be perceived as paving the way for a particular reception of Osborne's play, it was Kenneth Tynan's review of *Look Back in Anger* that first stated a belief in its unique potential.[135] Although Tynan introduced the play as a voice already heard in Kingsley Amis's *Lucky Jim*, he nevertheless insisted on its innovative contribution to the field of drama and strove to promote it in accordance with his own left-wing political and social inclinations.[136] His most significant role, however, in the rise to fame of *Look Back in Anger* lay in his ratifying the perception of the play's major concerns. Tynan's review, in fact, corresponded with the existing expectations cultivated by most theatre critics in response to the newly formed ESC: that new British playwrights should be concerned with issues of their day. Published at the close of the first week of the play's production, his review laid out the sociopolitical coordinates for the critical discourse that began to build around the play between July and November 1956, a period that began with Fearon's "angry young man" remark and ended with Granada's broadcast of the play just as the critical discourse caught up with the reviewer expectations pronounced upon the founding of the ESC. It was likely the aftereffect of Tynan's mediating influence on the evolving critical discourse that explains the impact retrospectively attributed to his review. His influence on the critics' perception of the play was indeed apparent in their enthusiastic responses several months after the play's initial performances. Moreover, his impact on the way *Look Back in Anger* was perceived is further evident in the film version of this play. Equally important is the manner in which his review became a recurring component of the narratives constructed around the play, to which

Tynan himself further contributed by reiterating the significance of the play over the course of many years.[137]

If Tynan's initial promotion of *Look Back in Anger* contributed to making this production a key cultural event, John Russell Taylor's 1962 study of contemporary British drama, *Anger and After*, was one of the first attempts to place that event within a developing narrative.[138] Tynan's review laid the groundwork for the perception of the play as revolutionary; Taylor's study, published six years after the play was first performed and offering the first overview of contemporary British drama to date, presented the play as the beginning of a new era of writing. For Taylor, the first performance of *Look Back in Anger* on May 8, 1956, was "the event which marks 'then' off decisively from 'now.'"[139]

Taylor chose to challenge Tynan's legendary role in the promotion of the play, presenting its critical reception as "almost uniformly favourable ... with a couple of exceptions."[140] Tynan's enthusiastic review was merely one of several factors—and probably not the most dominant one—that helped change the production's fortunes. Taylor acknowledges the impact of other factors, such as the October 16, 1956, TV broadcast, but he does so in his later study, *The Second Wave*.[141] In his earlier study, *Anger and After*, he attributes the play's eventual public success first to its extended run and then to its revival at a time when Osborne's next play, *The Entertainer*, "was already on the horizon, with a firm undertaking from Sir Laurence Olivier to play the lead."[142] Taylor maintains that the theatre-going public remained initially unaffected by the critics' tendency to present the play as revolutionary. It was, he argues, the company's decision to allow *Look Back in Anger* to "run continuously for some ten weeks"—a decision taken "more as an act of faith than anything else"—which together with the timing of its revival, turned the play into a box-office success.[143] Taylor's description of the play's success as a gradual process that began with the critics' recognition of its innovative qualities is consistent with his overall narrative, which reviews the ongoing changes taking place in Britain's theatrical scene at the time.

If Taylor's narrative belittles Tynan's role as the lead promoter of Osborne's play, it also enhances, albeit indirectly, Taylor's own reputation as the principal champion of both play and playwright. Taylor's attempt to downplay Tynan's role could have undermined Tynan's or indeed his own claims, thereby reducing the overall effect of the Osborne campaign. Ultimately, though, Taylor's narrative supplemented Tynan's advocacy and helped enhance Osborne's position in future studies. Here again, an unexpected dynamic was at play: like Fearon's "angry young man" remark, Taylor's challenge of the Tynan legend worked in favor of Osborne's play and career. Taylor further cultivated the view of the unique significance of *Look Back in Anger*, as well as his own gate-keeping stance with regard to it, by editing a case book on the play in 1968.[144] He maintained this gate-keeping role in his 1971 study of what he called the second wave of British drama, beginning with the author's retrospective view of the play's eventual impact.[145]

Yet factors and processes beyond their control contributed to the influence exercised by Kenneth Tynan and John Russell Taylor. The impact of Tynan's review was facilitated by the cumulative authority of the media (radio, literary journals, and the press) as the Movement emerged, subsequently manifested in the promotion, particularly by the press, of the AYM cult. As Guillaume Parmentier claims: "In 1956 the [British] press rather than television still remained the major means of communication between the general public and the opinion formers."[146] Additionally, in the 1950s newspapers were much smaller and had no separate review sections. Consequently, reviewers like Tynan and Hobson possibly had far greater influence on public opinion and discourse than their counterparts in the following decades.

What reinforced the impact of Taylor's study was, however, the series of cultural developments that took place, particularly in theatre and education between the late 1940s and early 1960s.[147] The major marker of growing institutional support of the arts was the establishment of the Arts Council of Great Britain on August 9, 1946, announced in the House of Commons in June 1945. Among other things, the Arts Council encouraged and subsidized emerging repertory theatres around the country,[148] which in turn expanded the availability of training grounds for theatrical practitioners. Another significant 1946 event was the founding of the first academic drama department at Bristol University, which helped establish an institutional presence for academic studies of drama. Also noteworthy were the founding of the Society for Theatre Research in 1948; the founding of new drama periodicals and magazines such as *Theatre Notebook* in 1946, *Plays and Players* in 1953, and *Encore* in 1954; the first Edinburgh Festival in 1947; and the founding of the National Youth Theatre in 1956.

The Society for Theatre Research and its associated journal, *Theatre Notebook*, were primarily devoted to theatre history, whereas the magazines *Plays and Players* and *Encore* dealt with emergent theatre. *Plays and*

Players, which first appeared in October 1953, was one of a series of seven monthly magazines on the arts published by Hansom Books, a company owned by Philip Dosse.[149] *Encore,* which bore the subtitle *The Voice of Vital Theatre,* began as a student magazine edited by Clive Goodwin at the Central School of Speech and Drama. Among its early contributors were Kingsley Amis and Sean O'Casey. In 1957, when Owen Hale joined *Encore* as patron and business manager, it was launched as a bimonthly magazine. Until its discontinuation in 1965, *Encore*'s contributors introduced and debated the merits of new dramatists, appraised new books on drama, and wrote reviews of new productions, articles on the policies of both new and established theatre companies and institutions, and essays on innovative theatrical practices, methods, styles, and critical approaches. In addition, the magazine dealt with a range of social and cultural concerns. *Encore,* in fact, provided a forum for a number of the most prominent theatrical and cultural mediators of the era, including Kenneth Tynan, Charles Marowitz, Peter Hall, Peter Brook, George Devine, Lindsay Anderson, Richard Findlater, Raymond Williams, Stuart Hall, Irving Wardle, Martin Esslin, and John Russell Taylor, the latter two of which were also regular contributors to *Plays and Players. Encore* was thus a crucial intersection that linked the academic, the critical, and the practical faces of theatre. During the years of its existence the magazine charted significant developments in the theatrical field in Britain. The developments in the theatrical field are further linked to the changes taking place in the educational system in Britain during the 1960s, reflected in the considerable broadening of education, the increasing support for the arts, and the growing interest in drama.[150]

In October 1963, the Robbins Committee on Higher Education urged the expansion of Britain's higher education system, with particular emphasis on the promotion of scientific studies in the universities. The main impetus of the Robbins report, however, went to encouraging the arts and social sciences.[151] As a result, investment in higher education rose significantly, with some of the money going toward the expansion and development of drama studies. Additionally, academic English studies during the 1960s had shifted toward Modernist texts.[152] The orientation of drama studies coincided with processes already underway in the theatrical field, leading to a further emphasis on contemporary British drama and dramatists. Taylor's *Anger and After,* described on its cover as "the first comprehensive study of the movement which began in May 1956," addressed precisely this emphasis. John Bull, assessing Taylor's study from the perspective of the

year 2000, claims that, "John Russell Taylor's 'guide to the new drama' ...
is still the first resort for students anxious to acquaint themselves with
the period"[153]; a judgment upheld by the fact that by 1969 the book had
gone through six editions.[154] Taylor's guide seems also to have had appeal
beyond academic readers, considering its popular style and its rapid appearance in paperback form. In 2000, Dominic Shellard made a special
point of noting those writers who in recent years had challenged "the he-
gemony that has built up around John Russell Taylor's hugely influential
work of the sixties, *Anger and After*, the bible of the Angry Young Men Fan
Club."[155] Until studies in the 1990s challenged Taylor's views, the impact
of his mediation extended far beyond university students, thus governing
historical views of developments in British drama and theatre in the 1950s
and 1960s,[156] and establishing Taylor as a major authority on the subject.
In sum, both Tynan and Taylor were external mediators who employed
differing media in order to advance their views of the significance of *Look
Back in Anger*.[157] In the process, Osborne gained two leading benefactors,
and Tynan and Taylor in turn further enhanced their own authoritative
positions in the cultural arena.

If *Look Back in Anger* turned Osborne into a celebrated playwright,
the 1981 publication of his autobiography, *A Better Class of Person*, followed ten years later by a second volume, *Almost a Gentleman*, earned
him a reputation as a prose writer. On July 1, 1985, a 120-minute extract
from the first volume was broadcast on television.[158] Highly acclaimed for
their literary merit by most critics, both autobiographical volumes further contributed to enhancing the celebrity status of the author and of his
renowned play, *Look Back in Anger*.[159] Many of the obituaries published
upon Osborne's death in late 1994 reveal that even after forty years, the
production of his first play retained its status as a key cultural event.[160]
Michael Billington, for instance, wrote: "So how important a writer was
John Osborne? Without a shadow of a doubt, he helped to change the face
of post-war British theatre, and nothing can take that away from him. He
also wrote at least half-a-dozen plays that will have a claim on posterity.
But I suspect he will be remembered as well for his two volumes of autobiography ... , which reveal him as one of the most incandescent prose
writers of his generation."[161]

In his eulogy at Osborne's memorial service in June 1995, David Hare,
a prominent playwright himself, asserted: "John knocked down the door
and a whole generation of playwrights came piling through, many of

them not even acknowledging him as they came, and a good half of them not noticing that the vibrant tone of indignation they could not wait to imitate was, in John's case, achieved only through an equally formidable measure of literary skills."[162] Hare pointed to "the two exceptional, illuminating volumes of autobiography, which prove—if proof was needed—that his celebrated gift for analysing the short-comings of others was as nothing to his forensic capacity for making comedy from his own failings. If he could be hard on others, he could be almost religiously brutal on himself."[163]

A 1997 casebook on John Osborne reflects the extent of interest in this playwright's dramatic works, and usefully brings together a wide range of critical approaches dealing with his most renowned play.[164] In it, Austin Quigley states: "Forty years after it made its historic appearance on London stage *Look Back in Anger* is widely regarded as a very important but not very good play. . . . This apparent disjunction between the quality of the play and the scope of its impact remains something of a puzzle."[165] This puzzle has elicited various critical explanations. As early as 1968, Raymond Williams contended that although Osborne's play had the appearance of a breakthrough in 1956, this perception was "essentially a delayed recognition of an already altered style" that was known outside the theatre, but until then had not broken through to the stage. Indeed, Williams claims that only a play of genuine power can achieve this public alteration of style, adding that it "gets a historical weight, a representative of importance, which is often more than in itself it can bear."[166] Some of the play's critics, however, attribute its lasting success primarily to its intrinsic merit. Simon Trussler, for instance, suggested in 1969 that as a study of a lonely man, the play "is a work of a real psychological insight and of unsentimental compassion."[167] In the same year Martin Banham argued that the play's impact was primarily the result of its revolutionary content, noting as well the passionate nature of Osborne's plays and their "great theatricality," which attracted many notable actors and directors to his work.[168] Ronald Hayman's 1969 book discussed the playwright's considerable influence over the new theatrical movement that emerged in the mid 1950s, maintaining that while the "revolution" in the English theatre did not occur overnight, Osborne "did more than anyone to popularise the new type of hero and the new type of actor."[169]

Several other studies seek to answer the puzzle by relating to Osborne's poetics in general. In Katharine Worth's 1972 view, for example, the power of Osborne's drama springs from its distinctive mix of and shifts between the old and the new styles—traditional elements and new forms—with the result that "the sense of the past and the spirit of change tend to be equally strong in it."[170] According to Austin Quigley in 1997, the nature of the puzzle becomes clearer in light of Osborne's sequel play, *Déjàvu* (1991), because in it, Jimmy Porter's dilemma, like the implications of the larger cultural concerns with which *Look Back in Anger* resonates, has "become clearer with the passing of time.[171] In 1995 Stephen Lacey offered the view that the impact of the play is rooted in the particular circumstances of the time—the sociocultural, economic, and political factors that contributed to the change in Britain's postwar theatrical arena.

In addressing the conundrum of Osborne's play, many studies draw on more than one critical approach, some of the more typical being, especially of late, archival, contextual, or sociocultural in nature. Most studies reflect a state of general confusion concerning the criteria for periodization in theatre history,[172] and in particular the criteria for establishing turning points. The numerous attempts to elucidate the puzzle regarding the unique status of *Look Back in Anger* are in themselves part of the apparatus that facilitates the narratives surrounding this play. The mediating modes and operations deriving from various behind-the-scenes motivations, all of which lent this play its singularity, have consequently fueled the production of the numerous and diverse critical views and historical narratives.

Look Back in Anger served as a turning point in several cultural developments simultaneously—literary/theatrical, educational/academic, and media related. Its significance draws on its placement within an era of turbulent transformation, which is a necessary backdrop to a play that, for all its ascribed innovation, is also seen as rather conventional in form. Its outstanding success resulted from the combined actions of various participants in and commentators on its cultural significance. Leading figures such as Devine and Richardson acting as in-house mediators, or Tynan and Taylor acting as external mediators, endorsed the play because it met their own aims or needs. Their modes of operation and the particular impact of their mediation were born of pre-existing conditions favorable to the play, and of emergent constellations of agents—members of the ESC council, producers, members of award committees, reviewers, theatre critics, literary critics, film critics, interviewers on television or in the press, academics, publishers, journalists—whose pursuit of their own discrete interests led to their forces being joined in collaboration.

THE LINKAGE OF COMPANY AND PLAY

Royal Court: Believed to be a literary theatre by the literati, a left-wing theatre by the Socialists, and an art theatre by the aesthetes. Its geographical location is particularly relevant; it stands facing Chelsea with its back to Belgravia and has a direct route to the West End.—Charles Marowitz, 1961

The cultural significance attributed to *Look Back in Anger* is irrevocably bound up with the subsequent trajectory of the company performing it. The immense success of the play enhanced the ESC's reputation and its financial standing but also set in motion a new company agenda. Coupled with the failure of Duncan's plays, the unprecedented success of Osborne's play disrupted the balance between various competing agendas. Now under the fortified directorship of Devine, the company, which prior to the success of *Look Back in Anger* had vacillated between several aims, would embark on a particular course. Devine had initially opted to promote a sort of European art theatre and sought to persuade British novelists and poets to write plays for the company, but the success of *Look Back in Anger* convinced him of the designated path for the company in the years ahead.

Gresdna Doty and Billy Harbin's edited proceedings of a conference held in Louisiana in 1981, devoted to the ESC's production practices and legacies to that date, reinforces the above claim.[173] Referring to the aftereffect of Osborne's play on the ESC, Doty and Harbin claim: "Devine recognized that the ESC's commitment must be to Osborne's contemporaries, the unestablished, young, and iconoclastic writers."[174] Especially significant is William Gaskill's view on the subject. Gaskill, one of the major participants in the conference, had joined the ESC in 1957, became associate director of the company in 1959, was the artistic director from 1965 to 1969, and from 1969 to 1972 one of the three artistic directors of the company, with Lindsay Anderson and Anthony Page. According to Philip Roberts (1999), Gaskill was the director favored by Devine. Gaskill testifies that during the formative phase of the ESC, Devine and Richardson's quest for new writing had targeted European art theatre and that the success of *Look Back in Anger* "swung the whole movement in a completely different direction"[175] in which "the writers themselves would dictate the character of the new theatre. The writing, directing, acting, and design talent began to come from a rather different social class and a regional background different from what was usual at the time." It was Devine's greatness, Gaskill further suggests, to recognize "what was actually going to work and that conditioned, and . . . has continued to condition, the life of the Court."[176] Devine's chosen path for the ESC, manifested in the company's policy, coincided with the cultural aims promoted by the establishment, a correlation also revealed by his three-year appointment as a member of the Drama Panel of the Arts Council in 1956–1957, and his being honored with the CBE (Commander of the Order of the British Empire) in 1957. According to Wardle, Devine explicitly recognized his usefulness as a member of the establishment: "I knew my country and I knew that we ourselves had to become part of the establishment against which our hearts if not our faces were set."[177] Gaskill recounts, however, that Devine never gave up his original dream and continued his attempt to return to the European art theatre, either by setting up workshops for the ESC's writers in which they studied the work of foreign theatres, or through his choice of repertoire, in particular the works of Beckett and Ionesco, which had a distinct presence in the Court's repertoire. Two of Devine's later projects further prove that he did not give up his initial interests: the Royal Court's Writers' Group, which met weekly for two years starting in 1958, and the Sunday Night Production without Décor, which began in May 1957—both projects that constituted a training center for theatrical experiments and learning.

The list of new playwrights associated with Devine's term as artistic director, following the ESC's first season, demonstrates the policy he adopted: dramatists such as Ann Jellicoe, Arnold Wesker, N. F. Simpson, Wole Soyinka, John Arden, and Edward Bond. At the time their plays were first performed at the Court, all of these playwrights were young and mostly unknown. Devine was explicit about his commitment to these playwrights, unwilling to compromise his support even when their plays proved to be box-office disasters or caused public or critical scandals. Ann Jellicoe, another major participant in the Louisiana conference, recalls Devine's supportive and encouraging attitude throughout her years at the Court, despite the failure of her first play.[178] Devine's dominant role in the promotion of the careers of these dramatists, especially in light of his initial premises and beliefs,[179] indicates that the direction he endorsed following the success of Look Back in Anger was focused on Osborne's contemporaries even though he continued to incorporate works by other playwrights, notably Beckett and Ionesco.[180] New playwrights greatly benefited from the opportunity they were provided by the Court, but the Court in turn benefited from its association with these new writers. As Wardle suggests, the effect of the Court was derived from "the impact the writers made collectively."[181] The Court is presented as a cornerstone in the emerging theatrical map of the 1960s by another key mediating figure, Martin Esslin, another participant in the Louisiana conference, whose influential position was established during the era in question. Esslin claims that "the coming of the National Theatre and the transformation of the Royal Shakespeare Company, and all that, radiates outward from the Royal Court experience."[182]

As confirmed by the commentaries of the participants in the Louisiana conference, Osborne's legacy—reflected in the course upon which the ESC embarked—bestowed on this company its association with innovative theatre. It is this legacy rather than the poetics of *Look Back in Anger* that appears to underlie many of the narratives presenting the play as a turning point.

The issue of Osborne's legacy echoes in yet another mediatory turn fifty years after the first production of *Look Back in Anger*.

In 2006, John Heilpern published a biography of Osborne.[183] David Edgar, a prominent playwright himself, published a review article of it in the *London Review of Books*. Describing the biography as "drawing heavily on Osborne's two-volume memoir (the glory of his later writing)," Edgar points out that "Heilpern's deeper purpose is not only to reaffirm Osborne 'as the unyielding advocate of individualism in conformist times,' but also 'to reclaim the place of *Look Back in Anger* in British history from recent revisionists who would have us believe that its impact was somehow minor or even negligible.'"[184] Edgar finds Heilpern's counterargument to the revisionists unsatisfactory. Moreover, he claims that although Heilpern "doesn't quite answer" the question of what was radical about Osborne's play,[185] "David Hare does" in three speeches he delivered on Osborne.[186] Hare's argument, Edgar says, revolves around three major points: First, that Osborne "brought emotional intensity back to the English stage"; second, that he "found a new audience"; and third, that by putting the playwright back at the center of the theatre—Osborne opened the door to wave upon wave of socially engaged new theatre writing, from 1957 all the way to the present." Concluding his review, Edgar asserts that "Osborne's real legacy is not the continued life of his own plays, but those of generation after generation of writers of whom he would doubtless disapprove (and who might well disapprove of him), which would not have been written for the theatre, or for any medium at all, without *Look Back in Anger*."[187]

In conclusion, the breakthrough narrative linking company, play, and playwright is the by-product of the multilayered network that constitutes the processes of mediation. The course of events recounted here illustrates the workings of different mediating agents and the effects of various constellations, exemplifying the accumulated impact of converging forces. This account also reveals unexpected developments at play, proving again that history is more than the sum of its constituents, and consequently that it is far easier to analyze events in retrospect than to predict them in advance.

2 | Divergent Forces
Theatre Workshop

Theatre Workshop could have reshaped English theatre—almost did.
They offered the theatre profession new possibilities between 1954 and
1965 which stemmed most notably from a European tradition of radical
theatre especially active between the two world wars. . . . But in the
absence of sufficient signs of continuity for Theatre Workshop's idea,
it becomes harder to persuade young people that Joan Littlewood's
work was significant, let alone to describe it in any meaningful way.
She is history now, this tough-on-the-surface Mother Figure of modern
theatre.—Derek Paget

The turns in the theatrical reputation of Theatre Workshop during its active years, as well as the shift in scholarly assessment of the company in the decades following its demise, present an intriguing case. This chapter explores the processes of mediation that shaped Theatre Workshop's reputation, centering on its first decade in the Theatre Royal at Stratford East, London. Given that its policy and objectives reflected its origins and evolution during the years preceding the company's move to Stratford East, a brief review of this early history is necessary. The concluding section illustrates the shift in the scholarly assessment of Theatre Workshop in the last two decades, repositioning both the company and its key production as defining contributions in theatrical and cultural history. Exploring this shift also demonstrates the modification (or rejection) of the narrative constructed around the significance of the English Stage Company's production of Osborne's *Look Back in Anger* discussed in chapter 1.

ORIGINS: THEATRE OF THE PEOPLE

The origins of Theatre Workshop are rooted in the Workers' Theatre Movement of the late 1920s, with its upsurge of theatrical activities following World War I and the General Strike. Theatrical groups, formed primarily by young unemployed workers, had sprung up in the northwest of England, creating a theatre chiefly concerned with daily issues of the class struggle. Performing for working-class audiences in a style that became known as "agitprop" (agitation and propaganda), these groups used theatre as a weapon in the class struggle. In the early 1930s Jimmy Miller, who was to change his name to Ewan MacColl, helped establish Red Megaphones in Salford, and Red Cops in Rochdale. In 1934, with agitprop groups all over the country, Red Megaphones became the Theatre of Action in Manchester.

Early that year, in Manchester, MacColl met twenty-year-old Joan Littlewood through his work on radio as an actor and singer. Littlewood had just fled France following the anti-government riots there, where she had intended to join Gaston Baty's company. Born and raised in the East End of London, Littlewood had attended the Royal Academy of Dramatic Art, but left before completing her studies in protest against the pedagogical tradition in which she was being trained, then the reigning theatrical practice manifested by the West End theatre. She met MacColl following an invitation from Archie Harding at the BBC to participate in the radio show *Tunnel* and subsequently joined Theatre of Action. Her professional collaboration with MacColl, whom she married in 1936, was to last until 1953.

Theatre of Action pursued a radical agenda on various levels. Its performances in working-class districts reflected the workers' lives and struggles, but MacColl recalls that he and Littlewood were also seeking to create a new theatre language: "One thing we felt was that the theatre that we saw, done by local reps or visiting companies, was incredibly static, in terms simply of the physical involvement of actors. It struck us merely as a series of monologues or dialogues, taking place without people doing anything that was particularly relevant on the stage."[1] In their theatrical work, MacColl and Littlewood integrated their study of Meyerhold (in particular his formulation of a system of biomechanics); the dance theories of Rudolf Laban, Piscator, and Bodenwiser; and the stage-lighting theories of Adolph Appia, a Swiss scenic designer. MacColl attributes his discovery and reading of Appia's theories in 1933 to Alf Armitt, one of the members of Theatre of Action, who built a switchboard that he would operate in front of the audience before the performance started. Appia's theories of lighting were to be further used in Theatre Workshop's many other productions.[2] Seeking, as MacColl recounts, "to try and find a theatrical language and style that people understood, which would move them but not talk down to them,"[3] Theatre of Action produced works that were concerned with the social issues of the time, developing a theatrical language that integrated into the production highly skilled acting techniques, movement, sound and light.[4]

Littlewood's fierce commitment to practicing and developing her theatrical work freely was already apparent in this early phase. Although clearly committed to politics, the innovative theatrical modes pursued by Littlewood and MacColl—both members of the Communist Party—did not correspond with the party's belief that plays should express direct propaganda for the cause. A conflict consequently ensued and the two were expelled from the Party. Strict demands and tough working conditions finally led to the break-up of the group. In 1935 MacColl and Littlewood left for London to await their visas for Moscow, where they had been granted a scholarship. While there, however, they set up a theatre school and subsequently exhausted their financial resources. Returning to Manchester in 1936, they staged a production of *Miracle at Verdun*, by Hans Chlumberg, recruiting a huge cast, from which they selected enough young people to form a new group they called Theatre Union.

According to Howard Goorney, Littlewood and MacColl had been inventing theatrical techniques and—through experimentation—solving problems regarding timing, movement, sound, and lighting since their first collaboration in Theatre of Action's production of *Newsboy* in 1934.[5] Their experiments were greatly shaped by the study of theatrical traditions and styles world-wide; as MacColl recounts: "We believed that all great theatre of the past had been popular theatre."[6] The group developed a training program that reflected their rejection of the conventional theatre of the time and their search for a new aesthetic and philosophy of theatre, drawing on the ideas of Stanislavsky, Meyerhold, and in particular Vakhtangov. One great influence on their work was Leon Moussinak's *The New Movement in the Theatre*, published in English in 1931, which introduced modern staging.[7] Theatre Union's 1938 production of *The Good Soldier Schweik*, which relied on Piscator's adaptation of Jaroslav Hasek's novel, produced in Berlin in 1928, was inspired by Moussinak's book.[8] *The Good Soldier Schweik*, later to be revived several times by Theatre Workshop, was its first production to be transferred to the West End—in 1956—after the company's move to Stratford East.

Between 1936 and 1942, the repertoire of Theatre Union, also called Theatre of the People, included classics such as Lope de Vega's *The*

Sheep Well, Aristophanes' *Lysistrata*, and *Schweik*, as well as new works that confronted social or political problems of the time.[9] Performing in Manchester and other provincial towns, Theatre Union concentrated on intensive training and on further development of theatrical techniques which laid the groundwork for the future of Theatre Workshop. One of the most successful Theatre Union productions was a documentary written by MacColl, *Last Edition*, a sort of "living newspaper" in which the scenes changed every week according to the most recent news, current events that led to World War II. Summing up those years, MacColl comments: "We were beginning to get a group of people together who were used to working together, who had a common vision of the theatre, and a common vision of the world"[10]—a description that clarifies the emergent nature of Theatre Union. According to Goorney, Joan Littlewood was the driving force of Theatre Union, particularly after the late 1930s. In 1940, after seeing the performance of *Last Edition*, Gerry Raffles joined the group. Raffles, who became Littlewood's life partner, would fill a key position in Theatre Workshop in the years ahead, serving as the company's general manager.

Wartime conditions between 1942 and 1945 prevented the company from continuing its active work. Littlewood and MacColl chose the best ten company members, each to be responsible for studying the theatre of a particular era. The members remained in contact with one another throughout the war years, although two were killed in the war. In 1945 a core of survivors of Theatre Union founded Theatre Workshop. One of the new members was John Bury, who at first acted in a number of productions, but soon became interested in design and eventually became a key figure in the company. After more than a decade with Littlewood, Bury later served as chief designer at the Royal Shakespeare Company (1963–1973) and then as head of design at the National Theatre (1973–1985).

During the first eight years of Theatre Workshop the company's base had alternated among the towns of Kendal, Ormesby Hall, Manchester, and Glasgow. In addition to intensive training the company toured throughout Britain, mainly staging one-night stands, taking theatre to the people. Between 1945 and 1953, the company also toured outside the country: in 1947 to West Germany, Czechoslovakia, and Sweden, and in 1951 to Scandinavia, where its work was highly acclaimed even though it remained relatively unknown in Britain.

The company's repertoire relied on both new works such as *Johnny Noble* and *Uranium 235* written by MacColl, and classical works such as Shakespeare's *Twelfth Night* and *As You Like It*, Chekhov's *The Proposal*, and Lorca's *Love of Don Perlimplin for Belisa in his Garden*. Theatre Workshop, pursuing the declared intentions of Theatre Union, aspired to create a theatre of the people, explicitly referring in its manifesto to Aeschylus, Sophocles, Shakespeare, Ben Jonson, Molière, and the Commedia dell'Arte as primary sources of inspiration.[11] The company's work and practice relied on their belief in a collective effort involving all members in the various aspects of production. Goorney recounts that in 1952 Michael Redgrave and Sam Wanamaker, who had watched the company's rehearsal of *Uranium 235*, arranged a short season for it at the Embassy Theatre in London, May 12–24, 1952. Redgrave introduced the company in the publicity leaflet for the production, praising its innovative and unique work.[12] The manager of the Embassy Theatre at the time, Oscar Lewenstein, recalls being impressed by the production's qualities and consequently introducing Gerry Raffles to the owner of the Comedy Theatre in the West End, to which *Uranium 235* was further transferred on June 18, 1952. Lewenstein remarks, "Thus I met this extraordinary theatre group, many of whom became my friends in the years that followed."[13] Lewenstein, who notes that it was the first transfer of a Theatre Workshop production to the West End prior to their move to Stratford East would prove to be a key mediator in their other, future transfers.

The tough working conditions on the road, combined with mounting financial losses, eventually led the company to change direction.[14] In his 1990 autobiography, MacColl sums up the company's state at that time: "It was plain that we had reached the point where we would either have to disband or find another way of working. . . . Our aims could not be achieved by touring, at least not unless we were subsidized. We had made countless appeals to a deaf Arts Council; we had approached trade-unions and government agencies. . . . And we had gone on working, postponing the inevitable decision. Now it could no longer be postponed. We had to put down roots."[15] At a meeting in Glasgow in 1952, the majority of the company members decided to lease the Theatre Royal in Stratford in the East End of London in a quest to achieve financial and artistic stability. The locale was perceived as not only complying with Theatre Workshop's objective of performing for working-class audiences but also bringing the possibility of broader recognition for the sort of theatre the company offered. MacColl opposed the decision, opting for Glasgow as a base, an option explored and deemed unfeasible. He saw the London locale as a potential threat to Theatre Workshop's basic aims. "It was argued," he remarks in his autobiography, "that there is no reason why critics and working-class audience shouldn't coexist peacefully." Littlewood, according to MacColl's account, opposed the move at first but later consented, and his objection was outvoted.[16] According to Goorney, Gerry Raffles, who was in charge of the company finances—mainly by default, since the other members were reluctant to fill the post—was the primary advocate of the move. Raffles saw it as a necessary step toward providing Littlewood with suitable working conditions, which was "always his main consideration."[17] Although MacColl continued to take part in the company productions after the move, his involvement with Theatre Workshop had essentially come to an end.[18]

In retrospect, the move to Stratford East marked a major reorientation of the company's agendas, reflected in MacColl's resignation. The company's new objective, to conjoin theatre directed at a working-class audience with the achievement of critical recognition, did eventually succumb to the tensions predicted by MacColl. Littlewood's own position on the matter at the time, particularly when read through MacColl, can be seen as an attempt to contain these seemingly incompatible agendas, while her conduct in the following years reveals her efforts to devise a mode that would resolve this incompatibility. In light of her subsequent conduct, Littlewood appears from the outset, as a matter of both belief and personal temperament, to have been bound by and committed to the original nature of the company, its declared theatrical aims, and its singular modes of theatre practice.

STRATFORD EAST: STRUGGLE ANEW

In 1953, Theatre Workshop moved to the Theatre Royal, Stratford East, with Gerry Raffles as the general manager. Prior to its arrival, the show at the Theatre Royal had been a striptease revue, *Jane of the Daily Mirror.* The theatre itself, which had been a wheelwright's shop until 1880, was in need of massive repair. Because it took all the company's resources just to pay off the purchase price—which took them two years—the members were required to make essential repairs themselves, in addition to the long hours of training and rehearsals. They recall how financial constraints led them to sleep in the dressing rooms and to cook their meals in a tiny room off the theatre's gallery, when they were not patronizing neighborhood café's like Café L'Ange, "where extra large helpings and credit were always available."[19] It became clear that a public subsidy was needed. At a meeting with representatives of local councils, it was agreed that the theatre should receive one, but until the first grant from the local authorities came through in 1957, the cast had to make an appeal for money after each show.[20]

The early period of Theatre Workshop at Stratford East commenced with the struggle to establish a local audience on the one hand, and the non-supportive response from the critical community on the other. The company, under Littlewood's direction, further developed and practiced a theatrical conception that integrated movement and sound; took an innovative approach to stage design and lighting, largely through John Bury's influence; and displayed a clear indebtedness to Brecht and Stanislavsky. Littlewood's foremost commitment was to theatre production as collective work, as Derek Paget suggests: "The 'Stratford East method' sought to replace the characteristically individualistic means of production which has tended to hold sway in theatres and publishing houses since the late seventeenth century with a collectivist version in which the individual effort is still fully present, but firmly subordinated so that the whole is greater than the sum of its parts."[21] Theatre Workshop's attitude to the text can be traced to the years of Theatre Union, as MacColl remarks: "We never stopped working on any of the scripts. And this went on right through Theatre Workshop."[22]

According to Paget, the persistent interest of Theatre Workshop's founders, MacColl and Littlewood, in the European radical tradition was the root of the company's famous and revolutionary production of *Oh What a Lovely War* in 1963.[23] The ideology underlying the company's policy, as well as the methods of work endorsed and practiced by Theatre Workshop during its Stratford years, were clearly rooted in the 1930s, when the members of the group, then Theatre Union, were united by a common vision of the theatre and of the world. Unlike the founding of the English Stage Company, which was an outcome of a particular momentum when varying agendas of different forces appeared to intersect, Theatre Workshop, upon its move to Stratford East, was an outgrowth of a gradual evolution borne of the interactions of committed individuals who shared common agendas. Membership was of course fluid, since established members of the company left and new ones joined. Many individuals originally affiliated with Theatre Union as well as members of Theatre Workshop during its touring years either dropped out of the company or went their separate ways. Two were killed during the war and others resigned. By 1953 the company comprised only a small core of veteran members, and even this relative continuity was unsettled by the move. Inevitably there were arguments and rivalries, but generally the in-house dynamics established by the company's founders did not degenerate into disputes over major issues. During the Stratford years, according to Goorney, major decisions over the company's policy were primarily made by Raffles, the general manager; Littlewood, the producer and director; and Bury, the artistic director.[24] Their decisions, when presented to the other company members, were nearly always approved. Consequently, when Littlewood—most probably in counsel with Raffles and Bury—endorsed a path and policy that may have stemmed from her ambivalent position upon the move to Stratford, she was on the whole backed by the members of her company. But Theatre Workshop's united front was not a source of unambiguous advantages; in some sense its very unanimity weighed the company down and would hamper its flexibility in interactions with external mediating forces.

ACQUIRING RECOGNITION AGAINST THE ODDS: PRODUCTIONS OF CLASSICS

Theatre Workshop's location in Stratford East, an unfashionable working-class area, put the company on the metropolitan margins. Furthermore, its interactions with external mediating forces were always conditioned by ideology (i.e., placing the working class at its center) and working ethos (e.g., collaborative work and improvisation). During 1953 and 1954, Theatre Workshop's many productions, each of which ran for two to three weeks, received little critical attention except for Littlewood's adaptations of *A Christmas Carol* on December 8, 1953, and *Treasure Island* on December 26, 1953, both intended for children and greatly enjoyed by their young audiences.[25] The production of Charles Fenn's *The Fire Eaters*, which won the Arts Council Award, also received favorable notices,[26] and in 1954 and 1955, the company's innovative approach to the classics drew the critics' attention. The company stressed ensemble work, revised texts to highlight the plays' contemporary relevance, and used minimalist settings rather than historical ones. The productions of Shakespeare's *Richard II*, *Arden of Faversham* by an unknown Elizabethan dramatist, and MacColl's adaptations of Hasek's *The Good Soldier Schweik* and Ben Jonson's *Volpone* received especially favorable reviews, which marked a new phase in the company's trajectory.

In the reviews of *Schweik*, for example, most critics called attention to Littlewood's choice of black-and-white settings drawn from the woodcut illustrations for the story, or to the device of the small revolving stage. Particular praise was reserved for the actor in the lead role, Harry H. Corbett. Kenneth Tynan's notice in the *Observer* expressed the view that "with half a dozen replacements, Theatre Workshop might take London by storm."[27] Tynan, then beginning his *Observer* career, would become a major theatrical figure over the next few years. His favorable notice of *Schweik* was to be only the first of a series of enthusiastic appraisals.

When Theatre Workshop's production of *Richard II* was presented on the same night as the Old Vic's production of the same play, on January 17, 1955,[28] a notice in the press presented the timing as an intentional challenge: "Coincidence? 'No,' says Theatre Workshop, 'a challenge. Our production is a complete departure from the Old Vic style.'"[29] This "provocation" indeed elicited critical response. A review by the influential critic Harold Hobson, comparing the two very different productions, emphasized Theatre Workshop's approach of ensemble playing, "not in the least devised in order to exhibit the graces of the leading actor (Mr. Harry Corbett)." Hobson also related to John Bury's set, and though he found the Theatre Workshop production on the whole less successful than that of the Old Vic, he viewed the former as "the more interesting, controversial and subtle."[30] Tynan, in contrast, clearly preferred the Old Vic production.

Theatre Workshop's nontraditional approach to classics was further manifested in its production of Jonson's *Volpone*, presented in modern dress on March 3, 1955. The drama critic of the *Daily Telegraph* expressed his reservation regarding "the fashion of playing classics in modern dress," yet described the production as "so beautifully brought off in this way that the sight of bicycles, and strangely enough even the sound of boogie-woogie rhythm failed to strike an incongruous note."[31] In Tynan's view, this production "rightly refuses to impose the 'Shakespeare voice' on Jonson's versified prose. Deprived of tights, ruffs and declamation, the actors have to act; and how keenly the present cast accepts the challenge!"[32] Tynan's favorable response to and promotion of the company's nontraditional approach was already apparent at this initial stage. The talented cast was also singled out for praise in other reviews, such as the one in the *Times*.[33]

In hindsight, it is possible to discern how these productions of classics resonated with the company's experience during its formative years as a touring company. Despite the move to London, which forced the company to meet the new demands such as filling the house and attracting critical attention, Theatre Workshop remained loyal to its underlying ideology, reflected also in its insistence on maintaining cheap seats to attract working-class audiences. Its innovative productions of classics seemed to weld past commitment to new conditions yet in practice attracted a growing nonlocal audience while stimulating critical interest and curiosity regarding the new theatrical language the company offered.

A new factor entered the mediatory arena in May 1955 when Theatre Workshop participated in the International Theatre Festival in Paris with productions of *Arden of Faversham* and *Volpone*, receiving high critical acclaim. About two weeks prior to the festival, Hobson had published an article in the *Sunday Times*, primarily expressing his annoyance with the British theatre. Whereas "enthusiasm for and interest in this festival have been shown in most parts of the world," he contended, leading players and major theatre companies in England had not accepted the invitation to go to Paris. Consequently "the solitary English representative in Paris will be Theatre Workshop, honourably known near Bow and on the fringe of the Edinburgh festival, but a stranger to the central tradition of English theatre." Hobson attacked the various organizations in England for not arranging "proper national representation at this festival."[34] By focusing on the English attitude and indifference toward the Paris Festival, Hobson's piece ignored Theatre Workshop's unique attributes as a company.

Equally important is the manner of Theatre Workshop's participation in the festival. Although struggling with immense financial difficulties, the company received no financial assistance for the trip. Moreover, the British Ambassador in Paris neither sent official greetings nor attended opening night.[35] Theatre Workshop's productions were nonetheless an enormous success, and the highly enthusiastic French critics praised the company's innovative style. Subsequent reports in the British press describing this enthusiastic critical reception reflected confusion—or perhaps embarrassment. "What is the meaning of this?" read the notice in the *Sunday Times*. "Are we wrong when we pass Theatre Workshop by, and also wrong when we praise it? Can English critics, poor fellows, do nothing right, or have the French gone entirely mad?" . . . "Most of us, most of the time, have ignored the activities of Theatre Workshop, which take place in an unfashionable part of London."[36] A notice in the *Times* recalled "passing references to the company's work appearing in the British press—not without the usual misgiving about the 'experimental' character of its production. These experiments have failed to frighten the French. On the contrary, they have filled them with rapturous delight."[37] In yet another notice, the *Times* described Theatre Workshop's success in the festival as "far exceeding that accorded to any other British company in France since the war" and provided an ironic counterpoint to Hobson's view of the company as an improper national representative: "French audiences and critics seem to derive much satisfaction from the fact that Theatre Workshop is a popular theatre."[38]

The press coverage of Theatre Workshop's success at the 1955 Paris festival sheds light on the relatively precarious position of the company in Britain at the time. With the exception of critical recognition of several of its productions of classics, the company's achievements were the object of official disregard. Press coverage tended to emphasize particular factors that would apparently affect the company's future, including its unfashionable location and the experimental/popular nature of the company's work. The glowing critical responses to the Theatre Workshop productions at the Paris festival nonetheless constituted, for London critics, a major catalyst in their growing recognition of the company's innovative work. It is surely significant, given the company's initial experiences and lessons of Paris, that Theatre Workshop would participate in four more International Theatre Festivals there in 1956, 1959, 1960, and 1963.

In July 1955, Theatre Workshop's productions of Bertolt Brecht's *Mother Courage* and Shakespeare's *Richard II* were performed at the Devon festival at Oscar Lewenstein's invitation. Lewenstein recounts that when Littlewood and Raffles told him that they had obtained the rights to produce Brecht's play, he suggested to Ronald Duncan that he and his partner, Wolf Mankowitz, present the Theatre Workshop Company at Devon.[39] Lewenstein had re-obtained the British rights for *Mother Courage* on the premise that Joan Littlewood would act the lead role.[40] The resulting production of *Mother Courage*, however, was fiercely attacked by the reviewers, in particular Tynan and Hobson.[41]

In his memoirs, Lewenstein expresses regret at having suggested to Brecht that Littlewood play the role of Mother Courage, which had "turned out to be such bad advice," and notes that Littlewood was never again to direct a Brecht play. He cites, however, Hobson's retrospective assessment that "even in the lamentable proceedings of that only half-rehearsed first night it was evident that *Mother Courage* was a work of quality,"[42] and quotes Hobson's view that "the theatrical revolution . . . really began . . . with the first British professional production of a play by

Brecht."[43] "In other words," Lewenstein comments, according to Hobson the revolution had started with "Joan's production at the Devon Festival of *Mother Courage*."[44] In terms of Theatre Workshop's critical reception, while the company's success at the Paris festival had clearly contributed to enhancing its reputation in Britain, its subsequent participation in the Devon festival—even though unfavorably reviewed—was a contributing factor to the company's growing visibility.

Goorney's account reiterates that the Devon festival marked a significant phase in the evolution of Theatre Workshop. His insider perspective (he had been an actor in the company since 1938) corroborates the view that the dynamics resulting from their newly acquired position affected them more than anticipated. In this respect, his account illustrates that even an apparently homogenous company was not impermeable to the effects of external mediatory forces. The balance between the company's pursuit of its agendas and the related constraints—aspirations and demands—became disrupted to a certain extent, which impacted on the company's inner structure and work methods from this point on.

Goorney lists several changes occurring after the festival that affected the longterm stability of the company and its working methods. The first relates to the cast, particularly to the decision by Harry Corbett and three other actors of the original nucleus to leave the company. The second change was a reduced emphasis on the training and discussion that had previously formed an integral part of its work, a change deriving partially from the different theatrical training and experience of the new actors and becoming more apparent in 1958 with the corresponding growth in the number of contemporary plays in its repertoire. These plays did not require the dance and movement abilities and social awareness essential to the actors who had participated in the company's early productions, such as MacColl's *Uranium 235*. The changes in both the cast and the training program also affected the working relationships among the members of the company, according to Goorney, manifested primarily in the growing influence of Joan Littlewood, whose role in the guidance of new members transformed her formerly key role into a position of dominance.[45]

Before dealing with Theatre Workshop's new repertoire of contemporary plays, beginning with *The Quare Fellow* by Brendan Behan in 1956, two of the company's productions of canonical plays deserve mention. The first was the successful restaging of *The Good Soldier Schweik* on October 25, 1955, a few months after the Paris and Devon festivals, and the second was Theatre Workshop's April 19, 1956 production of *Edward II*. *Schweik*, as already noted, was the first company production during Theatre Workshop's Stratford years to be transferred to the West End, a notable benchmark even though its run there lasted only three weeks, and achieved less success than anticipated. Tynan's favorable review of Theatre Workshop's production of *Edward II* enthused: "In the judgment of Paris, Theatre Workshop is our equivalent to the T.N.P (Theatre National Populaire). Anyone who visits its revival of Marlowe's masterly *Edward II* . . . can see why." He concluded: "Theatre Workshop has put itself on the map too, and honour in its own country is overdue."[46]

By 1958, Theatre Workshop had thus not only attracted critical attention but also been recognized by a few major critics for its unique theatrical contribution. Referring to the company's early critical acclaim for its productions of classics, Stephen Lacey contends that this was the point at which the company's policy "intersected with the interests of the literary critical establishment."[47] Lacey further suggests that the production of Behan's first play "brought wider critical acclaim and a much higher public visibility"[48] to company and cast alike. Arguably, Lacey's observations need modification. It seems that it was only when Theatre Workshop began to produce contemporary plays that its policy intersected with the emergent interests of the critical establishment. Confirming this view are the favorable responses of most critics to the declared aims of the newly founded English Stage Company (noted in chapter 1), particularly the intention of the ESC to provide a stage for new dramatists concerned with contemporary social or political problems. The expectations regarding new British playwrights are further revealed in the subsequent enthusiastic responses to Osborne's play toward the end of 1956. But Theatre Workshop's productions of classics, its participation in the two festivals, and its acclaim outside Britain were necessary preliminaries in shaping critical attitudes to the company's productions of contemporary plays.

The change in the company's repertoire, so obviously manifest by 1958, can possibly be attributed to Littlewood, whether alone or in counsel with Raffles and Bury. Although still reliant on the company's newly acquired visibility, Littlewood opted for a repertoire that would correspond to the critics' expectations. By choosing contemporary plays that preserved the company's historical agendas with respect to the playwrights selected, the themes of the plays, and the means of their production, Littlewood devised a mode that would resolve the contradictory

THEATRE ROYAL

ANGEL LANE, STRATFORD, E.15

Licensee and General Manager ... ... GERALD C. RAFFLES

Box Office open from 10.30 a.m.
(Miss Monica Patterson)
Telephone : MARYLAND 5973/4

6/-, 4/6, 3/6, 2/6, Res. : 1/6 Unres.

THEATRE WORKSHOP

presents

The Good Soldier Schweik

adapted from the novel of Jaroslav Hasek by
EWAN MACCOLL

PRODUCED BY
J O A N L I T T L E W O O D

HASEK'S PREFACE

A great epoch calls for great men. There are modest unrecognised heroes, without
Napoleon's glory or his record of achievements. An analysis of their characters would over-
shadow even the glory of Alexander the Great. To-day, in the streets of Prague, you can
come across a man who himself does not realise what his significance is in the history of the
great new epoch. Modestly he goes his way, troubling nobody, nor is he himself troubled
by journalists applying to him for an interview. If you were to ask him his name, he would
answer in a simple and modest tone of voice : " I am Schweik ".

And this quiet, unassuming, shabbily dressed man is actually the good old soldier Schweik ;
that heroic, dauntless man who was the talk of all citizens in the Kingdom of Bohemia when
they were under Austrian rule, and whose glory will not pass away even now that we have a
republic.

I am very fond of the good soldier Schweik, and in presenting an account of his adventures
during the World War, I am convinced that you will all sympathise with this modest,
unrecognised hero. He did not set fire to the temple of the goddess at Ephesus, like that fool
of a Herostratus, merely in order to get his name into the newspapers and the school reading
books.

And that, in itself, is enough.

TUESDAY, OCTOBER 25th, 1955—SATURDAY, NOVEMBER 19th
TUESDAY—FRIDAY 7.45   **SATURDAY 5 30 & 8 30**
Sunday Club, Oct. 30th at 7 p.m.   Discussion, Nov. 4th at 7 p.m.

Program cover of The Good Soldier Schweik, *Theatre Royal, October 25, 1955.*
Courtesy of Theatre Royal Stratford East Archives Collection.

objectives of loyalty to the company's ideology and the achievement of significant critical recognition. Omnipresent financial constraints could also have affected this repertoire shift. In 1955, the year of the Paris festival, the Arts Council had granted the company a very small subsidy of five hundred pounds conditional on the local authority doubling the sum. Although grants from the local authorities were secured in 1956, Theatre Workshop received no substantial funding either from the Arts Council or from local authorities until the 1957–1958 season.

SUCCESS ON A SHOE-STRING:
THE BIND OF CRISIS AND ACCLAIM

Theatre Workshop performed *The Quare Fellow* by the Irish playwright Brendan Behan on May 24, 1956, about two weeks after the English Stage Company's legendary production of John Osborne's *Look Back in Anger*. Behan's play, set in an Irish prison, deals with the last twenty-four hours of a condemned axe-murderer—"a quare fellow"—and with the effect of the death sentence on his fellow prisoners. The play depicts the prisoners' daily existence: the physical restrictions, the tensions, the boredom, the dark humor, and the power relations. Noteworthy among the play's favorable notices is Tynan's review, which praised the playwright's "supreme dramatic achievement," John Bury's sets, and the highly skilled actors. As Joan Littlewood's "best advertisement for Theatre Workshop," Tynan concluded, "*The Quare Fellow* will belong not only in such transient records as this, but in theatrical history."[49] The pronouncement marks the point at which Tynan, already an enthusiastic advocate, becomes a key agent in the promotion of Theatre Workshop and of Littlewood's contribution to the theatre.

In their reviews of *The Quare Fellow*, several reviewers elaborated on the playwright's personal experience, including his eight-year imprisonment for IRA activities, and commented with varying degrees of amusement on the reaction of the many Irishmen present at the production's first night in Stratford. Goorney relates that "when the Irish national anthem was played in the course of the action, half the audience stood to attention," adding that "Brendan became overnight the darling of the media."[50] This media attention was reflected in a televised interview between Malcolm Muggeridge and the playwright Brendan Behan. Mentioned by both Littlewood and Goorney, the appearance of the drunken playwright caused a terrible scandal and generated a great wave of publicity.[51] *The Quare Fellow*, performed on tour outside London, was the second Theatre

THEATRE ROYAL

ANGEL LANE, STRATFORD, E.15

Licensee and General Manager   ...   .   GERALD C. RAFFLES

Box Office open from 10.30 a.m.
(Miss Monica Patterson)
Telephone : MARYLAND 5973/4

6/-, 4/6, 3/6, 2/6, Res. : 1/6 Unres.

THEATRE WORKSHOP

presents

THE ENGLISH PREMIERE OF

THE QUARE FELLOW

A New Play by
BRENDAN BEHAN

PRODUCED BY

JOAN LITTLEWOOD

Early in the morning, the screw was bawling
Get out of bed and clean up your cell.
And that old triangle went jingle, jangle
Along the banks of the Royal Canal.

The screw was peeping at the lag who was sleeping
Weeping as he dreamt of his girl Sal.
And that old triangle went jingle, jangle
Along the banks of the Royal Canal.

In the female prison there are seventy women
I wish that amongst them I did dwell.
Then that old triangle could go jingle, jangle
Along the banks of the Royal Canal.

THURSDAY, MAY 24th at 7 p.m.

afterwards

TUESDAY - FRIDAY 7.45   **SATURDAY 5.30 & 8.30**

Sunday Club, May 27th at 7 p.m.

Program cover of The Quare Fellow, *Theatre Royal, May 24, 1956.*
Courtesy of Theatre Royal Stratford East Archives Collection.

Workshop play to be transferred to the West End. Though lasting some-what longer than the first transfer, it had only a three-month run at the Comedy Theatre, from July to September, 1956. Goorney remarks that the West End transfers became the company's financial salvation.

In July 1956, Theatre Workshop had again participated in the Inter-national Theatre Festival in Paris, performing *The Good Soldier Schweik* without financial support from the British Council. Apparently, the growing critical appreciation for Theatre Workshop's work had had little effect on the attitudes of governmental authorities toward the company. The performance, though less successful than the 1955 productions, was nonetheless one of the highlights of the festival.[52]

During the next two years three new contemporary plays joined The-atre Workshop's primarily classical repertoire.[53] The first, *You Won't Al-ways Be on Top*, written by construction worker Harry Chapman, deals with a day of work on a building site and includes the construction of an entire brick wall during each performance. The October 9, 1957, pro-duction received favorable notices on the whole, although Hobson ex-pressed reservations regarding the naturalistic style. In contrast, Tynan commented that "the extraordinary thing about this production is that it makes ordinariness fascinating. We are always hearing that the era of nat-uralism is over; Miss Littlewood proves that in this country it has never begun." Tynan particularly praised Bury's set, calling it "an astonishing achievement."[54] The production of Chapman's play, however, drew public attention primarily due to the court proceedings that followed the perfor-mance. The company's management was accused of performing a play, or rather particular segments of it, without obtaining permission from the lord chamberlain, whose office required a written script to be submit-ted for any new play. Such rigid censorship rules presented a problem for Theatre Workshop, which relied upon improvisation and changes to the text right up to and often even after the first performance. The funds to finance the company's defense were raised by such prominent figures as the Earl of Harewood, Kenneth Tynan, George Devine, and Peter Hall. Harold Lever, MP, who had been the business manager of Theatre Union in 1938, conducted the company's defense (with Gerald Gardiner, QC) free of charge. Though a minimal fine was imposed on the company for its offence against the censorship law, this case—as well as Theatre Work-shop's battle against censorship in general—contributed to the eventual dismantling of the lord chamberlain's office in 1968.

Major theatre figures recognized Theatre Workshop's attempt to advance its innovative agendas in spite of the difficulties and obstacles posed by governmental authorities, and they often voiced their views in *Encore* magazine, a significant channel of theatrical mediation through the 1950s and 1960s. Theatre Workshop's agendas at this juncture intersected with the underlying policy of *Encore* to encourage new, innovative, and experimental approaches in theatre. Throughout the company's most active years, *Encore* published articles and reviews that advocated, supported, and promoted the group's singular aims and work. Lindsay Anderson, a major film and theatre director, published one in 1957 titled "Vital Theatre" in which he surveyed the state of London theatre and concluded: "Working within the established framework of the West End, upper class theatre, the English Stage Company has accomplished wonders. Yet this framework is also a prison. The Theatre Workshop tries to work outside it; yet the penalty they have to pay, of exclusion, of an audience just as ungrateful, of finally a certain inverted snobbery, is equally frustrating."[55]

After *You Won't Always Be on Top,* the next two contemporary plays performed by Theatre Workshop in 1958 were *A Taste of Honey,* by Shelagh Delaney, and *The Hostage,* by Brendan Behan. Before *A Taste of Honey* appeared, the *Daily Mail* announced Theatre Workshop's discovery of a new talent, Shelagh Delaney, a nineteen-year-old photographer's assistant, formerly a factory worker from Salford. The reporter further revealed that Delaney, who had seen only one play (Rattigan's *Variations on a Theme*) before writing her own, introduced herself to the company's management as "The English Françoise Sagan." In conclusion the reporter quoted Gerry Raffles, the company's general manager, as saying, "Quite apart from its meaty content, we believe we have found a real dramatist." This report reflected the company's new marketing strategy on the one hand, while showing precisely what this strategy endorsed on the other: promotion through the device of "discovery" itself. Retrospectively, the recruitment of Shelagh Delaney for both these ends proved to be effective.

The production of *A Taste of Honey* on May 27, 1958, was unconventional on many levels. In the play, Jo, an eighteen-year-old illegitimate daughter of a former prostitute, is left alone when her mother marries a young upper-class alcoholic. Jo then has an affair with a charming black sailor and becomes pregnant. After the sailor leaves, she finds comfort in the company of a vulnerable, gay art student, who wants to look after her and the baby she is about to have, but who himself leaves upon her mother's return following the break-up of her own marriage. The initial critical response was divided. Most reviews described the production of the play—its fast-paced scenes, black-and-white set, jazz trio, and many asides to the audience in the manner of music hall—as highly stylized, though a few contended that the stylized production did not complement the play's simple realism. Shelagh Delaney, however, became the focus of media attention, which occupied itself with Delaney's factory background and youth.[56]

Some reviewers attacked the playwright's inexperience. Milton Shulman and Edward Goring, for instance, recommended to the young playwright that she see more plays before writing her next one.[57] Most reviews, however, even the less favorable ones, attributed the play's effect primarily to its authenticity and freshness, a direct result of the playwright's youth. Tynan perceived the playwright's inexperience as endowing the play with "the smell of living." "Happily," he further claims, "Miss Delaney does not yet know about us and our squeamishness, which we think moral but is really social. She is too busy recording the wonder of life as she lives it. There is plenty of time for her to worry over words like 'form,' which mean something, and concepts like 'vulgarity' which don't."[58] Most notices, favorable and unfavorable, found the production very well acted. Lindsay Anderson's review explicitly promoted Theatre Workshop's agenda. "To talk as we do about popular theatre, about new working class audience, about plays that will interpret the common experience of today—all this is one thing, and a good thing too," he began. "But how much better, even how much more exciting, to find such theatre suddenly here, suddenly sprung up under our feet!"[59] Anderson went on to suggest another perspective from which to view the young playwright's first play: "One of the most extraordinary things" about it is "its lack of bitterness, its instinctive maturity. This quality was emphasized by Joan Littlewood's production, which seems to me quite brilliant."[60] The production of *A Taste of Honey* was a success and, as Littlewood recounts, "the audience arrived along with agents and newshounds, anxious to get the low-down on this teenage wonder."[61]

A Taste of Honey, one of Theatre Workshop's greater successes, was followed by one of its more acute crises. When the company failed to raise the requisite grants from the local authorities, the Arts Council withdrew its offer of a thousand pounds for 1957–1958. As the Arts Council's annual report for those years notes: "Soon after the reopening of the season it was clear that the company was in serious financial difficulties and

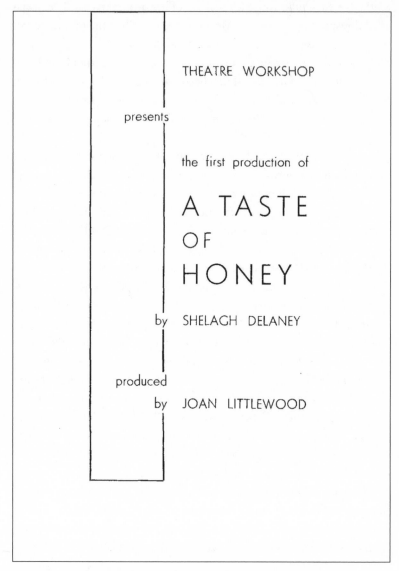

THEATRE WORKSHOP

presents

the first production of

A TASTE
OF
HONEY

by SHELAGH DELANEY

produced
by JOAN LITTLEWOOD

Program cover of A Taste of Honey, *Theatre Royal, May 27, 1958.*
Courtesy of Theatre Royal Stratford East Archives Collection.

discussions between representatives of seven local authorities, the Arts Council and the Company took place in an effort to find a solution to this problem. But no real solution was found and the problem persists more acutely than ever."[62]

Nadine Holdsworth discusses the council's contradictory tendencies toward the company: namely, its acknowledgment of Theatre Workshop's contribution yet its reluctance to provide the company with adequate financial support. In Holdsworth's view, the antiauthoritarian stance and nonaccommodationist conduct of the company, often seen as impertinent, contributed to the suspicious attitude and eventual hostility of financing bodies such as the Arts Council and borough councils.[63]

News of the company's crisis reached the public with the publication in the *Times* on June 26, 1958, of Graham Greene's letter suggesting that he and nine others would contribute a sum amounting to the Arts Council's withdrawn offer.[64] A response from M. J. McRobert, deputy secretary of the Arts Council, appeared two days later, followed by a letter from Littlewood. This correspondence, recounted by Goorney, Littlewood, and Holdsworth in varying detail,[65] calls attention to a particular issue in dispute: whether Theatre Workshop had achieved a viable local audience. The view expressed in the deputy secretary's letter was that during the company's five years at Stratford East, in effect a trial term, it had failed to achieve this aim. This issue ties in with another repeatedly raised with regard to the company in various contexts: the theatre's unfashionable location. The Arts Council—though it officially denied this—had repeatedly urged Theatre Workshop to "move west."[66] Whatever the case, the financial crisis resulted in the closure of the Theatre Royal in July 1958. A note enclosed in the program of *A Taste of Honey* announced that the theatre would reopen in the autumn of 1958 if economic circumstances permitted.[67]

Encore, as might have been anticipated, voiced its support for the company. In a 1958 article, Tom Milne, who was to join Clive Goodwin as coeditor of *Encore* the next year, presented the unique achievement and nature of Theatre Workshop, describing the company's impressive repertoire of seventy plays during its thirteen years of existence, as well as its highly accomplished productions since taking over the Theatre Royal.[68] "In spite of this," Milne asserted, "Theatre Workshop has rarely been able to command a full house in London (although unlike the English Stage Company, the audience it does have is faithful)." Milne did not spare the critics, stressing that when praise is given it is "with an air of surprise that this enfant terrible (a *leftist* enfant) should actually have produced something worthy of mature consideration, needing no excuse or special allowances." Milne explained that attitudes toward Theatre Workshop should be attributed to the company's "double sin," the first being its belief that "the theatre must be in direct contact with life"—a belief that dictated the company's choice of new plays, or rather playwrights, and even worse, the company's "having no respect for the classics as classics." The second resided in its method of work, in particular its belief in the theatrical production as a collective enterprise. Milne referred to the Arts Council's refusal to continue the subsidy under the present conditions and discussed the issue of the theatre's location and the option of a move to another part of town, suggesting that "if Stratford is impossible, perhaps there is much to be said for a move into town, where, provided it could preserve its own qualities intact, Theatre Workshop might begin to impose those qualities on the West End theatre, driving out the Old Vicery, *Dry Rots* and *Touch of the Suns*, and establishing the *Taste of Honey* and *Arden of Favershams*."[69]

The correspondence in the *Times* as well as Milne's explicit support for Theatre Workshop's nontraditional approach and methods, reflect the polar positions elicited by the company's work and rationale. In this case however, the crisis with the financing bodies was resolved. Whether due to public pressure or other factors, the local councils promised increased funding and the Arts Council decided to renew the company's subsidy.[70] The Theatre Royal reopened after three months with the production of Behan's play *The Hostage* on October 14, 1958. A notice in the *Times* announcing the production explained the decision to reopen the theatre as largely due to the expectations generated by the company's meeting with representatives of the local authorities.[71]

If Delaney's script of *A Taste of Honey* had undergone deletions and additions at the hands of Littlewood and the cast, the final script of *The Hostage* was generated over the rehearsal period through a process of collective rewriting by the playwright and the company. Given Behan's fondness for drink, which would eventually lead to his death, the narratives surrounding this process have become part of the theatre's mythology.

In *The Hostage*, set in a Dublin brothel, an English soldier is held by the IRA as hostage for an IRA soldier sentenced to be hanged in Belfast. The hostage is accidentally killed at the time of the hanging. Goorney recalls that "the Saturday night of the first week of *The Hostage* was the first completely full house the company had ever had." The Full House

Theatre Royal
Stratford e.15

the

theatre workshop
presents

produced by
Joan Littlewood

Brendan Behan's

OSTAGE

Program cover of The Hostage, *Theatre Royal, October 14, 1958.*
Courtesy of Theatre Royal Stratford East Archives Collection.

sign unused up to this point, "was to stand outside the theatre many times during the next few years."[72] Most reviews were highly favorable, those by Hobson and Tynan especially so. Hobson referred to the performance "given by the inspired, chuckle-headed, aggravating, devoted and magnificently alive company Theatre Workshop at the Theatre Royal Stratford," describing the play as one which made "the impression of a masterpiece" and was "an honour to our theatre."[73] Tynan enthusiastically stressed the radical and innovative nature of the production, foregrounding its innovativeness through his own self-conscious rhetoric: "Mr. Behan's new (careful now)—Mr. Behan's new play. I use the word advisedly, and have since sacked my advisers—for conventional terminology is totally inept to describe the uses to which Mr. Behan and his director, Joan Littlewood, are trying to put the theatre. The old pigeonholes will no longer serve." He added, "Nor can one be sure of how much of the dialogue is pure Behan and how much is gifted embroidery; for the whole production sounds spontaneous, a communal achievement based on Littlewood's idea of theatre as a place where people talk to people, not actors to audiences." Integrating an explicit promotion of Theatre Workshop's unique aims and contribution, he concluded: "Miss Littlewood's production is a boisterous premonition of something we all want—a biting popular drama that does not depend on hit songs, star names, spa sophistication, or the melodramatic aspects of homosexuality."[74]

It is significant that both Hobson and Tynan exercised their authority as prominent critics to position Theatre Workshop solidly within the theatrical field. Hobson bestowed on the company an honorable standing, while Tynan assigned it a major position by virtue of its innovative nature, allocating it a radical niche instead of one of "the old pigeon-holes." In highlighting the production's radical nature, Tynan was apparently pursuing his agenda to encourage innovative contemporary theatre.

On January 20, 1959, A Taste of Honey was revived with the original cast at Stratford as a run-in for its transfer to the West End—first at the Wyndham Theatre on February 10, 1959, and thereafter at the Criterion Theatre on June 8, 1959. Oscar Lewenstein, who initiated the production's transfer, recounts that when he watched A Taste of Honey he forgave Littlewood the disastrous affair surrounding the Brecht production. Meeting Donald Albery "on the steps of the theatre he owned," Lewenstein told him about the production and added that he wanted to bring it to the West End. Albery went to see the play and subsequently proposed to Lewenstein that they present it together.[75] Littlewood has noted that Albery was "the first West End manager ever to approach [them]."[76] In view of her remark—especially when considering the company's future West End transfers—it is worth mentioning that, according to Goorney, she resisted the demand to recast with star names.[77] In 1959, the production became a London hit and ran for almost a year, experiencing a highly successful run on Broadway. Also that year, Delaney was the focus of press reports elaborating on the playwright's year of success, fame and money.[78] Screen rights were sold to Woodfall, the film company owned by Osborne and Richardson, and the film version, directed by Tony Richardson, came out in 1961.[79]

The next West End transfer for Theatre Workshop was *Fings Ain't Wot They Used t'Be*, by Frank Norman, an ex-convict. Littlewood turned the original script into a musical for which Lionel Bart composed the music and lyrics. Littlewood met Bart through Lewenstein, who had worked with him in Unity Theatre. The musical, opening February 17, 1959, was set in a gambling den in the Soho underworld, full of gamblers, thieves, pimps, and prostitutes. The production was a great success, with a full house throughout most of its seven-week run, but notices were mixed. A few reviewers praised the production on the whole but found the script too thin,[80] while others found it entertaining but not as good as the company's previous productions.[81] Most reviewers mentioned the authenticity of setting and atmosphere, elaborating on Frank Norman's background, as did Croft in a review in the *Observer:* "He has been in the nick, or more properly, in and out of the nick, during a goodly part of his twenty-eight years."[82]

These Theatre Workshop successes rendered visible yet another mode of mediation: press articles about founder-director Joan Littlewood. In March 1959, the *Observer* published a profile that introduced her as a long-term enthusiast who was "becoming accepted as the possessor of one of the most genuine talents in our theatre to-day."[83] The profile highlighted Littlewood's beliefs, in particular her aim "to create in Britain a people's theatre" that informed her innovative approach to theatre practice. She was described as having a "salty vocabulary," an "aggressive disbelief in 'great art,'" and a dislike "of theatre as it is practiced almost everywhere." Her first condition of theatre, freedom, included "freedom from censorship by the Lord Chamberlain's office." Nonetheless, in contrast to the many media profiles of Littlewood that were to come, the

Observer presents her as relatively tame and ends with an accolade: "Few people in the theatre today doubt that Miss Littlewood is among the most brilliant directors now working in Europe." Such press exposure clearly reflects the position Littlewood had attained by 1959, while also reflecting her growing willingness to collaborate with the press. Becoming more evident in the next two years, her use of the press as a public stage enabled her to critique the reluctance of governmental authorities to support her company's work.

A representative of the Arts Council responded to the profile in a letter, published in the *Observer*, specifying that the Arts Council had been the first public body to contribute, in 1954, to the needs of Theatre Workshop, thereafter increasing its help and acting to persuade five local borough councils to grant funding. The letter mentioned the Arts Council's subsequent efforts to secure larger contributions from the borough councils. The *Observer*'s response to the letter referred to the profile's mention of the Arts Council's initial subsidy to the company, stressing "that it was never keen on the location of the theatre, and decided to stop the grant last year, changing its mind only when nine East London councils agreed to increase their subsidies."[84]

Theatre Workshop's production of *The Hostage* represented Britain at the Paris festival, April 3–6, 1959. At this third participation in the festival of Theatre des Nations, the company was provided with financial support by the British Council, in apparent recognition of their status as a formal representative. Nevertheless, in a report on the festival, Leslie Mallory remarked that "at home in Angel Lane, in the East End of London, the 30 young actors and actresses of Theatre Workshop could drop dead for all the British Government would care. Here in Paris they were suddenly somebody. . . . The foreign office . . . sent no handshakers to the airport. Not even a rose for Joan, the producer." Mallory described the company's arrival at the Sarah Bernhardt Theatre where the production was to take place and the festival director's warm reception of Littlewood and Raffles, then noted: "Sir Gladwin Jebb, the British Ambassador, who had turned up after all half-way through the play, congratulated the author."[85] *The Hostage* won first prize as the best production at the festival.

The London press pulled out all the stops to report on the prize and on Littlewood's receiving the 1959 international Olympics Prize for Theatre. This Italian award went to Littlewood for being an "untiring and genial promoter of juvenile forces and new character in the art of theatre." The *Daily Telegraph*'s theatre columnist listed, in addition to the

French and Italian awards, four other awards given to members of the company, the result of the 1959 *Variety* critics' poll.[86] The issue of the Arts Council's withdrawal of the company's grant was not missing from this notice. Gerald Raffles was quoted as attributing the withdrawal of the Art Council's grant to "the prosperity of the group," though the reporter also noted that "negotiations are still in progress."[87] It is worth noting that the Broadway production of *The Hostage* in September 1960 (in which several roles were played by U.S. actors), and in particular the consequent attention the media bestowed on the playwright, Brendan Behan, also received wide coverage by the London press.[88]

In June 1959, following a short-run revival of *The Hostage* at Stratford, Lewenstein and Albery arranged a transfer of the production to the Wyndham Theatre, where it replaced the production of *A Taste of Honey*, which had transferred to the Criterion Theatre after a run of almost a year. *The Hostage* ran from June 11, 1959 to July 18, 1960. Lewenstein remarks that he considered this production "the best Joan did," further commenting that in 1959 he presented four productions in the West End at Albery theatres, three of which were directed by Joan Littlewood.[89]

Littlewood now began "starring" in the press. A broad-canvas article by Robert Hollis, appearing several days before the opening of *The Hostage* in the West End, deserves particular mention.[90] The timing of Hollis's article and his many citations of Raffles on various matters point to its being initiated either by, or in collaboration with, the company's management as a marketing strategy. Titled "The Woman Who Is Shaking Up the Theatre," it centered on Littlewood. Hollis stressed the company's continuous financial struggle and focused on Littlewood's singular and innovative approach to theatre practice, promoting her work by providing a context within which to view her company's accomplishments. He reviewed the company's repertoire of contemporary plays—written by a construction worker (Harry Chapman); a razor-scarred ex-convict (Frank Norman); a "beer swilling Irish playwright" who had served several years in various prisons "as a result of his activities as an IRA terrorist" (Brendan Behan); and a nineteen-year-old Salford girl (Shelagh Delaney)—disclosing through various anecdotes the unorthodox working methods Littlewood brought to each production. Since the success of Behan's and Delaney's plays, Hollis revealed, Littlewood had been bombarded by scripts and by hundreds of actors applying to join the company, yet "the public is so far uncommitted." Finally, Hollis alluded to the contrast between audiences in Stratford and the West End, recounting that soon after *A Taste of Honey* was transferred "one liberal-minded supporter of the company arrived in the second row of the stalls in his shirt sleeves. His neighbours complained to the management. He was politely requested to leave." By tracing the company's recent successes and simultaneously drawing attention to its financial state his article appears to be calling upon the public to endorse a more active and committed stance in support of Theatre Workshop. However, the highlights chosen as well as the anecdotes selected, suggest that the groundwork was also being laid for subsequent narratives of the company's evolution and methods of work.

In July 1959, *Plays and Players'* choice for Personality of the Month was Joan Littlewood. The magazine portrayed her as a rebel, emphasizing her company's continuing "fight against lack of money, public mistrust and official apathy," along with the difficulties the company had yet to overcome. *Plays and Players* chose Alfred Lynch, who had played the title role in Behan's *The Hostage* performed in the West End, as Tomorrow's Lead.

Theatre Workshop's evolution after its production of *The Quare Fellow* thus encompassed a range of mediators, individuals, and organizations, from theatre critics, journalists, and funding bodies to producers and the company manager and director. The various modes of mediation employed by external or in-house mediators included reviews, articles in periodicals and in the press, reports on the company's productions and operation, initiatives of production transfers (exemplified by Lewenstein), interviews on television or in the press, and awards, as well as marketing tactics in press notices and production programs. The company's visibility and reputation developed via such channels as the press, television, theatre magazines, film, production programs, and theatre festivals. Examining these factors against the state of Theatre Workshop at given points in time reveals that the company, as the hostage of divergent forces, managed to attain its position despite its precarious location within a divided theatrical and public terrain.

RESTING ON SHAKY GROUND

The next musical to be produced by Littlewood at Stratford, on October 17, 1959, was *Make Me an Offer* by Wolf Mankowitz, with music and lyrics by Monty Norman and David Henker. Set in Portobello Market, it was produced from the outset as a potential West End transfer, according to Goorney, who notes that few of the company's actors played in the musical, which "was in no way a product of the continuing work of the company," and was therefore "difficult to regard . . . as a Theatre Workshop production."[91] Several of the new actors recruited for the musical however, in particular Sheila Hancock, Wally Patch, Victor Spinetti, and Roy Kinnear, would remain in close contact with Littlewood, collaborating with her in future Theatre Workshop productions. In spite of the tension between Mankowitz, who disliked the changes made to his script, and Littlewood, who rejected his interventions and protests, *Make Me an Offer* was a success. Highly praised by most reviewers,[92] it was transferred after an eight-week run at Stratford East to the Albery Theatre (then the New Theatre), where it received favorable notices and ran for six months.[93] In 1959 it won the *Evening Standard* Drama Award for best musical.

Lewenstein's mediating involvement with the transfer of *Make Me an Offer* ended his collaboration with Littlewood. He recalls that he had turned down the opportunity to transfer *Fings Ain't Wot They Used t'Be* in collaboration with Donald Albery partly because he did not like it as much as the company's other productions—in whose transfers he was involved—but primarily because he felt that "Joan herself was very ambivalent about the transfers, complaining that they broke up her company."[94]

The section relating to the company in the Arts Council's annual report for 1958–1959, begins: "Theatre Workshop has sprung from the direst straits to considerable success in rather less than a year." With reference to the previous year's crisis:

> The Arts Council was concerned by the company's failure to attract sufficient local support and decided to discontinue its own grants unless the neighbouring local authorities would offer much more effective help than they were giving. Eventually ten local authorities agreed to take part in discussion with the Arts Council on the future of this company, of which nine were persuaded to increase, and in some cases double, their support in 1958/59. The company's fortunes were also happily turned by the success of its productions of *A Taste of Honey,* by Shelagh Delaney, *The Hostage,* by Brendan Behan, and *Fings Ain't Wot They Used t'Be,* by Frank Norman, all of which received a great deal of publicity and drew the town to such an extent that two have been successfully transferred to the West End, and the third is on its way.[95]

It should be mentioned that 10 percent of the profits made by the successful transfers of *A Taste of Honey* to the West End and to Broadway, as well as of the sale of the film rights, went to the Arts Council. Raffles tried without success to negotiate with the council to reduce the sum. Although the council's acknowledgment of the company's success was reflected by the appointment of John Bury as a member of the Drama Panel in 1960,[96] the council's subsidy granted to Theatre Workshop for the 1959–1960 season remained a mere 1000 pounds. In contrast, the Arts Council subsidy to the English Stage Company that year was 5000 pounds, down from 5500 pounds awarded to them for the previous season.[97] Toward the end of 1959 Theatre Workshop invested some of its remaining profits in essential repairs and renovations to the Theatre Royal.

The Arts Council's tight-fisted policy toward Theatre Workshop contrasts with the critical acclaim acquired by the company at this stage of its development, the appreciative assessments of its singular contribution by major theatre periodicals (such as *Plays and Players* and *Encore*), and the continuous press coverage of the company's successes. By 1959, however, divergent forces from within were further threatening the company's contested position in the theatrical/cultural arena. Of the period when three Theatre Workshop productions were playing simultaneously in the West End, Littlewood complains: "I had to spend my time running from one to the other reviving tired performances, playing all sorts of tricks to combat the artist's deadly enemy—slowness, milking the part. Mounting a show is easier than keeping it alive. Success was going to kill us."[98]

The Arts Council's attitude toward Theatre Workshop, as well as Littlewood's own assessments, clarify that although the company had achieved the critical recognition and acclaim it sought, its other aspirations—financial and artistic stability—remained out of reach. Rather than resting on its laurels, the company still stood on shaky grounds. It had now entered a closed circuit that called for a complete change of policy rather than further accommodation. Goorney's account of *Make Me an Offer* (a tellingly double-edged title), produced as a potential West End transfer with few of the company's own actors, suggests how Littlewood may have sought to resolve the impasse between relying on permanent ensemble work and achieving financial stability. By producing a musical intended for transfer that relied on imported actors, the company's continuity of work, already disrupted, could have been maintained to some extent. But Littlewood would not choose this path, possibly because it implied further compromise of her commitment to noncommercial theatre. It would not be long before the Theatre Workshop paid the price for this commitment.

In the meantime, at the beginning of 1960, another West End transfer—*Fings Ain't Wot They Used t'Be*—was on its way. This production, received rave reviews and the *Evening Standard* Award for the best musical of 1960.[99] After it had run for a year, the lord chamberlain ordered twenty cuts in the script, an intervention that received wide press coverage.[100] The play went on to complete a two-year run at the Garrick Theatre, February 11, 1960 to February 18, 1962.

Nadine Holdsworth claims, "West End success was not only creatively detrimental, but financially disabling." Discussing the company's no-win situation as revealed in the minutes of a meeting of representatives of the local council on March 4, 1960, she reconstructs the figures showing the company's supposed profitability, which resulted in the withdrawal of local authority support.[101]

AN AFFLICTED COMPANY

Theatre Workshop revisited the Paris festival in 1960 with the production *Every Man in His Humour* by Ben Jonson, June 27–30. Three days before the company was to leave, Victor Spinetti, the lead role, announced that he would not be able to join them due to his commitment to another show. There was also a problem with the set.[102] In spite of these obstacles, the Theatre Workshop production received favorable notices at the festival, though when the play was performed later at Stratford East the notices were less favorable.[103]

In August, the company produced *Sparrers Can't Sing* written by actor and former bricklayer Stephen Lewis, about a street in the East End. A great success at Stratford, it ran for only two months when transferred to Wyndham's Theatre. Goorney claims that the characters, "deeply rooted in the East End" where Lewis had lived all his life, "did not appeal to the more sophisticated taste of the West End audience."[104]

Critics and audiences alike panned Theatre Workshop's production of *We're Just Not Practical* in January 1961, an adapted stage version of Marvin Kane's television play about the bad luck of a young couple working as housekeepers in a boardinghouse. The playwright, an American writer living in London who blamed the failure of the play on changes made to the script by Littlewood and the company's cast, expressed his protest in the press. Tom Hutchinson, in the *Daily Express*, cited the playwright's critique of the actors' improvisations during rehearsals: "The whole play was going off in a completely different direction." The playwright also complained that after Littlewood attacked his suggestions, she said it would be better if he didn't attend any more rehearsals. Kane criticized the production, stating that "the audience was kind. I felt like offering their money back." He concluded: "No wonder the critics panned it. But it wasn't my play." Hutchinson defended Littlewood by citing the praise that playwrights Behan and Delaney had for her, as well as dramatist Alun Owen's statement that he had had no complaints. Hutchinson's article concluded with Raffles's explanations that Kane and his wife "were only asked to leave rehearsals when their presence proved unhelpful" and that although Kane could not break his contract, he could "have his name taken off the playbills and his original script back" if he wanted.[105] David Nathan's *Daily Herald* article on Littlewood answered Kane's public attack by describing Littlewood as "one of the world's most brilliant and unorthodox producers." Nathan quoted Littlewood's admission that the new show was a disaster but that the company was still working on it, and further that most of the playwrights with whom she collaborated worked like journalists in that "they can write as we go along," but "with Mr. Kane, this was not possible." Nathan concluded: "Miss Littlewood has done too much great work for the theatre to be accused of being unfair to writers. But she must pick her playwrights more carefully in the future."[106]

Littlewood left for Berlin soon after *We're Just Not Practical* was produced, returning after six months to direct *They Might Be Giants* by James Goldman, a U.S. playwright. This fantasy about a former judge who believes he is Sherlock Holmes was produced in association with Robert E. Griffith and Harold S. Prince, the latter the U.S. producer and director of *West Side Story*.[107]

Goorney retells the events surrounding the opening night of *They Might Be Giants*, June 28, 1961, disclosing the tension behind the scenes. Littlewood, who believed in long periods of rehearsal and continuous work on productions throughout their run, was expected to have the production ready after a relatively short rehearsal period. She wished to postpone the opening night but was overruled by Harold Prince, who had invited Princess Margaret; the press too was due to arrive. The production, opening as scheduled, was unfavorably received, notwithstanding the critics' praise of Bury's set. Most reviewers directed their attack primarily at the producer-director, Joan Littlewood. Milton Shulman, for example, remarked that "even more disturbing than the juvenilia of the symbolism is the gauche and awkward manner in which Joan Littlewood has directed this odd offering."[108] Ronald Hastings found that "Joan

Littlewood's surprisingly clumsy production and much of the playing did not help us to follow the author through his changing moods and dramatic styles."[109] And a *Times* reviewer noted that the play, "workable enough in itself," was nonetheless "completely destroyed by a totally unsuitable production."[110]

In her recollection of this play Littlewood remarks that the initial script "presented many problems set-wise, and the author was uncompromising. . . . Unfortunately, the company was already in love with the damn play and there was that financial backing." According to various accounts, she greatly believed in *They Might Be Giants* and expressed her disappointment at the critics' disapproval: "At first, I raged against the critics, then I gave them up. London was finished anyway. We could do better anywhere else. We couldn't do worse."[111]

All of Theatre Workshop's productions during the 1960s were undermined by problems inherent in the state of the company at the time. Many of the actors were also committed elsewhere rather than devoting themselves solely to the ensemble. Moreover, theatrical offerings about the East End, while strictly in line with the company's professed concerns, held little appeal for a West End audience. Littlewood had lost the freedom to determine the length of a production's preparation process and was pressured into scheduling opening night according to extraneous demands. It became increasingly difficult to bridge the company's former agendas and the pressures now ensuing after eight years in London. Furthermore, given that the grants awarded to the company were clearly inadequate for its needs, no solution seemed forthcoming.[112]

The process of critical recognition and subsequent growing appreciation of Theatre Workshop's unique contribution to theatre corresponded with a gradual shift of attention to Littlewood herself. The company's great success with Behan's and Delany's plays had led the media to shift these playwrights to center stage, possibly as a result of the company's marketing strategies. However, in 1959, with three of the company's productions running simultaneously in the West End, Littlewood became the primary source of attraction. The preoccupation with her would mushroom in the years to come, underlying the attitudes to the company's subsequent development.

The evolution of Joan Littlewood as a phenomenon was the subject of an article published in the July-August issue of *Encore* in 1960.[113] "Working with Joan," consisted primarily of actors recounting their experience of collaborating with Littlewood throughout various phases of her career.

Especially relevant to the present context is the article's framing. The authors, Clive Goodwin and Tom Milne—coeditors of *Encore*—introduced Littlewood as someone "who after fifteen years in the wilderness, has changed the face of London's West End, and *forced acceptance on her own terms.*" Their account reviewed the process of Theatre Workshop's acceptance by critics and audience, shifting between her and the company. "The breakthrough proper began with the success of Brendan Behan's *The Quare Fellow*, and the ground gained was consolidated by the runaway triumph of *A Taste of Honey*. At last London was waking up to the fact that a home-grown genius was sitting on the doorstep. *The Hostage, Make Me an Offer* and *Fings Ain't Wot They Used t'Be* followed in rapid succession. Theatre Workshop was in." Describing the powerful effect of these productions on their audiences, Goodwin and Milne noted that "people began to talk about this fresh and robust style. How did she do it? What were her methods? The curiosity spread to the profession. . . . The myth snowballed."[114] Littlewood's move to the center, according to these authors, had thus been a direct consequence of the company's success. Several citations from the closing paragraph clarify the authors' intent: "The group and the training of the group—these are the things most important to her. . . . Now her actors are scattered over four different theatres. Other ex-members are off in the world of television and films. A re-gathering of forces seems commercially impossible. We already have a long and disgraceful record for the neglect of genius in this country. But in this case there is still time, brother, there is still time." The article concluded: "Of course in any sensible community, the Government would stand up and say to Joan 'Look, here's a handsome subsidy, go and do what you want to do,' and she would build a theatre group that would make London the envy of the world."[115]

Encore's support neither activated public pressure nor convinced the government to approach Littlewood. In 1961, facing a dead-end, Littlewood decided to leave the company. Although the press notices stated that her departure was temporary, her decision caused a sensation.

MEDIA AFTER THE FACT

The massive media coverage of Littlewood's departure is hardly surprising considering the position she had acquired by that time. Press reports such as the ones entitled "Genius Quits" (*Reynolds News*) and "Blow to the Theatre from Our Leading Director" (*Stage*), which paid her tribute and lamented the great loss to British theatre, indeed confirm that Littlewood's reputation as a director, established on the achievements of Theatre Workshop, had come to be seen on its own terms. Littlewood exploited the opportunity, using the various media to state her views in general and the reasons motivating her departure in particular. She expressed her frustration and rage in a blunt, unrestrained fashion, further cultivating her image as a provocative rebel possessed of genius who challenged the authorities, the establishment, tradition, and theatrical conventions. In an interview with Malcolm Muggeridge on Granada Television, Littlewood blamed her departure on "the old ladies who run the Arts Council, sipping their teas and deciding what is good for people." She claimed she could not work with the "dozens of West End managers looking over [her] shoulders. They grab my actors."[116] Littlewood's accusations against the Arts Council and her rage and frustration regarding the critics' dismissive notices of *They Might Be Giants*—the Workshop's most recent production—repeatedly appeared in press notices covering her resignation.

Many press reports of the angry and puzzled reactions of members of the company and of others who had worked with Littlewood attempted to present her viewpoint in a way that would justify her decision.[117] In particular, the press dwelled upon Littlewood's inner conflict born out of the company's golden phase, for example, her 1961 statement that she found herself in "an impossible position, a sort of rope being tugged between commercialism and real theatre."[118] She was described as becoming increasingly worried and upset by the course of action forced on the management of Theatre Workshop by economic circumstances beyond her control, in addition to being continuously tortured by self-critical doubts when she compared the company's work with what she perceived as its much better work during the early years. In other words, these reports suggested, what was at stake in the decision were Littlewood's beliefs and agendas, since the company's financial constraints and the wish of her actors and writers to raise their earnings to a position of equality with their colleagues elsewhere, an aspiration with which she sympathized, compelled her to work contrary to her principles. One cannot help recalling Goorney's interpretation of Raffles's considerations in advocating the move to Stratford East: namely, to provide Littlewood with more suitable working conditions. Recognition of the success of Theatre Workshop was almost always bound up with a reference to the unfashionable location of the Theatre Royal.

The news of Littlewood's departure surprised the company's remaining members and others who had worked with her, the press reported.

Most journalists predicted that her departure would bring about the end of Theatre Workshop. Goorney reviews the responses of several company members, including John Bury—"We'd burned ourselves out"—and remarks on the willingness of several members to rebuild the company. He references Littlewood's great fatigue, suggesting that she had not consulted the company before announcing her decision. If Goorney's description of other, less significant, events in the company's evolution offers an engaged account, which at times includes his judgment and commentary, his manner when recounting Littlewood's departure is remote. Refraining from judgment or accusations, Goorney reports that, "following a season of visiting companies, Oscar Lewenstein took over the lease of the theatre in November 1961."[119]

In interview titled "Littlewood and After," published in *Reynolds News* on March 3, 1962 just prior to the opening of the spring program at Stratford East, Lewenstein said he had discussed his move to the Theatre Royal with Littlewood and emphasized that he wanted his "policy to be in line with her tradition."[120] Considering Lewenstein's expertise as a mediator and his familiarity with the field, his pronounced respect for the company's founder and former director also reflects both his attempt to advance the season after Littlewood—by virtue of his new function as an in-house mediator for Theatre Workshop—and his anticipation of the company's diminished appeal due to her departure.

Littlewood, exploiting the various channels of the media to express her anger and protest, did not overlook her debt to *Encore*, which had consistently voiced its support of the company's work. Her letter, titled "Goodbye Note from Joan," was published in the September 1961 issue. She addressed *Encore* writers directly, noting that they had "always given serious consideration to the problems facing people working in the English theatre," restating her primary beliefs, and explaining the reasons motivating her departure. She responded indirectly to various issues regarding her company that had been raised in articles published in *Encore* through the years, writing, for instance: "My objective in life has not changed; . . . I do not believe in the supremacy of the director, designer, actor or even of the writer. It is through collaboration that this knockabout art of theatre survives and kicks. . . . Each community should have a theatre; the West End plundered our talent and diluted our ideas; cannot each district afford to support a few artists who will give them back some entertainment, laughter and love of mankind?"[121]

In "The Breakthrough That Broke Down," Tynan questioned the

breakthrough in theatre that he himself had identified several years earlier. Reviewing the state of the theatre in the fall of 1961, he presented Theatre Workshop's unfulfilled promise and Littlewood's departure as further confirmation of his viewpoint.[122]

CELEBRATED RETURN/DEPARTURE?

Two years later, Littlewood returned to the Theatre Royal, Stratford. The enormous success of Theatre Workshop's musical satire of World War I, *Oh What a Lovely War* on March 19, 1963, celebrated her return. Many notices explicitly welcomed her back. Bernard Levin, for example, exclaimed: "She's back! For far too long Miss Littlewood, the Mother Courage of Theatre Workshop, has been away from home."[123] Another reviewer, Ronald Hastings, asserted that "the air of excitement was there once more."[124]

Oh What a Lovely War was inspired by Charles Chilton's 1961 radio program "A Long Long Trail." Raffles, as various accounts testify, had first broached the idea. The complex compositional process of the musical, as well as its source materials, pose issues much discussed and debated among scholars.[125] In his glowing review of the production for *Encore*, Charles Marowitz, critic, playwright, director, and coeditor of the magazine,[126] called attention to the immense theatrical innovation of the show. "Stylistically," he claimed, "the show is an astounding achievement, for it creates a context which accommodates—naturally and without strain—a number of different and often antithetical styles." He described the show as the culmination of Theatre Workshop's explorations over the years, for "the technique which produced this result grew out of the Living Newspaper productions of the thirties, the English Music Hall in its pre-war heydays, the satirical reviews of the early Unity Theatre, the Pierrot tradition of the English seaside resorts, the socialistic convictions of the Manchester school (the city where Littlewood began), and the tardy influences of Piscator and Brecht." Comparing Theatre Workshop's *Oh What a Lovely War* to works produced by the Royal Shakespeare Company and by the National Theatre Company, he proclaimed: "Joan Littlewood's company is the only experimental aggregation in the country. . . . Littlewood is finding the really creative way of saying things because, of all English producers, she is the one with most to say. The equation here is obvious, but it can never be said too often."[127]

The press coverage of the production's success included a report on Princess Margaret and the Earl of Snowdon attending the play and on

THEATRE ROYAL E 15

a musical entertainment based on an idea of Charles Chilton
designed by John Bury

'OH WHAT A LOVELY WAR'

Program cover of Oh What a Lovely War, *Theatre Royal, March 19, 1963.*
Courtesy of Theatre Royal Stratford East Archives Collection.

offers from at least ten theatre managers for *Oh What a Lovely War*.[128] After a four-week run at Stratford the show was transferred to the Wyndham Theatre, where it ran for a year. In 1963, it shared the prize for best production at the Paris festival with the Royal Shakespeare Company's production of *King Lear*, directed by Peter Brook. In 1964 *Oh What a Lovely War* was performed in Philadelphia and thereafter in New York, running for six months on Broadway. It was performed in East and West Germany in 1965, and in 1969 came the film version, directed by Richard Attenborough, in his debut as a film director, with a cast that included Dirk Bogarde, John Gielgud, Laurence Olivier, Michael Redgrave, Vanessa Redgrave, Ralph Richardson, and Maggie Smith. The film was received favorably by most critics,[129] and became a box-office success.

Theatre Workshop's *Oh What a Lovely War* was the company's most successful and influential production,[130] widely revered as its most revolutionary and greatest achievement. There were dissonant voices too, however. Among them was Chilton's accusation regarding changes made in the posters and program after the play had proven a success, in particular his claim that Littlewood's name had been "given prominence over his own in publicity."[131] The acclaimed Frances Cuka, one of the company's actresses, recalled her shock at the changes made to the play's ending to accommodate the production to West End "taste."[132] But most decisive was MacColl's perception of the company's West End production as representing "the climax of a long period of betrayal of the original aim of Theatre Workshop to create a theatre for working people."[133]

MacColl's critique is hardly surprising, considering his earlier uncompromising attitude, yet for all its success, *Oh What a Lovely War* also marked a detrimental turn in the company's developmental trajectory.[134] In line with the tendency that had dogged the Theatre Workshop throughout its first decade at Stratford East, the company's greatest success was once again followed by a series of severe crises. Its ongoing struggle with financing bodies resulted in an artistic instability that seeped through to the level of in-house dynamics. The immense success of *Oh What a Lovely War* did not change the Arts Council's attitude. In fact, their reluctance to increase Theatre Workshop's subsidy for its 1964–1965 season discouraged the company from applying for a grant. For the next seven years, Theatre Workshop received no financial support from the Arts Council.[135] During those same seven years, the grant awarded to the English Stage Company was increased from 32,500 pounds to 99,596 pounds. In addition to financial struggles, Theatre Workshop also battled against censorship.[136] And, in 1970 a development scheme by the Newham authorities threatened the Theatre Royal with demolition. Due to these external forces, the company gradually lost the cohesiveness provided by a unified inner structure. Cast members continued to commit to non-Theatre Workshop plays, as they had done through the company's "golden phase"[137] and especially during Littlewood's absence, a practice that damaged the company's continuity of work and eventually resulted in varying casts from play to play.

Although involved in several of the company's subsequent productions, Littlewood[138] gradually withdrew from the theatre and concentrated instead on her project of creating Fun Palace.[139] Intended as a popular center of activities, learning, and entertainment centered on the arts and sciences, the Fun Palace was an outgrowth of Littlewood's and Theatre Workshop's socio-cultural agenda. According to Goorney, however, Littlewood's close colleagues John Bury and Gerry Raffles neither believed in this project nor offered their support. Trustees for the Fun Palace Trust were Buckminster Fuller, the Earl of Harewood, Lord Ritchie Calder, Yehudi Menuhin, and Littlewood herself. Holdsworth concludes that she "had evidently learnt from the experience of English Stage Company, and hoped that prestigious trustees would convince the institutions to support this radical cultural enterprise."[140] Due to funding difficulties that were in part the result of local and institutional objections, Littlewood abandoned this project in 1970.

Nevertheless, she appears to have learned the power of mediation, partially through her experience with the company's transfers to the West End. Her exploitation of the media channels upon her departure in 1961 suggests a transformed attitude. "The West End Littlewood is a different animal," Marowitz noted in *Plays and Players* in 1965. "She has not only learned the Impresarios' game; she has beaten them at it. Her independent control over *Lovely War* in the face of countless offers was a major coup."[141] He concludes: "Given a choice between a Super Arts Council loaded to the point of hernia with 150 million pounds, and Joan Littlewood working with a handful of under-nourished actors in an open lorry, I, with a confident perversity, would unhesitatingly choose the latter."[142] But considering the company's state of affairs through the decade following *Oh What a Lovely War*, Littlewood's decision to decamp appears inevitable.

Littlewood directed her last production at Stratford in 1973, thereafter leaving the Theatre Royal. In the view of actors who had worked with her for many years, during this final period "the theatre was being run on anarchic and immature lines, and Stratford as an area no longer held joys for Joan Littlewood."[143] Gerry Raffles resigned from Theatre Workshop in 1974 and died the next year while on holiday in Vienne, France. In 1976 Littlewood left for France, never to resume her theatrical career. And in 1978, in a final closing note, the name Theatre Workshop was dropped from the Theatre Royal.

REIGNING (FOR A TIME)

Nadine Holdsworth remarks that "Littlewood, exhausted by the continual battle to secure institutional recognition for her work, ironically retired from British theatre at the moment when her unique contribution to performance training, creative working processes, and dynamic theatre products was being acknowledged by a new generation of theatre workers."[144] This belated recognition had no effect on Theatre Workshop's fate, but voices emerging out of critical and historical accounts decades later would alter, in retrospect, the judgment of the company's position.

Critic John Russell Taylor, who served as a cultural (external) mediator, is perhaps the key figure in the battle of accounts that followed. The first edition of his study was published in 1962, after Littlewood's first departure, and the revised edition was published in 1969, after Theatre Workshop's production of *Oh What a Lovely War* but before Littlewood's final withdrawal from the theatre. Given Taylor's intention to introduce, present, and advance a view regarding new figures in the changing theatrical scene—primarily playwrights and second-order "producers, directors, impresarios, and policy-makers"—his study develops a narrative that exemplifies yet another channel through which a mediatory mode may be explored. His book, subtitled *A Guide to the New British Drama*, identifies the 1956 production of *Look Back in Anger*—performed by the English Stage Company (Royal Court)—as the significant turning point marking a new era in British theatre. But, he acknowledges: "If the Royal Court unmistakably took the lead in the field of new drama with *Look Back in Anger*, it was not long before a rival appeared on the scene," the rival being Behan's *The Quare Fellow* produced at the Theatre Royal, Stratford. Taylor describes Theatre Workshop in its pre-Stratford phase as "Joan Littlewood and a small band of fellow enthusiasts," summing up those years as "a wandering on-and-off sort of life on tour in Wales, the industrial north and elsewhere." Since his main topic is new dramatic writing, Taylor deals primarily with the new playwrights that Littlewood encouraged and her singular "free" approach to texts.[145] "Of all the producers and directors intimately connected with the staging of the new dramatists," he claims, "Joan Littlewood has had the most far-reaching effect on the actual texts we know on the stage and in volume form."[146]

Although Taylor presents Littlewood as a new force on the theatrical scene, he pays little attention to her theatrical innovations as a director, clearly reflected in her productions of classics. With respect to the company's productions before *The Quare Fellow*, he downplays the "series of political journalistic pieces by Ewan MacColl," mentioning in passing that "it was generally agreed that its best work was done with classical revivals . . . and staging of modern classics.[147] Even if Taylor's scanty presentation of the company's productions of classics can be explained by his study's focus on new drama, his downgrading of its early work is significant, especially in light of Marowitz's review of the production of *Oh What a Lovely War*, which presented this work as an innovative new dramatic form born of the company's experimentation throughout the years.

Although Taylor discusses in detail the plays of Brendan Behan and Shelagh Delaney, Theatre Workshop's "new playwrights," he underplays both Littlewood's overall contribution and Theatre Workshop's role in the changing landscape of British theatre. He views Littlewood's effect as a short-lived phenomenon in British theatre: "Her actors are dispersed, her theatre taken over by others, and only some uniquely exciting memories and a couple of, after all, rather remarkable plays remain to commemorate the splendours of Stratford E."[148] Even though Taylor's perspective of Theatre Workshop as a passing phenomenon can be seen as grounded in the company's reduced state from the mid-1960s on, and granted his study's declared intention to focus on new playwrights, the selective nature of his account is nonetheless striking. Because new dramas and authors matter to him, Taylor's account suppresses Theatre Workshop's radical left-wing orientation and agendas, advocated repeatedly in *Encore* and promoted by prominent critics, notably Tynan. Absent from Taylor's account too are the company's visits to the Paris International Festival, the critical acclaim it won outside Britain, and its ongoing financial struggle, especially with respect to Arts Council subsidies.

Taylor explains that "to understand precisely why Joan Littlewood's departure should set up such a violent reaction, one must look a little more closely at her company and its policy."[149] In this way Taylor deflected from the start any consideration of the financial difficulties that had played a crucial role in the development and demise of Littlewood's theatrical career and the developmental course of Theatre Workshop itself. His views run exactly counter to Littlewood's own, stated in her television interview with Malcolm Muggeridge, in which she related her departure directly to the company's financial struggles: "For the past few years I have had dozens of West End managers breathing down my neck. The money from the West End was put into Stratford but we can pack the Theatre Royal to the roof and still cannot make it pay. I cannot accept any more a situation where I am unable to work with a company freely."[150] Taylor also chooses to overlook the press coverage of Littlewood's departure, such as the *Daily Mail* headline announcing: "Curtain Down! Joan Littlewood quits Theatre Workshop and blames 'the enemy with money.'"[151] Consistent with his intention to concentrate on new dramas and playwrights, however, he neither omits Wolf Mankowitz's objections to changes made in his script, nor ignores the press coverage of Marvin Kane's disgust with Theatre Workshop's production of his play as being "a travesty of his original intentions."[152]

Taylor's study, on the one hand, and the media coverage of Littlewood's departure in 1961 exemplified by the television interview and press articles, on the other, offer another illustration of the divergence in the mediators' views of Littlewood and Theatre Workshop. Taylor's take on the transient nature of the company's effect also diverges from the views held by other prominent critics, such as Tynan and Hobson, and by dominant theatrical figures such as Anderson and Marowitz, all of whom recognized Littlewood as a highly influential theatre director and perceived Theatre Workshop's innovative work as far-reaching in its influence. Taylor's view of the English Stage Company, founded in the mid-1950s and operating around the same period as Theatre Workshop—remembering that the 1969 edition of his study was published before Theatre Workshop's final demise—appears in sync with the attitudes of governmental authorities. Lionized by Taylor in his book, the English Stage Company was posited as the theatrical company that revolutionized British theatre and won the establishment's ever-growing support.

But Taylor's was not the only voice in evidence. In 1963 Kenneth Tynan chaired an International Drama Conference at the Edinburgh Festival, assembling such major theatrical figures as Peter Brook, Joan Littlewood, Harold Pinter, John Osborne, Eugene Ionesco, Lillian Hellman, Wole Soyinka, and Joan Plowright.[153] A year later, Tynan would introduce

Littlewood as "the most original and unpredictable director in British theatre today" and discuss the talk she had delivered at the conference in light of her singular beliefs and theatre practice. He also promoted her conception of the Fun Palace and highlighted her overall radical approach, predicting that "when the annals of the British theatre in the middle years of the twentieth century come to be written, Joan's name will lead all the rest."[154]

It was, however, Taylor's view of Theatre Workshop, not Tynan's, that reigned—for a time at least—over the story of British theatre in the 1950s and early 1960s, as the critical accounts and historical narratives of British theatre published in the following two decades reflect. Where the convergence of Tynan's and Taylor's viewpoints had been a major factor in the perception of *Look Back in Anger* as a breakthrough, their conflicting views in the case of Theatre Workshop manifest the split in the theatrical/cultural terrain. Indeed, the divergence of mediating forces underlying the evolution of Theatre Workshop outlived the company's existence and survived until the 1990s.

The evolution of Theatre Workshop, from its roots to its demise, demonstrates the interactions between a unified company and divergent external mediating forces. The company's developmental course displays its resolute and unchanging commitment to its radical agenda in the face of the continued indifference of funding bodies, combined with the pressure of internal modification and accommodation, concomitant with a growing critical acclaim.

In view of its decline between 1965 and 1975, it is perhaps worth recalling that the contrasting attitudes toward the company were already in evidence during the first year of its existence. Dan Rebellato's 1999 study recounts the attempts made to influence the Arts Council's policy toward Theatre Workshop as early as the mid 1940s. He details the many recommendations from major public figures, "an illustrious delegation to the Arts Council," and "a series of glowing endorsements in the theatre press," all of which had failed to impress the Arts Council.[155] Throughout the years of Theatre Workshop's existence, the Arts Council's policy toward it proved unchanging, despite the company's increasing reputation, thereby deepening the division within the cultural arena. Critical recognition, high acclaim, press coverage, awards, and even popularity with the audience had little effect on the council's funding policies. But the case of Theatre Workshop also demonstrates that financial backing is by no means a sufficient condition in itself to determine a company's fate, unless the backing is consonant with the company's ethos and agendas. The West End successes of Theatre Workshop that saved the company in the short term eventually led to its demise. Unwilling to move from Stratford East, maintaining a cheap seats policy and a repertoire of plays that critiqued the existing system, Theatre Workshop's aims and agendas were anti-establishment. Though compromised to some extent by the need to survive, these agendas constituted its raison d'être and were not subject to further negotiation. It seems certain that if the cultural developments taking place in the East End through the 1980s and 1990s—specifically the plan for opening a new Performing Arts Center in Stratford East in 1999—had occurred three decades earlier, Theatre Workshop could have embarked on a completely different course. Prominent critics advocating the company's causes were not enough to counteract the opposing forces. The critical evaluations of the company's achievements, however, laid the foundation for later scholarly assessments of the contribution of Theatre Workshop.

VOICES OFF: THE PENDULUM SWINGS

Joan Littlewood is a genius, a Cockney bastard who transformed British drama. Her Theatre Workshop was one of the boldest attempts to create a people's theatre, the first of its kind since Shakespeare.... The authorities feared her, the Arts Council snubbed her and the BBC banned her as a communist and refused her entry when she arrived to record a radio play. Now she is 80 and they all revere her.— Times, 1995

In the 1960s, partly because of the influential writings of John Russell Taylor, many observers felt that the English Stage Company was the most innovative theatre company in England. This perception was based upon four major factors: the correspondence between the ESC aims and the emergent expectations of critics; the reputation of the ESC artistic director, George Devine; the association of the Royal Court's playwrights with the highly publicized Angry trend; and the acclaim and fame of *Look Back in Anger* and its author, John Osborne. By the 1990s, however, scholarly assessment of modern British theatre had shifted its evaluation. Many scholars, including Derek Paget, Stephen Lacey, Dan Rebellato, and Dominic Shellard, had concluded that Theatre Workshop had actually been a far more innovative company than the ESC.

Scholarly accounts of British theatre published in the 1970s and 1980s demonstrate the assessments of the two companies and their key productions that emerged in the two decades following Taylor's *Anger and After*.[156]

John Elsom's 1976, *Post-War British Theatre* provides a more complete account than Taylor's of the singular contribution of Theatre Workshop and of its evolution. Elsom describes the "particular gifts" of the ensemble since its early and trying years at Stratford-atte-Bowe. He emphasizes that Behan's *The Quare Fellow* was first performed in the same month as Osborne's *Look Back in Anger*.[157] He notes Littlewood's singular directing style and claims that she "began to stimulate a new tradition of British theatre."[158] Elsom's concise discussion of Theatre Workshop recounts its founding, its production of classics through the early years, and its financial difficulties that led to its crisis in 1961, the year of Littlewood's first departure.[159] The production of *Oh What a Lovely War*, Elsom believes, set an example that "encouraged the growth of local 'documentaries' in Britain," a genre, that "became particularly popular in the late 1960s" and that "remains Littlewood's great contribution to British theatre."[160] Elsom's highlighting of the contribution of *Oh What a Lovely War* no doubt affected the studies that were to follow, yet Elsom, like Taylor, claims that "the revival of post-war British theatre was substantially due to the group of writers and directors who gathered around George Devine; while the spring board from which the English stage company dived into the cold and treacherous waters of sponsoring new plays was *Look Back in Anger*."[161]

Ronald Hayman's 1979 *British Theatre since 1955* offers a critical survey of theatrical achievements since 1955's London premiere of *Waiting for Godot*. Hayman refers to Littlewood's unconventional dramatic work, her "most strenuous and serious attempt to create a theatre for the people," and the Arts Council's reluctance to help her company.[162] He stresses Littlewood's innovative approach as a theatre director, focusing in particular on her production of *Oh What a Lovely War*, which "represents a turning point in the history of the English theatre." For corroboration he cites Charles Marowitz's 1963 review in *Encore* magazine.[163] Littlewood, Hayman asserts, "must be recognized as the great pioneer of the growing collaborative flexibility we now enjoy. In the early Sixties she was the only important director in England to allow actors to contribute creatively to a text."[164] Hayman's reassessment advances the view of the "new era." He presents Jimmy Porter in *Look Back in Anger* as "the paragon of articulacy in contemporary British drama," but regrets that this play "has dated rather badly, partly because of its topical references."[165] Still, he elaborates on John Osborne's innovations as a dramatist, such as his use of monologues.[166]

Taylor's influence is more apparent in Richard Courtney's study, which aims to outline the entire history of British drama,[167] and like Taylor's, centers on the new plays produced by the English Stage Company and by Theatre Workshop. Comparing the two companies, Courtney highlights the contribution of the ESC to modern drama but ignores Theatre Workshop's innovative productions of classics. Unlike his relatively elaborate discussion of the ESC, Courtney's treatment of Theatre Workshop's work is rather brief, including a short account of Behan's *The Hostage*, in which he refers to Kenneth Tynan's 1958 review.[168] Yet, on the whole, Courtney attempts to maintain a balance in accounting for the theatrical contributions of the two companies. "Joan Littlewood's political Theatre Workshop was a left-wing 'collective' with brilliant acting," he comments, whereas "Devine encouraged different production styles," and "both Devine and Littlewood built superb ensembles."[169] Courtney's assessment is that "although Littlewood's plays contained direct social criticism, more often the criticism came from antisocial characters (as with Osborne) or was oblique (as with Pinter)."[170]

John Russell Brown, associate director and repertoire adviser at the National Theatre, published *A Short Guide to Modern British Drama* in 1982. In it, he draws on a series of talks he had given on Radio 4 in 1981 called *Up to Now: Drama*. This dual media exposure—of radio and print—may have increased the influence of his views. Brown attributes "the first unmistakable change" in the modern British theatre to the performance of John Osborne's *Look Back in Anger*.[171] He notes the provocative nature of this play, its critical reception, and its immense impact with an enthusiasm that makes his description of Littlewood as "a person who did most to give post-war British theatre a renewed sense of the pleasures of performance"[172] seem tepid by comparison. Theatre Workshop, he claims, "brought to the West End a series of plays that were written for the company and owed more to vitality of performance than to the individual originality of a writer." Brown finds *Oh What a Lovely War* "the fullest example" of Littlewood's work, a "vital" production that critiqued "the generals and politicians for their inhumanity."[173] Brown, like Courtney, highlights Theatre Workshop's productions of new plays by Delaney and Behan as well as *Oh What a Lovely War*, and ignores the company's repertoire of classics. However, in his introduction to a collection on modern British dramatists published two years later, Brown does comment on

Theatre Workshop productions of British and European classics, noting they "lacked the glamour and historicity for which other directors were still striving but put in their place Joan Littlewood's own notions of contemporary relevance and innovative interpretations."[174]

Unlike Courtney's and Brown's studies, accounts by Howard Goorney, a member of Littlewood's company for thirty years, and Mike Coren, a freelance journalist, foreground Theatre Workshop's radical and innovative work and the company's continuous struggle for existence. As Howard Goorney acknowledges in his preface to *The Theatre Workshop Story*, published in 1981, an "Arts Council grant was the starting point for this long task and in my criticism of the Arts Council I am aware that I have bitten the hand that fed me. But, short of suppressing the facts, there seemed to be no alternative."[175] Articles in the *Sunday Telegraph* and the *Guardian Women* in the early to mid-1980s also reflected renewed interest in Littlewood's work.[176] As Coren remarks in *Theatre Royal,* which appeared in 1985, "in the mid-1980s, Joan Littlewood's name was on everybody's lips."[177]

Alan Sinfield's 1989 cultural survey of postwar Britain—a milestone in the field of cultural studies—was a major influence on the growing tendency to reassess the postwar era. Sinfield identifies the disillusionment during the postwar era and traces among other cultural practices the rise of the New Left. He discusses the seminal role of Osborne's play within the context of the 1950s cultural transformation and distinguishes "the Royal Court and *Look Back in Anger* as "points around which new-left perceptions were organized." As a consequence of "the combative significance of left-wing plays," he comments, "theatre became a place where new-left attitudes could be explored. The magazine *Encore* was founded to develop the connection, and the work of Joan Littlewood and Theatre Workshop, marginalized hitherto for its socialist policy, was celebrated."[178]

In the 1990s the pendulum swung to the opposite extreme, as the theatrical establishment paid tribute to Littlewood's innovative contribution. If a shift in the establishment's stance toward the contribution of Theatre Workshop was already underway in the mid to late 1980s, a sequence of events in the mid-1990s evoked cumulative media operations that were affected by and in turn instigated this overall transformation.

Following the 1994 publication of her provocative memoirs, *Joan's Book: Joan Littlewood's Peculiar History as She Tells* It, Littlewood returned to Britain for a visit. The book received wide media coverage, providing an opportunity to review her theatrical career in retrospect.[179] It was at this time that Littlewood rejected the National Theatre's offer to produce the play *Oh What a Lovely War*, scheduled for that fall; she also disapproved of the BBC radio version of the play scheduled for June 11. But the synchronous publication of *Joan's Book* and the press coverage it received,[180] the BBC documentary on Littlewood,[181] and the publicized attempts of the National Theatre in March 1994 and the BBC to attain her consent to revive *Oh What a Lovely War* all roused the public's attention. The public became curious once again about the controversial theatre director who had disappeared from view for two decades. Although Littlewood vehemently refused the offers to revive her play, the BBC went ahead with its radio version despite her disapproval. Furthermore, the BBC, possibly counting on the public's growing interest, announced their intention to serialize Littlewood's memoirs.[182] These media operations suggest an emergent narrative of belated recognition—the formulaic story of an artistic genius whose radical work was banned in her own time, yet recognized forty years later for its immense contribution to the theatre.[183]

The cultivation of Littlewood's image as a rebel, an image validated by her own conduct, only enhanced her reputation.[184] A case in point is the behind-the-scenes story of the 1998 revival of *Oh What a Lovely War* by the National Theatre. This mobile production, directed by Fiona Laird, took place in a tent on a hill in Milton Keynes. Littlewood finally gave her consent to revive her play, with conditions that the NT had to respect, that "the National, the RSC, and the West Yorkshire Playhouse were no-go areas."[185] In fact, as Jeremy Kingstone recounted it, the National Theatre production was not to be played at the Cottesloe, its logical home, because Littlewood famously detested that organization. "Indeed," Kingstone notes, "to persuade her to let the NT mount a production at all must have required the diplomacy the Allies notably lacked in 1914."[186] The National Theatre's 1998 revival of *Oh What a Lovely War* marked a concluding episode in Littlewood's interactions with the established institutions of the London stage.

The *Observer* announced the death of Joan Littlewood on September 21, 2002, in an article titled "Littlewood, First among Radicals, Leaves Stage." In the lead paragraph Vanessa Thorpe described Littlewood as "the legendary theatrical director who launched many of Britain's brightest stars and founded the groundbreaking Theatre Royal in London's Stratford East."[187]

By the 1990s the perception that Theatre Workshop had been a more radical, innovative company than the English Stage Company prevailed in scholarly assessments of modern British theatre, as exemplified by Derek Paget's essays, which center on *Oh What a Lovely War*. In "'*Oh What a Lovely War*': The Texts and Their Contexts," published in *New Theatre Quarterly* in 1990, Paget asserts that "for many people, it was not *Look Back in Anger* but *Lovely War* which was the theatrical event 'marking *then* off from *now*' in post-Second World War theatre revolution."[188] This statement challenges Taylor's view in the lead paragraph of *Anger and After*.[189] Paget discusses the extraordinary effect of *Lovely War* on British theatre, which had been acknowledged by many theatre practitioners. He sets out to illuminate the collective work involved in the Stratford East's production, drawing on interviews with the original participants, on the printed edition from Methuen, and on source materials. In tracing the creation of this work Paget aims to refute the critical notion that *Lovely War* "is somehow a play which feeds off nostalgia" and to replace it with a view that this key work originated as "a critique of war as the greatest of all capitalist 'enterprises'," and as such should be given the status it deserves.[190] He further explores the contribution of the play in another essay published in 1990,[191] in which he claims that it "transformed English theatre post-World War Two by making available a European style of production, which had more to do with figures such as Meyerhold, Piscator, and Brecht than anything English, and which was to influence profoundly the new 'Fringe' of the 1960s to 1970s."[192] Paget examines *Lovely War* as a product of "a wider post-war cultural reorientation." He comments that "the time was ripe for work which deconstructed official accounts of the Great War, and in the public arena of the theatre *Lovely War* achieved this by giving access to the 'new histories.'"[193] In a 1995 essay published in *New Theatre Quarterly*, which develops the perception presented in a 1990 study, Paget suggests that "Theatre Workshop was the Trojan horse through which European radical theatre practices from the 1918–1939 period entered post-war Britain. Inside this Trojan horse was a set of critical, political attitudes and a theatrical methodology more capable of sustaining a critique of issues and events than dominant naturalistic forms. Once smuggled into the cosily conservative world of British culture, these elements were well used by the oppositional theatre of the 1970s." The effect of the collective methods and European tradition of Theatre Workshop on alternative theatre, in Paget's view, "brought about a real theatrical revolution in the UK, which had nothing to do with the cosmetic alterations of the Osbornes and Pinters in 1956."[194]

Christopher Innes's 1992 book *Modern British Drama* similarly presents Theatre Workshop's work as a major influence on oppositional theatre. Innes examines, for example, the various ways in which Littlewood and MacColl used agitprop theatre, concluding that the effects sought—mainly political—were only partly achieved and the results, on the whole, proved mostly disappointing, as MacColl himself admitted. "However," Innes comments, "by developing Agitprop elements within the resources of the conventional stage, the Theatre Workshop remained a model for counter-theatre. When radical playwrights emerged in the early seventies with the aim of making drama a weapon for class conflict, they turned again to Agitprop."[195]

Stephen Lacey's 1995 study *British Realist Theatre* identifies a range of socio-economic, political, and cultural factors that effected changes in the postwar theatrical arena. It argues "for the centrality of a version of the period that has *Look Back in Anger* as the defining theatrical event and which privileges a complex understanding of realism."[196] Lacey locates the success of *Look Back in Anger* within the overall context of the socio-cultural and political transformations of the 1950s, particularly deriving from the critical context established with respect to the Movement and the role of the media. He notes the influential figures involved with the ESC's founding and discusses this company's various aims and policies, particularly its emphasis on encouraging new writers and new themes. The ESC provided new writers with opportunities that, in Lacey's view, corresponded to the interests of the press at the time and to the then prevalent cultural tendencies or tendencies in the making.[197] "The Court," Lacey comments, "was never in real opposition to the theatrical establishment after 1956."[198] The Arts Council "showed little enthusiasm for entering some more contentious areas of theatrical debates," Lacey remarks, and he adds that the Arts Council "had neither the will nor the resources to effect radical changes within the cultural profession."[199]

He further emphasizes that "unlike the ESC, Theatre Workshop was not a 'new' company, nor did it appear in its structure and origins, like any other theatre of the period." Moreover, the company was "in almost every area of its activities an alternative to the then dominant forms of commercial theatre,"[200] and "Littlewood's search for radical theatre forms and working-class audiences led her away from formal theatre entirely." He also makes it clear that it was the crippling financial problems that the company faced and the compromises Littlewood was forced to make due to the ailing theatre system that drove her out of the theatre.[201]

Dan Rebellato's 1999 study *1956 and All That* takes Lacey's reassessment of the "New Wave" further, adopting an ironic and critical approach toward misleading historical notions.[202] The author himself declares that his book offers "a counter-reading of this period" but also that he wants neither to shift the turning point nor to suggest an alternative. Although Rebellato acknowledges that there was change, he argues that it "has been badly misunderstood."[203] He identifies the crucial role filled by "the sense of cultural and imperial decline, the structure of arts funding, and the 'problem' of homosexuality" in the construction and establishment of the narrative associated with the postwar theatre revolution. He also discusses the motivations underlying the differing attitudes of government authorities toward the two companies during the era in question.

Rebellato's critique is directed at "history as fairy tale."[204] He challenges "the picture routinely offered to us" that "Royal Court to the West End is as David to Goliath." Exploring the various reasons for the Court's success, Rebellato claims that Devine, founder and director of the ESC, "was not a break with the previous structures, he was a link with them"[205] and that the ESC board "as a whole was made up of just the sort of people that the Arts Council liked."[206] The Arts Council's attitude to Theatre Workshop, Rebellato comments, reflected its general refusal to recognize and support the activities of theatre of the Left.[207] He recounts the difficult financial struggle of Theatre Workshop, and relates the various unsuccessful attempts to change the Arts Council's policy toward it. Referring to Theatre Workshop's early years at Stratford East, he suggests that "while their political stance was certainly an issue . . . it was their refusal to become docile objects of the Council's gaze that was the problem."[208] He further comments that the Council liked the company's repertoire of "semi-forgotten classics" and acknowledged its success at the Paris festivals of 1955 and 1956; however, he remarks, "after twelve years of work," Theatre Workshop was still being offered only a very small subsidy "with the condition that the Local Authority match it."[209] The Royal Court, on the other hand, "was everything the Arts Council had been waiting for, in its project of national-cultural renewal."[210]

Dominic Shellard, in his 1999 study *British Theatre since the War*, aims to provide a "first and useful map" of the history of postwar British theatre. Of the two theatre companies, Shellard suggests: "If George Devine's English Stage Company at the Royal Court was a 'writers' theatre, Joan Littlewood's Theatre Workshop at Stratford East on the other side of town was a practitioners' one."[211] Like Lacey and Rebellato, Shellard attempts to revise Theatre Workshop's historical record and incorporates data from Goorney's account. Referring to the company's broad and rich classical repertoire during the early 1950s and to the low cost of its productions, Shellard argues that this company, predating the ESC in London by three years, "foreshadows George Devine's project. This offers further confirmation that the reorientation of post-war drama did not begin with a 'big bang' of 'Anger.'"[212] Reassessing Littlewood's position in the context of her own era, Shellard extends Hayman's earlier assessment and attributes to Littlewood a major role in what he perceives to be the renaissance of British directing, which paralleled that of British playwriting.[213]

Shellard recounts in detail Theatre Workshop's consistent and unsuccessful attempts to apply to the Arts Council for grants from the 1940s to the early 1960s and to secure a subsidy. His detailed table of subsidies, which compares the Arts Council grants awarded to Theatre Workshop and to the English Stage Company relies on Goorney's 1981 account.[214] Shellard quotes a letter from Jack Reading, vice president of the Society for Theatre Research, in which Reading refers to the 1958 production of Shelagh Delaney's play.

> A Taste of Honey has been overlooked as an example of a new theatre in advance of its time. . . . In addition to all these new-at-the-time aspects the staging of the play was equally revolutionary. Littlewood's direction methods resulted in a style, acceptable, workable, but more direct and real than any acting to be seen further to the west in London. . . . A Taste of Honey was being considered at about the same time as Look Back in Anger but reached the stage later, but it has an equal, if not greater, claim to be a break point of the British theatre. Alas, it had no banner-title to wave and, after all, was in the East End poor relation theatre.[215]

Advancing the view that Look Back in Anger was not the most radical of the plays associated with the change of British theatre in the postwar era, Shellard argues that this play should be reassessed in the light of other significant theatrical events that occurred prior to and around the same time as its first performance. In an essay published in 2000, Shellard points to the significance of other theatrical events occurring between 1945 and 1954 that were "important for the subsequent development of British theatre and obscured by the clamour of the Angries."[216]

Reflecting this same turnabout in scholarly evaluation, Nadine Holdsworth writes in her 1999 essay:[217] "It is now commonplace to suggest that

Joan Littlewood and Theatre Workshop were ill treated by the theatrical establishment and also circumscribed by their reliance on the commercial sector. Indeed this theatre 'fact' has reached the status of cultural myth yet very little evidence is in the public domain."[218] In contrast to Lacey, Rebellato, and Shellard, whose studies revise Theatre Workshop's historical record, Holdsworth presents the establishment's ill treatment of Littlewood and the Workshop as a "theatre fact," which serves as a point of departure in her own attempt "to document the problematic relationship that existed between the Arts Council and Joan Littlewood's Theatre Workshop between 1945 and 1975." To this extent Holdsworth's essay both reflects and advances the revisionist agenda underlying critical and historical studies of postwar British theatre published in the 1990s.

More recently, in "British Theatre, 1940–2002," Baz Kershaw discusses the state of the theatre in light of the reform initiated by the "neo-Conservative" government elected in 1979 and led by Prime Minister Margaret Thatcher.[219] He claims that even "if the new Right's policies were abhorrent to most theatre enthusiasts, their actual effects in the 1980s were by no means entirely bad news."[220] Further, in the 1990s, "in exactly the same period as the theatre was enjoying an efflorescence of aesthetic and institutional creativity there were mounting cries of 'crisis' from both practitioners and commentators."[221] He goes on to suggest that "perhaps the sense of crisis in the British theatre industry as the millennium turned was produced by its apparent inexorable incorporation into market consumerism."[222] Dominic Shellard remarks, in his 1999 study, concerning the challenges taken up by the theatre during the years of the Conservative government, that "whilst the period between 1979 and 1997 has been one of struggle, it has also been one of achievement against great odds."[223] The threatened state of the theatre in the 1980s and the 1990s described by Shellard and by Kershaw may have been conducive to the production of revisionist histories. Clearly, key journals such as *New Theatre Quarterly* and key publishers like Routledge, which provided a stage for the revisionist views, played an essential role in the major reassessment of postwar British theatre that occurred in the 1990s.

In 2004, lionized by *The Cambridge History of British Theatre*, Theatre Workshop was granted recognition of its revolutionary and enduring contribution to the British theatre. Theatre Workshop and the English Stage Company are discussed in volume 3, edited by Baz Kershaw. In his introduction to the years 1940–2002, Kershaw claims: "Conventional histories routinely cite John Osborne's *Look Back in Anger*, staged by the

English Stage Company at the Royal Court Theatre in its first season in 1956, as the play that unleashed a new age of great British drama. But the first literal foundations of the success of the 'new wave' playwrights were laid two years later and 100 miles further north of Coventry City Council, which opened the brand-new Belgrade Theatre in 1958."[224]

Theatre Workshop's production of *Oh What a Lovely War*, rather than the English Stage Company's production of Osborne's *Look Back in Anger*, is given the more elaborate discussion in the 2004 Cambridge volume. Derek Paget's "Case Study: Theatre Workshop's *Oh What a Lovely War*, 1963," is one of the ten essays comprising the 1940–2002 section. Another of the ten essays, John Bull's "The Establishment of Mainstream Theatre, 1946–1979," refers to the singular reception of the ESC production of *Look Back in Anger*. Bull comments that "part of the significance is the effect that Osborne's play had on subsequent drama, which was substantial. But the immediate reaction to Osborne's play disguised what was to become a far more influential development, which was related to the incorporation of *non*-British theatrical models into the main stream."[225] That is, Bull perceives "the key importance of *Look Back in Anger* in the creation of a new kind of mainstream British theatre." He refers to the development of the Royal Court "as a major venue for new writing and, furthermore, a venue that learnt from the outset the necessity of transferring productions into the commercial theatre in order to survive economically."[226] Bull finds the transfer of *Oh What a Lovely War* to the Wyndham Theatre in 1963 as yet another indication of what he calls the "emergent trend."

Paget presents the transfer of *Oh What a Lovely War* to the Wyndham Theatre as "a landmark in British theatre; a theatrical methodology that had been thirty years in the making had finally arrived in the cultural mainstream."[227] He discusses the innovative nature of Theatre Workshop; the formative influences of European political theatre, Brecht's methods, and Erwin Piscator's plays; the working-class entertainment traditions integrated into the company's work and the way in which the company hit back "at the dominant class and its ideology" but "took a robust attitude to bourgeois hypocrisy and working-class sentiment alike."[228] He focuses on the revolutionary production *Oh What a Lovely War*, contending that although this production "was Joan Littlewood's last major contribution to British theatre, it can be seen as a culmination of the Theatre Workshop project."[229] In his account of the achievements of *Oh What a Lovely War*, Paget cites Charles Marowitz's 1963 review. Paget's detailed description of the Stratford East production highlights the innovations of the show, the "new multi-media theatre" and "new dramaturgy" it introduced. "Although," he claims, "radical views became fashionable in both theatre and society in the 1960s (and the play benefited from this), West End success muted the play's original radicalism. Criticism and commercial pressures combined to decrease the political commitment of the show as it moved into the mainstream."[230] Paget concludes with the National Theatre production of *Oh What a Lovely War* in 1998, stating that "all theatre productions are locked into their historical moments." He maintains that at the end of the millennium, *Oh What a Lovely War*'s "oppositional values, displaced and relativised, were consequently enfeebled."[231]

Philip Barnes's perception of Joan Littlewood, in *Companion to Post-War British Theatre*, stems from the notion that each era needs its own rebel: "Her flair for unconventional theatre, her radicalism and her anti-establishment position-taking made Joan Littlewood a very necessary *enfant terrible* of post-war British theatre."[232] Kenneth Tynan, a major proponent of Littlewood's work, acknowledged the state of affairs in his amused remark that "a few centuries ago such a woman might easily have been burnt as a witch."[233] Tynan, it should be recalled, also predicted that "when the annals of the British theatre in the middle years of the twentieth century come to be written, Joan's name will lead all the rest."[234] He would have been indeed amused, though hardly surprised, to learn that his prediction had come so close to realization by the end of the twentieth century.

3 | John Arden
The Playwright Who Wouldn't Play Ball

> *The curse of John Arden is that he simply won't play ball.*
> —Charles Marowitz

> *John Arden: So it's not as good as it was. I started off with bad notices
> and then after that they kept on saying "he doesn't live up to his
> promise." I'm not the only one who suffers from that.*
> *Margaretta D'Arcy: We were really quite shocked when we went
> to Canada, because we've found out that John has been totally
> removed.... He's only talked about as a personality of the sixties—
> that's the only time he's mentioned.... We'd just been
> wiped out.*[1]

John Arden's early plays are associated with the postwar London theatre, but even early in his career Arden had become involved with fringe and regional activities, eventually shifting the center of his activities outside of London. From the second decade of his career, he wrote most of his plays in collaboration with his wife, the actress and playwright Margaretta D'Arcy.[2]

There are puzzling turns in Arden's career. The reception of his early plays reflects the difficulties critics encountered with his theatrical work, making his rise to prominence in the mid-1960s intriguing. More puzzling still, considering his acknowledged merits as a dramatist and the prominence he achieved in the 1960s, is his later descent into oblivion. The role played by mediation in the London phase of Arden's career provides a possible explanation for this trajectory.

BEGINNING AT THE ROYAL COURT:
A CENTER OF CONTROVERSY[3]

*The English audiences were not ready for the Brechtian style, although they'd
had the Brechtian Company four years before. There was a dislike of that kind
of thing. —Arden interview*

The beginning of John Arden's theatrical career is associated with
George Devine and the English Stage Company at the Royal Court. But
Arden's first play, *All Fall Down*, was performed at the Edinburgh Fringe
Festival in 1955, staged by a student company from the College of Arts in
Edinburgh, where Arden had completed his training as an architect. The
first professional production of an Arden play, broadcast by BBC radio on
April 16, 1956, was *The Life of Man*, which won the Northern Region New
Play prize. According to various accounts it was this play that attracted
the attention of Devine. Arden recounts that following a letter of request
from Oscar Lewenstein, he sent the Royal Court a stage play based on the
legend of King Arthur, which was rejected. He then sent another play to a
drama competition run by Kenneth Tynan in the *Observer*. The winning
play would receive a one-night production at the Royal Court. Arden's
play "did not win, but it was commended."[4] *The Waters of Babylon*, directed by Graham Evans, was eventually presented at the Royal Court
on October 20, 1957, as part of the Sunday Night Productions without
décor.

When Devine then offered Arden the position of first reader, one of
the preliminary readers of submitted scripts, Arden left the architect's office where he had been working,[5] becoming a full-time writer by the end
of 1957. According to Irving Wardle, George Devine admired people with
verbal skill, partly due to his own "feeling he lacked it himself." Moreover, being "by temperament a teacher" and also "a team man," Devine
sought to involve writers in the team without infringing upon their work.
He devised the system of the "writer's pass," which gave the writers free
admission to the Court's rehearsals and performances. Arden regarded
the writer's pass and the Court's offer to read manuscripts, both of which
enabled him to spend all his time "in or around theatre," as the two most
important gifts he had ever been given.[6]

Although most reviews of *The Waters of Babylon* had been unfavorable, the Court commissioned another play from Arden. *Live Like Pigs*,
written in collaboration with Margaretta D'Arcy and directed by Devine
and Anthony Page, was performed by the ESC on September 30, 1958 and

it too was unfavorably received by reviewers. Arden's next plays were *Serjeant Musgrave's Dance*, directed by Lindsay Anderson and performed at the Royal Court on October 22, 1959, and *The Happy Haven*, directed by William Gaskill and also performed at the Royal Court, on September 14, 1960. Both plays, but particularly *Serjeant Musgrave's Dance*, elicited critical controversy. Two other dramatic works are also noteworthy: *When Is a Door Not a Door?* directed by Robert Cartland in 1958 at the Embassy Theatre (Central School of Speech and Drama), and *Soldier, Soldier*, which won the Italia Prize and was subsequently broadcast on BBC television in 1960, directed by Stuart Burge.

From the outset Arden's plays had offered a unique range of subjects and styles. *Waters of Babylon* presents an intricate story of municipal corruption, addressing the audience directly in music-hall tradition and using pantomime gags, song, dance, and verse monologues. *Live Like Pigs* exposes the problems of forcibly integrating a family of gypsies into a respectable council estate community. Although this play is ostensibly naturalistic, it actually portrays a violent, conflictual state of affairs in the style of music-hall entertainment, using ballads to introduce each scene and music-hall props. *Serjeant Musgrave's Dance* draws roughly on a newspaper account of an incident in Cyprus.[7] In the play, four deserters— Serjeant Musgrave and three soldiers—go on an apparent recruiting mission to a strike-bound mining town in the north of England in the late nineteenth century. Through violent and vindictive actions, "Black Jack" Musgrave and his soldiers are bent on bringing the facts of war to this somber town, the home of a dead comrade. In *Musgrave*, as in several of his later plays, Arden blurs the distinction between the historical and the contemporary, using popular dramatic tradition, song, verse, and dance. Albert Hunt describes the play as a combination of the Hollywood western and English ballad.[8] Hunt relies on Arden's own reference to the American film *The Raid* as one of the sources of the play's structure.[9] In contrast to *Musgrave*, with its serious topic and tragic ending, the next play, *The Happy Haven*, by Arden and D'Arcy, is a farce about an old-age home. According to the authors, "The Five Old People wear character masks of the commedia dell'arte type,". . . "following roughly the Elizabethan model."[10] It presents a mixture of high comedy and low farce, using masks and pantomime to cast young actors and actresses in the roles of the old people. In all four plays Arden employs highly sophisticated language and a variety of modified Brechtian devices.

The press notices on Arden's first play, *Waters of Babylon*, mainly reflected puzzlement. Primarily attacking the lack of order, or structure, the *Times* found that "Mr. Arden's theme, indeed his purpose in writing the play, remained obscure,"[11] and the notice in the *Daily Telegraph* concluded that "dialogue full of metaphors and similes echoing Dylan Thomas, songs à la Brecht and the appearance, but not the substance, of Shavian extravaganza were poor substitutes for order and style."[12] Kenneth Tynan, in the *Observer*, proclaimed the play to be "on the fringe of fantasy throughout; and when an author takes us into no-man's-land we are entitled to ask for signposts."[13] In spite of their disapproval, several reviewers related to the playwright's dramatic talent or presented him as promising. Tynan admitted that although the play "ended in confusion, the bumpy trip was full of memorable landmarks," while Cecil Wilson commented that "through the haze of words I glimpse a high promise."[14]

The reviewers' puzzlement, often manifested in their ambivalence toward Arden's dramatic work, was even more apparent following his next play, *Live Like Pigs*. An unfavorable review in the *Times* also pointed to some redeeming qualities: "The play has some good scenes. . . . Mr. Arden gives the impression that if he knew when to stop he could tell a good story for the stage."[15] The *Illustrated London News* reviewer was hopeful about Arden, "who before long will have something to say in the theatre."[16] Similar in tone was the notice in the *Sunday Times,* which concluded: "It looks as though the English Stage Company has discovered another new dramatist."[17] Wilson, in a favorable review, felt that "the play, written in the fashionable mixture of earthy prose and lofty poetry—far too lofty for these slobbering, illiterate mouths—is a specific sore in three acts; a dramatized cesspool. But it reveals a tremendous new talent."[18]

The initial critical responses to Arden's third play, *Serjeant Musgrave's Dance*, reflected a sharp division among the reviewers. Harold Hobson in the *Sunday Times* described the play as "another frightful ordeal,"[19] and the notice in the *Times* found it "an inordinately long-winded and rather foolish play."[20] The title of Felix Barker's review, however, proclaimed, "A Slow Fuse, but What an Explosion!"[21] W. A. Darlington asserted that, "John Arden is a dramatist of considerable ability, and his new play at the Royal Court, *Serjeant Musgrave's Dance*, has atmosphere and intermittent power,"[22] while Philip Hope-Wallace found it "something short of a great play. But wild horses wouldn't have dragged me from my seat before the end."[23] Wilson expressed disappointment yet concluded by addressing the playwright: "How about really getting down to it now, Mr. Arden, and writing that masterpiece?"[24] Caryl Brahms, in *Plays and Players*, stated: "For an outstandingly important play, *Serjeant Musgrave's Dance* has had a very mixed press. There have been those critics of Mr. John Arden's piece who have boasted that they could understand it but disliked it. Others have admitted that they could not understand it but disliked it. And so it has been left to an enlightened few—among whom I have the honour to make my stand—to salute the quality of greatness in it."[25] The reviews of *Happy Haven*, Arden's next play, once again reflected controversy. The play was described by one reviewer as "disastrous" and "hideous" and by another as "brilliant" and "haunting." Arden was presented in one review as "one of our most interesting new dramatists"[26] and in another as "more-than-promising."[27]

Overall, the critics responding to Arden's plays were baffled. Hunt perceives their confusion as rooted in their expectations.[28] Arden's theatre, he suggests, "rejects the basic assumptions the cultivated theatre-going public holds about what makes 'good' theatre." Frances Gray concurs that "to watch a play by Arden, or to participate in one, is to engage in a debate about theatre—what it is for, and whom it is for."[29] Elaborating on the critics' confusion, Gray remarks that "the notices are not only, on the whole, disparaging, they are also very uncertain about the nature of the plays." Strangely enough, as Gray notes, "critics acknowledged his power but aloofly rejected the actual plays."[30]

The singular nature of Arden's reception, as exemplified by the notices, lay not only in the division among critical responses or in the critics' ambivalence, but also and primarily in the reviewers' inability to decide on the position Arden should be assigned as a dramatist and the appropriate construct by which to typify his work. In other words, in the process of evaluating new playwrights, reviewers typically locate them in light of their affiliation with, or divergence from, recognized and established theatrical trends or schools, and they assess the newcomers' particular means of theatrical expression in terms of their potential contribution to the theatre.[31] The affiliation provides reviewers a familiar context from within which to view the new playwright's work, and their assessment of the particular means of theatrical expression enables them to differentiate the newcomer's contribution from that of established playwrights. Consequently, the new playwright is presented as continuing, while simultaneously enriching and expanding, the repertoire of a given theatre tradition. Throughout the process of a playwright's acceptance, reviewers devise a package of attributes that characterizes the new dramatist's work.

This package is subsequently formulated into the playwright construct, an aggregation of traits that recur in the works seen to typify the dramatist in terms of influences and innovation. This construct becomes the dramatist's trademark, serving the reviewers to further market the plays and the dramatist. The critics' formulation of the playwright construct is essential to their mediatory function: to make the work accessible and to locate the dramatist within the overall theatrical tradition.

Because Arden's range of subjects and styles differed from play to play, reviewers encountered an immense difficulty. Their attitude toward his work was ambiguous from the start. They were unable to devise an attribute package for his work, even though they recognized his dramatic powers, and this led to their inability to determine his placement as a dramatist. The reviewers' ambiguity was not resolved at this stage of Arden's career, and his dramas were consequently tagged as controversial.

If the critical controversy over Arden's works is apparent from the reviews, their commercial failure is verified by all accounts. Gray begins her study of Arden's work with this comparison: "The Royal Court Theatre made about 50,000 pounds producing the plays of John Osborne and lost 14,857 pounds producing those of John Arden."[32] The early stages of Arden's career were a mirror image of those of John Osborne. Both playwrights were commissioned by George Devine and the first plays of both were performed at the Royal Court Theatre. Both playwrights had the benefit of a promising start: a supportive artistic director and a rising theatre company, the ESC. Both playwrights won *Evening Standard* awards for the most promising playwright of the year: Osborne for *Look Back in Anger* in 1956 and Arden for *Serjeant Musgrave's Dance* in 1959. Though both dramatists were being presented as major playwrights by the end of the 1950s, Arden's position, unlike Osborne's, was rooted in controversy and relied primarily on the support and powers of a few in-house mediators, notably Devine and Anderson. Both men supported and promoted Arden's plays in the face of hostile criticism, and at times in the face of in-house objections too.

Devine, who perceived both Osborne and Arden as playwrights who justified the Court's raison d'être, provided them unlimited support. Various accounts concur that Devine recognized Arden's work as embodying the Court's objectives. That the Court continued to produce Arden's plays despite the financial losses involved suggests that the decision to provide the playwright with a stage should be attributed to Devine's influence. Philip Roberts comments on Devine's view of the two dramatists: "If Osborne had opened up the possibilities for the Court, Arden had stated unequivocally what the Court was for." Roberts refers to a letter Devine wrote to Greville Poke, in which he stressed that "all our trials and tribulations come from the fact that we are making these kinds of investments in artists because we believe in them. The dividends we will just have to risk, and they certainly won't be in terms of cash."[33] Following the reviewers' attack on *The Happy Haven*, Roberts reports, Devine wrote to Neville Blond in defense of the playwright: "Arden is probably the most important dramatist next to Osborne we have produced."[34] According to Gaskill, who directed *The Happy Haven*, the use of masks in the play developed out of the classes given by Devine to the Writers' Group, in which Arden had participated, and Arden later confirmed this in various interviews. Roberts remarks that "the development of a new writer like Arden was linked via Devine with Saint-Denis and Copeau," and he mentions Tony Richardson's aversion to "that Saint-Denis rubbish."[35] Roberts's view provides a possible explanation for Devine's personal commitment to Arden's work. Devine's initial agenda was to promote the European line, primarily the plays of Beckett and Ionesco. He continued to pursue this agenda even after the success of Osborne's play and explicitly declared his intention of shifting between these two lines.[36] Arden's work, as perceived by Devine, hence fully accorded with the sort of theatre he sought to promote. Peter Roberts conducted an interview with Devine in 1961 in which Devine spoke of the financial difficulties encountered by the English Stage Company, recalling the first season, in 1956, when "he was determined to keep the theatre open at all costs and bash his way through with quantity as well as quality to show that it *could* be done." Devine clarified that in view of the company's state in 1961, the Arts Council grant it received was clearly insufficient, saying it was "really nothing when you are doing an experimental work." The company then invented what they called the Pylon System in order to subsidize themselves; that is, they put on star pieces that packed the theatre for six weeks and between these successes they interspersed experimental work. Devine specified the sort of theatre the company sought to promote and singled out the work of a particular playwright. For example, he said, "a dramatist like John Arden, whom the English Stage Company absolutely believes in, has cost a lot of money. But they continue to invest in a man they believe in without any particular return, except the knowledge that they are doing what they think they ought to do."[37]

SERJEANT MUSGRAVE'S DANCE

Lindsay Anderson gave it a brilliant production, really a splendid production somewhat muddled in Brecht's style. . . . Lindsay wrote a letter to the press defending the play because he felt that the critics were so unfair to it, and this actually was a big help. It's extraordinary how one gesture like that can make a difference. It didn't really bring in more audience, but it brought in some.—Arden interview

The English Stage Company's support of Arden's work was most apparent in the case of *Serjeant Musgrave's Dance*, which initially garnered an especially hostile critical reception. The trajectory of this play calls for consideration not merely because it poses a unique case, but also because its gradually acquired stature contributed to the playwright's growing reputation in the years that followed.

Lindsay Anderson, who directed the first production of the play, was also actively involved in its promotion. Alan Pryce-Jones's second review of *Serjeant Musgrave's Dance*, in the *Observer*, began with a reference to the letter of protest he had received from Anderson. Anderson had reacted to the reviewers' comments on *Serjeant Musgrave's Dance*, protesting the "grave injustice being done to a work of . . . extraordinary talent and originality." In reply Pryce-Jones wrote: "Since Mr. Anderson is a director whose work in the theatre and in the cinema gives him every right to be heard I am glad to return to a play which has received opinions so strongly divided; some hating it outright, others (like myself) having strong reserves about it, and a few delighting in it wholeheartedly." In his second review of the play, Pryce-Jones held to his initial verdict: "While the incidents remain, the essential evaporates even before the fall of the last curtain."[38]

The director's choice to defend the playwright and the play seems significant not only with respect to Anderson's role as a mediator, manifest in other cases (such as Theatre Workshop), but also in view of this play's future canonical position. Interestingly, Roberts mentions that Anderson's public defense of Arden's play had alarmed the Court's publicity people.[39] Anderson's belief in Arden's work led to a particularly constructive and apparently effective collaboration between playwright and director, all the more remarkable considering that other directors of Arden's early plays were at times puzzled themselves[40] and given the playwright's interactions with the directors of his plays in the later phases of his career.

The English Stage Company was involved in the promotion of *Serjeant Musgrave's Dance* in several ways. In June 1959, four months before

22.10.1959

Royal Court
Theatre

Sloane Square S.W.1

THE ENGLISH STAGE COMPANY

present

SERJEANT MUSGRAVE'S DANCE

by JOHN ARDEN

First performance October 22nd, 1959

Programme—sixpence

Program cover of Serjeant Musgrave's Dance, *Royal Court, October 22, 1959.*
© V&A Images/Theatre Museum.

the Court's performance of the play, Arden received first prize for it in a competition organized by the Encyclopedia Britannica and the English Stage Company, sharing the prize with Arnold Wesker, for *Chicken Soup with Barley*. And while Anderson's letter reflected the director's own attempt to change the views of *Serjeant Musgrave's Dance* in the face of hostile critical notices, the company endorsed a mediating strategy that attempted to resolve the confusion of both press and public. *Musgrave* was scheduled for a three-and-a-half-week run. Ten days after the first performance, the theatre added a leaflet to the program entitled "What Kind of a Theatre?"[41] It begins by explaining: "This play had a confused press. But in spite of the criticisms, we believe it will be tragic if it is allowed to slip into obscurity. That is why we are printing this leaflet." Further clarification follows: "This is not a bid for commercial success. . . . The play will close as advertised on November 14th. But we are optimistic enough and proud enough of our work to believe that there are enough people alive to the excitement of good theatre to justify a full run." Citing two contradictory opinions—Harold Hobson's harsh attack on the play in the *Sunday Times* and Philip Hope-Wallace's favorable review in the *Manchester Guardian*—the leaflet asks the audience: "What kind of a theatre do you want?" It concludes with the comments of several well-known figures, such as Dame Peggy Ashcroft, John Osborne, Sir Michael Redgrave, Wolf Mankowitz, Karel Reisz, N. F. Simpson, and Arnold Wesker, all of whom expressed highly favorable opinions of the play. The leaflet states clearly that the aim in citing the comments of such people is to help the public decide. The press reaction, on the whole, was nonetheless hostile.

Serjeant Musgrave's Dance was published by Methuen in 1960 with an introduction by the author. In 1961 it was published in *Plays and Players*, and by Rowohlt Verlag in Germany. In 1962 the play was broadcast on BBC television and also performed in Switzerland and Germany. A revival was produced at the Court on December 9, 1965, directed by Jane Howell. The program note accompanying this latter production included a section, "Arden on Theatre" that comprised five extracts from an interview conducted with the playwright published in *Peace News* and an extract from Arden's introduction to the printed edition of his play.

Eric Shorter, in his reserved review, commented on these extracts: "Last night with copious notes by Mr. Arden himself in the programme for the Royal Court revival, we could consider ourselves properly tutored."[42] Overall, the reviews were mixed. Harold Hobson, who praised the production, began by expressing his dislike of the Royal Court production in 1959. He also mentioned Peter Brook's attempt to promote the play by presenting a production at the Athénée in Paris. Hobson referred to the actors playing Musgrave in the three productions and proclaimed that "what neither an Englishman nor a Frenchman has been able to do, a Scot has accomplished." The Scot in question in the 1965 Court revival was Iain Cuthbertson, who had acted in another Arden play, *Armstrong's Last Goodnight*, produced in Glasgow two years earlier. "Could he save *Serjeant Musgrave's Dance*? He could, and he did," Hobson asserted, adding: "I put the matter crudely in order to emphasize the extent of Mr. Arden's debt to Mr. Cuthbertson." The lead actor's "force, his authority, and his discretion," in Hobson's view, "dissipated the clouds of that boredom which is Mr. Arden's besetting danger, and thereby allowed us to see a landscape whose bleak strangeness and ascetic beauty are unique in the British theatre." Most other notices also praised Cuthbertson's performance.[43] From January 31, 1966, *Serjeant Musgrave's Dance* entered into the Court's repertory; also that year the play was staged in New York.

The next revival of *Serjeant Musgrave's Dance*, directed by John Burgess, was performed at the National Theatre (Cottesloe) on June 18, 1981. The program note this time included a relatively elaborate biography of John Arden and a chronology of his work, incorporating a brief extract from the playwright's introduction to the published text.[44] The National Theatre appears to have been primarily relying on the play's acquired stature by that time. Indeed most of the reviews referred to earlier productions of the play and to its acclaimed achievement. Although mostly favorable, the reviewers also expressed reservations. Ian Stewart related to the play's distinctive form and content, pointing out "its disdain of naturalism, its rather Brechtian use of ballads and its odd mixture of prose and verse. As to its matter, its ambiguous attack on war and violence, its demonstration of the absurdity of pacifism, pursued by violent means, it was as apt then as it is today."[45] Almost all the reviewers referred to the play's descriptive subtitle, "An Un-historical Parable," as a reference to the play being up-to-date. Although most still found the play strange, they stressed its powerful effect. J. C. Trewin commented that "*Serjeant Musgrave's Dance* seems to grow with every new revival: what one disliked in 1959 has established itself in the drama of the generation."[46] John Barber remarked on the production's commercial success: "*Serjeant Musgrave's Dance*, regarded as a modern classic but rarely produced. A favourite with amateurs and schools, it is attracting full houses and earnest queues for returned tickets.[47]

Albert Finney directed another National Theatre revival of the play, at the Old Vic in may 1984, and also played Musgrave. The reviews were mixed, many finding the production faulty. Worth noting is Michael Billington's review, which began: "John Arden's *Serjeant Musgrave's Dance* is an unsinkable masterpiece." He went on to say, "now at the Old Vic it survives a slightly undercooked production," which he primarily blamed on the management. He praised Finney's "startling performance." Billington's review, however, is an exception, because rather than stressing the production qualities, he highlighted the play's greatness, its use of language, and its depiction of a morally complex situation. Although he pointed to several production faults, he found it "held together by Finney's own doughty performance." In sum, he concluded: "Arden's work is one of the best post-war political plays and deserves to be seen as well as studied."[48] Irving Wardle also found the production faulty, but he too commented on the play's greatness: "Since its first appearance in 1959, the play has advanced toward us as if in a slow prophetic march."[49]

Sir Michael Redgrave, cited in the leaflet added to the program note of the Royal Court 1959 production of the play, predicted that "in years to come this play will be 're-discovered' as an important early work of a remarkable playwright." Redgrave's prediction would be fully realized even sooner than he had anticipated, but the views concerning the playwright were still to undergo major transformations. Uncertainty had already underlain the critical views of Arden's work in the early 1960s. Even those who were willing to acknowledge the merits of *Serjeant Musgrave's Dance* were uncertain as to the playwright's future work, suspecting that Arden would surprise them again with an utterly different kind of play. Laurence Kitchin's cautious judgment of the play in *Mid-Century Drama,* published in 1962, is typical: "Clearly this work is not to be defined as picaresque in a limiting way. It has a complexity of organization which cannot be fully described outside itself and I see it as a permanent addition to the national repertory. Nor is there any certainty that Arden will go on using the form."[50]

There is no doubt, however, as to the play's acquired stature. The many productions of *Serjeant Musgrave's Dance* inside and outside Britain and the play's inclusion in various collections and anthologies of drama of the 1960s and British drama in general, testify to its canonic standing. Initially faulted by the majority of reviewers for its structure, its preaching, and its indeterminate mixture of symbolism, evangelism, pacifism, and rough melodrama, this play is today perceived as a masterpiece, serving

Program cover of Armstrong's Last Goodnight, *Old Vic, October 12, 1965.*
© *Royal National Theatre.*

as a set text in English Literature syllabuses.[51] In an interview Ronald Hayman conducted with the playwright, Arden remarked: "I wrote a play attacking the complacency with which the British public was prepared to regard actions undertaken by the British Army in foreign parts. The play becomes famous. It is presented as an examination piece for schoolchildren. And the British Army continues to do exactly the same things in Ireland, and has been doing so for ten years."[52]

PARTICIPANT ON HIS OWN TERMS

The only paper I got real support [from] was Encore *magazine. [In the 1965 issue] there was a long interview with me which helped me a lot, sort of helped me get going. —Arden interview*

The English Stage Company production of *The Happy Haven* in 1960 was the last production of a new Arden play at the Royal Court and to this extent concluded the playwright's collaboration with this company, which can be seen as a major contributor to his theatrical career. The ESC not only introduced Arden's drama—providing a stage for his early plays—but also supported his work in the face of hostile critical reception. In this respect the ESC fulfilled an essential mediating role in the playwright's career. Indeed, where the mediation of his work was concerned, through the early stages of his career Arden primarily relied on his association with the ESC.

An article on Arden by Leslie Mallory[53] was published in the *News Chronicle* following the opening night of the Royal Court production of *The Happy Haven*. Mallory referred to the controversy elicited by Arden's work and presented the playwright as a victim of the Angry Old Men "who oppose truth in the theatre—or the gropings of a rebel dramatist to achieve it." Although other young dramatists such as Osborne and Pinter had also been victims of this "vicious fury," Mallory claimed that Arden had suffered an unfair share. According to Mallory, the playwright's attitude toward critical responses to his work seemed remote and indifferent. For instance, following the opening night of his new play Arden went back to Bristol University, where he had a year's fellowship in playwriting, leaving critics to argue the pros and cons of his latest work among themselves: "Not for Arden the ritual of other dramatists' opening week, which is to lunch at the Caprice where one may See and Be Seen." Arden, cited in the article, explained: "I find I can't work in London. People keep ringing up and coming round and I can't get on with my plays." He neither defended his work nor addressed the critical controversy elicited by his plays. His seeming aloofness at this stage of his career is noteworthy, especially compared with Osborne's cooperative attitude toward journalists or his willingness to explore other media exposure.

Although Arden was not involved directly in the critical controversy over his plays, he did express his concern and attempted to mediate his work. His concern, reflected in his conduct in the 1960s, was further demonstrated, though in a somewhat different manner, in later phases of his career. He never responded directly to critical attacks, nor did he engage in correspondence over his work. Instead, in interviews, most of which were published in *Encore*, and in his own essays,[54] Arden stated and explained the convictions underlying his dramatic art. He also clarified his motivation for employing particular theatrical devices as means to achieve his goals as a dramatist. Unlike his later essays, however, the earlier ones manifest the playwright's attempt to contribute to the understanding of his singular poetics, integrating, either implicitly or explicitly, his response to specific critical judgments of his work.

Arden's renowned article, "Telling a True Tale," published in *Encore* for example, deals with the function of the ballad in his work, which has baffled critics, producers, and directors of his plays. Referring to the ballad singer introducing each scene in *Live Like Pigs*, Hunt claims that "the directors never knew what to do with this man."[55] Apparently aware of the difficulty, Arden contended that "the bedrock of English poetry is the ballad." And since his concern (in view of the language he writes in and his intended audience) is to express his dramatic themes "in terms of . . . English British . . . tradition," and although he believes that regrettably the English public has lost touch with its own poetic tradition, Arden views this tradition as "the one that will always in the end reach the heart of people, even if the people are not entirely aware of what it is that causes their response." Arden presented the shift to formal language, in verse or song, as signifying emotional climaxes of the story, hence also serving as a segmentation device. He traced a line of writers "who have always built close to the bedrock" and referred to Brecht, who "consistently worked upon the same principle." Arden thus affiliated his own work with a poetic tradition and pointed out his particular theatrical direction. Moreover, he implicitly located his work at an intersection: it displays social criticism and is hence in line with contemporary playwrights such as Wesker, Osborne, and Arthur Miller; yet because it aims to have a weight and impact transcending contemporary documentary facilities, "it is expressed within the framework of traditional poetic truths." Arden concluded his article by addressing the issue of the author's "social standpoint," clarifying that "if the poet intends us to make a judgment on his characters, this will be implied by the whole turn of the story, not by intellectualised comments as it proceeds."[56]

An interview Tom Milne and Clive Goodwin conducted with Arden, published in *Encore* in 1961, also reflected the playwright's preference for mediating his plays on his own terms. For example, Arden explained his singular use of both prose and poetry in his plays: "I see prose as being a more useful vehicle for conveying plot and character relationships; and poetry as a sort of comment on them." On the characters in his plays who are not readily sympathetic, Arden stated: "I have grave objections to being presented with a character onstage whom you know to be the author's mouthpiece. . . . I cannot see why a social play should not be so designed that we may find ourselves understanding the person's problem, but not necessarily approving his reactions to them." Of the masks in *The Happy Haven,* he clarified that the use of masks, "a valid form of theatrical technique," had solved a problem arising from the nature of the play. To have elderly actors too near the age of the characters, in a grotesque comedy about an old folks' home, he said, "becomes cruel in the wrong sense." Putting young actors in masks solved the problem and was in keeping with the play's faster pace. Most significant were Arden's comments on the unpopularity of his plays, which he attributed partly to theatre audiences in London. Specifically of the reception of *Musgrave,* he remarked: "I suppose that to ask an English audience to accept a period play that is neither comedy, romance or even history *is* asking a lot."[57]

Arden's uncompromising approach as a dramatist, also manifested in his mediating conduct, is further reflected in a 1965 interview with Albert Hunt about his play *The Workhouse Donkey.*[58] The play, produced by Stuart Burge, was performed at the Festival Theatre, Chichester, on July 8, 1963. *The Workhouse Donkey* deals with municipal corruption, depicting the conflict between an appointed chief of police and the head of the party that runs a northern town. The town is torn between the two and the rivals are destroyed in the conflict. Hunt described the play as "a celebration of anarchy." Although the play was inevitably seen as referring to current local and national political scandals—it was the time of the Profumo affair—Arden ascribed its underlying dramatic conception to the medieval tradition of the Feast of Fools; it is, he said, "a straightforward classical comedy in structure." Of the donkey, he said: "I think that I had in mind the Golden Ass of Apuleius rather than the specifically Christian story." Arden referred to problems that beset the production, one of them being the lord chamberlain and his censorship office: "One of the prime functions of theatre has, since the earliest time, Aristophanes and beyond, been to inflame people's lust." He disputed the assumption that a playwright should "present the audience with a character that they can identify with," claiming that "plays are not public arguments. They are a presentation of life. I think that in a play like *The Workhouse Donkey* the action itself is the argument." In addressing the issue of intellectualization, Arden referred to the Dionysian origins of comedy and warned that as long as influential critics and writers "maintain that the highest form of theatre is the intellectual play, the theatre will be dead."[59]

These examples show that, in line with Arden's uncompromising stance as a dramatist, his mediatory conduct, rather than opting to accommodate, challenged the norms of critical discourse and audience expectations alike. In other words, Arden did not devise a marketing tactic for his drama; he neither made his work familiar by offering a relevant, contemporary context, nor packaged his plays with a catchy, accessible frame. Instead, he displayed his underlying intentions as a dramatist primarily by rooting his multilayered works in a theatrical tradition that made them even less accessible. One can recall in contrast Osborne's own publicizing of the catchphrase "angry young man" on television and in the press, which contributed to the perception of *Look Back in Anger* as a contemporary expression of the younger generation.

While in-house mediators such as Devine provided Arden with a stage and support, the external mediators who championed his work primarily exploited the channel of *Encore*. Aware, it appears, of Arden's uncompromising tendencies manifest in his mediating conduct, these critics relied on their own expertise to provide a framing or context within which to view the dramatist's innovative plays. Their efforts eventually helped construct and enhance his reputation.

As early as 1960, in *Encore*, Albert Hunt accused theatre critics of dismissing rather than facing the serious and "uncomfortable"—that is, political, critique—embedded in *Serjeant Musgrave's Dance*. Hunt's first target of attack was the notion of theatre Harold Hobson put forward in his review of *Musgrave*, including the remark: "It is the duty of the theatre, not to make men better, but to render them harmlessly happy." Protesting the separation of culture from politics, Hunt observed: "It's not really surprising" that Hobson—the theatre critic of the *Sunday*

Times—"should have little sympathy with the aims of the new Left." However, it was the view presented in the *New Statesman*, "the voice of Socialist humanism," that most infuriated Hunt. "John Arden," he wrote, "is making an attempt, however tentative, to break through to new values," whereas the tendency of the theatre critic, even in a paper such as the *New Statesman* that supposedly "carries on a political struggle," is to opt for theatre as entertainment.[60] Hunt concluded: "We still have some vital theatre left; for God's sake let's have some vital critics."[61] Hunt thus promoted Arden by presenting him as a dramatist who had broken new grounds, whose drama challenged the critics' assumptions on theatre and thereby provoked their objections. Hunt was to develop and cultivate this view in his articles and study of Arden's work in the years to follow.

By 1963, and before the National Theatre production of *The Workhouse Donkey*, Irving Wardle in the *Observer* had placed Arden "in the front rank of British playwrights," stressing that unlike the overnight success of most of his contemporaries, the dramatist's reputation "has grown slowly, and owes nothing to box office appeal or critical acclaim." Wardle explained that "partly because Arden has never repeated himself, and partly because he cannot be fitted into any obvious category, his work has been persistently undervalued at the time it appeared"; however, viewed in retrospect, his plays have "emerged as major landmarks of the modern theatre." Wardle thus relied on Arden's troublesome reception—unfavorable reviews and commercial failures—to claim the dramatist's merits. He also drew upon the playwright's own perceptions when commenting on Arden's original contribution to the theatre, stressing the innovative nature of the work. "Arden is the most literary of the new English dramatists," Wardle contended, "the first writer of the post-Fry generation to succeed in restoring verse to the stage, and the first to have assimilated Brechtian method into a style that is entirely his own."[62]

Charles Marowitz was another prominent theatrical figure who attributed the unfavorable views of Arden's plays to the reviewers' own shortcomings. In his 1965 *Encore* review of *The Workhouse Donkey*, Marowitz claimed: "Reviewers who do not know how to react to a playwright who builds no consistent image and refuses to pander to an audience's signal-responses are being told by a fervent claque that this man has got something. Not being able to define him with the clichés at their disposal, the critics cock a wary eye." Marowitz was highly infuriated at T. C. Worsley's dismissal of *The Workhouse Donkey* as "an ambitious piece that is both a downright failure and a muck-up and is far, far from interesting," and

Worsley's comment that "perhaps his young fans will now stop ruining his [Arden's] chance of a career as a dramatist by turning off the praise until he has earned it."[63] In rebuttal, Marowitz elaborated on the play's virtues and referred to Arden as "the writer least committed to sects and most committed to truth." Although pointing to a few problems in the production, which was praised by most critics for its high quality, Marowitz presented the play—in spite of its needing some structural revision—as a unique offering of "richness and fulsomeness."[64]

These examples show that external mediators who championed the playwright's case saw the troublesome reception of Arden's plays—in particular the reviewers' tendencies to undervalue his work—as deriving from the critics' own limited repertoire, their lack of suitable means for appraising a drama that does not accord with familiar and accepted theatrical norms, that is, drama that poses too great a challenge for them. The ambivalent attitude of most reviewers toward Arden's work—attacking his plays yet recognizing his dramatic powers, together with Arden's own attempts to explain his objectives and the policy endorsed by his champions all contributed to the construction of his image as a highly innovative dramatist whose work challenges both the widely agreed perceptions of theatre and the accepted borders of theatrical forms. Gradually, then, an "Arden" construct was being formulated that comprised adjectives such as "unconventional," "experimental," and "controversial." In other words, the reviewers, torn between fulfilling their mediating function and their inability to devise a construct conjoining characterizing dramatic traits, had resolved this difficulty by employing an aggregation of higher-level abstractions. They formulated an applicable "Arden" construct that circumvented the widely varying components of his plays. Arguably, it is this quasiconstruct associated with Arden's dramatic work that helped enhance his reputation toward the mid-1960s.

Another factor that in all likelihood contributed to the gradual buildup of Arden's reputation was the publication of his plays,[65] a channel the playwright himself had increasingly exploited. He added prefaces, introductions, and author's notes to the printed editions of his individual plays and to the published collections. Since the performance of a play preceded its publication, Arden could incorporate into his introductory notes his responses to reviews. He employed another mode of mediation—via a different channel—adding an author's note to the program accompanying his plays, for instance, to the program notes for *Armstrong's Last Goodnight* and *Left-Handed Liberty*.

UNDER THE WINGS OF THE ESTABLISHMENT

Between 1963 and 1965 Arden's career underwent a change: the productions of four of his plays were associated with established institutions. The National Theatre in Chichester staged *The Workhouse Donkey* on July 8, 1963. On January 29, 1964, *Ars Longa, Vita Brevis,* by Arden and Margaretta D'Arcy, was directed by Peter Brook and performed during the Royal Shakespeare Company's experimental season, the Theatre of Cruelty, at the LAMDA (London Academy of Music and Dramatic Art) Theatre Club. *Left-Handed Liberty,* a play commissioned by the City Corporation of London, was staged at the Mermaid Theatre on June 14, 1965, and in October of the same year the National Theatre performed *Armstrong's Last Goodnight.* Two of Arden's plays were also shown on television. On September 13, 1961, his television play *Wet Fish,* directed by Peter Dews, was broadcast by the BBC and on April 11, 1965, BBC2 aired a television production of his play *Ironhand,* directed by Rudolph Cartier.[66] In 1963, Arden and D'Arcy hosted a one-month Festival of Anarchy at their home at Kirbymoorside in Yorkshire. It had evolved from a film about Kirbymoorside that D'Arcy had begun upon the Ardens' move to the town. The advertisement in *Encore* on December 11 invited anybody who wished to join and take part in "a free public entertainment" and explained that "no specific form of entertainment is at present envisaged but it is hoped that in the course of it the forces of Anarchy, Excitement and Expressive Energy latent in the most apparently sad persons shall be given release." The response was enthusiastic and the festival was widely attended by metropolitan participants. It included films, plays, songs, readings, and performances by the Ardens and others.

The first play of the four staged plays, *The Workhouse Donkey,* was initially to have been produced by the Royal Court for a festival in Coventry, Arden recalled in our September 2001 interview. "The festival committee decided that it didn't want it, because they were having trouble between the corporation and the Church of England over the rebuilding of the cathedral, and they thought people would be offended by the argument in the play about the art gallery. So it wasn't put on in Coventry." Arden further recalled: "Laurence Olivier was running the Chichester Theatre when he was appointed head of the National Theatre and he started off by sort of organizing productions as the beginning of his National Theatre work. The play was then done at Chichester as a sort of joint management venture between Olivier, the Chichester Theatre, and the Royal Court."

The next year, the Royal Shakespeare Company staged *Ars Longa, Vita Brevis,* a play built around children's games. According to Sally Beauman's historical account, the 1963–1964 productions of *Wars of the Roses,* directed by Peter Hall (then the artistic director of the RSC) and designed by John Bury, "began the high noon of the RSC's existence that decade, one of those extraordinary periods that can happen to theatres when they suddenly make a breakthrough, and everything they touch turns to gold."[67] As RSC productions were performed concomitantly that season in London (Aldwych) and Stratford, Peter Brook and Charles Marowitz organized a series of club performances of experimental work under the title Theatre of Cruelty, [68] which included *Ars Longa, Vita Brevis.* The "Arden" quasiconstruct associated with the playwright's work at this stage of his career, along with Marowitz's view of the dramatist's plays, made Arden a natural choice. Predictably, the RSC with the production of *Ars Longa, Vita Brevis*—like the ESC with the early productions of Arden's plays, and possibly also like the joint venture of the ESC and the new National Theatre in the case of *The Workhouse Donkey*—provided Arden with a stage when his work was seen as complying with the company's aims. Beauman indeed stresses the new radicalism of the RSC's productions in the early and mid-1960s when compared with the work performed at the National, although she points to four productions that represented "the National's only forays into more controversial territory": Arden's *Armstrong's Last Goodnight* in 1965; Beckett's *Play,* Max Frisch's *Andorra,* and Brecht's *Mother Courage.*[69]

Interestingly, Tom Milne's review of the Theatre of Cruelty season, published in *Encore,* questioned the nature of this overall project. The full script of *Ars Longa, Vita Brevis* followed the review. Milne stated: "The Arden play is a corrosively funny, freewheeling examination of the relationships between Art, War and Education: it is an excellent piece, in a way a summary of his work to date, but neither more nor less experimental than his full-length plays." What he questioned was the purpose of the entire project: "There seems to be some uncertainty as to what the Theatre of Cruelty is—showcase or workshop." Rather than promoting the effort of staging plays such as Arden's, Milne chose to stress the experimental nature of the playwright's overall work to date.[70] His review implicitly suggested that rather than credit the RSC project for Arden's experimental work, the playwright himself should be promoted for his persistence in offering innovative drama.

Like Milne's, Hunt's view of the play reflects his disapproval of the

RSC experimental season as an appropriate venue. Hunt suggests that although this play was first produced by Peter Brook as part of the season "in which he [Brook] was exploring with professional actors the techniques suggested by Artaud . . . the Ardens' play belongs much more to the world of the children at their Kirbymoorside Festival."[71] The allusion is to the commissioning of the play for fourteen- to seventeen-year-old actors and its 1964 staging by D'Arcy with the Kirbymoorside Girl Guides.

Directed by David Williams and performed at the Mermaid Theatre on June 14, 1965, Arden's *Left-Handed Liberty* was commissioned by the City Corporation of London to commemorate the 750th anniversary of the signing of the Magna Carta. In the author's note included in the program, Arden clarified that the facts of the play were to a large extent based on history, while "the *opinions* are perhaps less historical." He continued: "It seems unlikely that any of the men concerned with drawing up the Great Charter had any conception of the reputation the document would have for future generations." In fact, the play centers on the apparent failure of the Magna Carta to serve its intended purposes, and, as Arden pointed out: "If this play has any direct message—and I am not normally an enthusiast for didactic drama—I suppose it is that an agreement on paper is worth nothing to anybody unless it has taken place in their minds as well."

The reviews of the production were mixed, although Arden's attempt to clarify his intentions helped, for several reviews drew directly on his program note. Philip Hope-Wallace in the *Guardian*, for example, asserted: "The simplistic view of history—that the Charter was a milestone and an enduring shield—is mere fairy tale. Agreements are not scraps of papers, they must come from the heart."[72] Milton Shulman's review implicitly employed the "Arden" quasiconstruct, referring to the decision of the City Corporation of London to commission for this particular event a writer like Arden, who "is not likely to produce anything conventional or orthodox," a choice he found "both imaginative and daring." Having mentioned the reputation of Arden's *Serjeant Musgrave's Dance*, Shulman declared that "if a play about Magna Carta had to be written" he could "think of no living playwright, with the exception of John Osborne, who would have tackled it with more zest and passion than has John Arden."[73] In the *Daily Telegraph*, Darlington directed his harsh critique at Arden's treatment of the historical material. He found (as did Bernard Levin) that the play reminded him of a lantern lecture.[74]

"The Theatre of Bewilderment," an article published in the *Guardian* in 1965, reflects Arden's peculiar standing at this stage of his career. Its author, Benedict Nightingale, said of the three recent productions of Arden's plays, "It seems like success." Yet he also remarked that the public "has still not accepted Arden" and claimed that the critics "remain perturbed" by him. "At first they mostly dismissed him out of hand.... Perhaps they were bewildered by the sheer bulk of ideas blandly served up, and chose to blame the author rather than themselves for the bewilderment. Slowly, they have been won over." But rather than offering a coherent overview of the dramatist's work, Nightingale, himself bewildered, pointed to the complex, confusing effect of Arden's plays—the main characters who "are not heroes, not villains," and the message that often seems to be "that there are no easy messages to be had."[75]

Arden's replies to these issues clearly established his criteria and objectives as dramatist. Addressing the issue of the critics, Arden emphasized that he "has his own self-criticism to face out: his plays, he finds, never match up to the ideal he had conceived." In response to Nightingale's question of whether Arden was interested in politics, Arden replied: "Yes, but in the dramatic side of politics, in the effect of political crisis on people.... I suppose I'm an anarchist with a small 'a,' and I subscribe to CND [Campaign for Nuclear Disarmament]; but find it hard to be committed to anyone." Arden admitted that he was not entirely satisfied with his plays as produced; he thought that rehearsal time should be extended and there should be an option of re-writing after the opening.[76] The publication of this article, which indicates Arden's standing as a dramatist at that time, served to further cultivate his reputation, while also confirming that even at this stage of his career many critics were still at a loss to judge his dramatic work.

Armstrong's Last Goodnight, directed by Denise Carey, was first performed May 5, 1964, at the Glasgow Citizens' Theatre and next in July, 1965, at the Chichester Festival Theatre, directed by John Dexter and William Gaskill.[77] Associated with the ESC since the late 1950s, both Dexter and Gaskill were at the time associate directors of the National Theatre.[78] In an interview with Tom Milne, Gaskill talked about considerations preceding the production of *Armstrong's Last Goodnight* at Chichester: "The thing about this play was that so many people whose opinion I trust, and so many ordinary people, non-theatre people, have been enthusiastic about it. And, before it opened, both John Dexter and I felt that it *might* make it with the critics—though from bitter experience of the past I wasn't disillusioned when it didn't."[79] Another production of the play—directed by Albert Finney, who also acted the lead—was staged by the National Theatre on October 12, 1965, at the Old Vic. An extensive program note accompanied this production.[80] Beginning with "The Ballad of Johnnie Armstrong," the program included citations from Sir Walter Scott, a graph of the power structure in the play, a broad introduction on Arden's previous dramatic work, and a note on the play written by the playwright. Although program notes commonly include a few words on the playwright, the extensive introduction by R. H. Bowden provided an overview of Arden's development as a playwright with respect to his subjects, themes, and techniques—an attempt to mediate not only Arden's work, but also his singular career. It cited the author's prefaces to various works and set forth an elaborate explication of his intentions and techniques in his best-known plays. Noteworthy are sentences such as: "In *Serjeant Musgrave* and *The Workhouse Donkey* we have, in fact, what has come to be a typical Arden protagonist"; "both plays . . . are typical of Arden's dramatic technique"; and "all these give added overtones to his work which, if at first not immediately assimilated, in retrospect seem to make the plays work with the proper yeast of humanity." The concluding sentence reads: "Arden's *Armstrong's Last Goodnight*, dealing as it does with problems of the Congo translated into terms of Scottish border conflicts in the early sixteenth century, suggests that he is developing further the thesis implied in *Serjeant Musgrave*: for each problem of the present there is an objective correlative hidden in the poetry of the past."

Arden's own note on the play follows the introduction, providing and explaining the play's historical context. He also traces the writing process, which included his reading of the book *To Katanga and Back* by Conor Cruise O'Brien, to whom he dedicated the play. He points out similarities between past events (Scotland in 1528) and recent political occurrences (the Congo in 1961). Identifying the aims and political agendas underlying the characters' actions, he distinguishes between the play's components that are founded upon historical facts and those that are his own invention. In clarifying his motivation to use a language from sixteenth-century Scotland (dog Gaelic), Arden refers to Arthur Miller's *The Crucible* as being, to some extent, the model for his play.

The reception of the Old Vic production of *Armstrong's Last Goodnight* was on the whole favorable. Most reviewers found the play much more effective on the proscenium stage at the Old Vic than in its open-stage production at Chichester, yet stressed that the production gained primarily from Finney's particular restaging of the play and from his own effective performance. Darlington, for example, greatly surprised at enjoying a play that he had not liked at Chichester, thought it was "pretty clear" that "great credit must go to Albert Finney."[81] The emphasis on Finney's role rather than the playwright's in this play's success is striking when compared to the *Daily Telegraph* review, which began: "The new season of the National Theatre opened last night with a play which should ensure for Mr. John Arden his long deserved status as a contemporary classic."[82] Finney, it appears, was not only a source of attraction—his reputation no doubt added luster to the production—but in the view of the reviewers he also made the play accessible, beyond the contribution of the program note. John Russell Taylor presents *Armstrong's Last Goodnight* as "Arden's nearest approach to genuine popular success, especially when it was allied in people's minds with *Left-Handed Liberty*."[83] Taylor's take is that Finney's "charismatic presence" attracted the audience and "once there they found that the ear became quickly attuned."[84] But if Finney's presence won over critics and audience alike, it was Arden's acquired status as a dramatist that almost certainly accounts for the overall success of this production. The association of Arden's work with established institutions finally outweighed the critics' inconclusiveness regarding his status as a dramatist, endowing him with a prominent standing. Noteworthy in this context is the *Encore* issue of September-October 1965, devoted to Arden's plays, which offered an overview of the playwright's work to date.[85]

Through the late 1960s and early 1970s, however, the mediating forces that had influenced Arden's growing reputation gradually underwent a process of elimination. This process, which involved Arden's and D'Arcy's open confrontations with the established theatre, subsequently took its toll, undermining Arden's acquired standing. The process culminated in Arden's break with the London theatre. It was clearly significant to this next phase of Arden's career that by the late 1960s *Encore* magazine, a major channel through which the dramatist's champions had voiced their support, ceased publication after October 1965.[86]

IN FACE OF THE ESTABLISHMENT

The problem with theory is that it puts plays into categories and once you're in a category, you're in difficulties, because you can't get out of it. . . . There is political drama, there is commercial drama, there is community drama— there are all these things. Now in real theatre, in live theatre, perhaps they flow in and out of each other. You can't separate your work into these sorts of categories. —Arden interview

In the late 1960s and early 1970s Arden continued to pursue new theatre forms as his perception regarding the playwright's responsibility to society changed. Among the champions of his work, views diverged regarding his course and the venues he chose for staging his plays. Repeated confrontations with theatre managements, the growing explicitness of Arden's political stance, and his increasing involvement with the Irish Troubles all were factors at play.

The opening night of *The Hero Rises Up*, by Arden and D'Arcy, marks the first direct confrontation between the authors and theatre management of a company in London. An ironic presentation of Nelson's life intertwining private and public events until his death at the battle of Trafalgar, the play takes a sardonic view of the hero cult. It combines the style of nineteenth-century melodrama with Brechtian detachment, using the form "both to celebrate and to question an English myth."[87] The Institute of Contemporary Arts (ICA), a leading artistic establishment, sponsored the 1968 production at the Round House. Heading ICA was Michael Kustow, an editor of *Encore* since 1964,[88] and a major promoter of Brecht in Britain, who had worked for a year in France with the director Planchon, known for his revolutionary work. Kustow's backing of *The Hero Rises Up* accorded with his interest in advancing political theatre.[89]

The authors and the ICA management had butted heads throughout their work on the production, according to Hunt. The conflict reached its climax on opening night, when the playwrights "threw open the Round House, and let the audiences in free."[90] Although the play was a popular success, most critics judged it harshly. Hunt stresses the playwrights' view that the final production, afflicted by bad lighting, chaotic seating, and difficulty in seeing and hearing the performance, was an inevitable result of their being "denied the co-operation necessary to make such a large-scale undertaking work."[91]

Hunt takes issue in particular with some of the views of *The Hero Rises Up* expressed by Simon Trussler in the *Drama Review* in 1969. Trussler first summarized Arden's dramatic work and critical reception up to 1969: "With Arden the talent-spotters never used to know where they were: turning his own declared pacifism topsy-turvy in *Musgrave* one minute, the next he'd be suggesting that the action of *Armstrong's Last Goodnight*, a play about medieval Scotland in dog-Gaelic, was tangential to the Congolese civil war. He'd toy with *commedia dell' arte* in the geriatric wards of *Happy Haven* as readily as with Aristophanic ribaldry in the council chambers of *The Workhouse Donkey*. There was no trusting him." Arden's dramatic work, however, "defined not dogmas but dilemmas; it was predicated by dramatic structure which was appropriate to an action rather than predictably idiosyncratic in an Osbornian manner. Arden was, in short, a consummate craftsman."[92]

Trussler focused on *The Hero Rises Up* and Arden and D'Arcy's *Harold Muggins Is a Martyr*, performed by CAST (Cartoon Archetypical Slogan Theatre) in June 1968 at the Unity Theatre. The audience at the Unity Theatre comprised primarily members of trade unions, while the Round House, owned, though seldom used, by Arnold Wesker's Center Forty Two, had often served to stage productions of an experimental nature that required a vast space at a low cost. Trussler claimed that these two projects were a continuation of Arden's (and D'Arcy's) experiments in community dramas. He referred to *The Business of Good Government*, a nativity play written and directed by Arden and D'Arcy, which was staged in 1960 as the Christmas play at the Church of St. Michael, Brent Knoll, Somerset, and to *Ars Longa*, written for schoolchildren and staged in 1964. Both plays were commissioned by local institutions, as was a later play by Arden and D'Arcy, *The Royal Pardon* (derived from bed-time stories), staged in September 1966 at the Arts Festival at Bedford Devon. Trussler also mentioned the Festival at Kirbymoorside in 1963. In his view, the earlier community dramas, produced between Arden's better-known works for the conventional theatre, *Musgrave* and *Armstrong*, were well-suited to their rural environments. The two later projects, *Harold Muggins Is a Martyr* and *The Hero Rises Up*, directed toward a more metropolitan audience, were immense failures.

In *Harold Muggins Is a Martyr* the employees of an old café rebel against their employer, Muggins, and against the gangsters who are taking over and modernizing the café. Trussler advanced several reasons for the failure of *Muggins*: the nature of the play, for instance, a "seemingly simple, actually elaborate political parable," and "typical Arden in its refusal to take sides"; the blunt, instrumental style of the production, inappropriate for a play "which needed to hint at complexity as well as to make propaganda"; and perhaps the audiences' expectations and lack of preparation. But "wherever the truth lay, the audience searched harder for it, as it turned out, than the newspaper reviewers, who were incensed by Arden's failure to conform even to his own brand of nonconformity." Despite the harsh reviews, the audience "packed the theatre for the duration of the play's run."[93]

Trussler attributed the failure of the next project, *The Hero Rises Up* primarily to the Ardens' choice to stage it at the Round House, which he considered an artistically unsuitable venue for the play that resulted in a misconceived production.[94] He pointed out three courses that had been open to the playwright at the time, two of which would have been suitable: returning to the fringe of the conventional London theatre (such as the Royal Court), or centering on community drama. He believed the course Arden had opted for in *Muggins* and *Hero*, which reflected "the attempt to discover a new play for each audience," to have been the least suitable, and one "destined to be a frustrating and unrewarding occupation."[95] Here, Hunt differed with him: "Trussler's argument implies that the Ardens are willfully rejecting professional theatre." Regarding the courses open to them, Hunt pointed out that "the professional theatre in this country has seldom been able to produce the 'style of entertainment' Arden's work demands."[96] Significantly, Trussler's article appeared in 1969, following the ICA production of *The Hero Rises Up*—five years before Hunt's study in 1974, two years after the RSC production of *The Island of the Mighty*, associated with Arden's break with the London theatre.[97] Both critics, however, acknowledged the uncompromising character of Arden's continuous search as a dramatist, manifested in his variegated objectives and in the demands his work made on both theatre professionals and audiences.

Another advocate of Arden's dramatic work was the influential critic, writer, and mediator John Russell Taylor, who in three editions of *Anger and After* in 1962, 1963, and 1969, devotes one section to Arden's plays. The section in all three editions opens: "Perhaps the biggest thing to stand in the English Stage Company's favour . . . will be their continued championship of John Arden in the face of a Press dubious to hostile and of almost complete public apathy." The elaborate account of Arden's dramatic work to date that also appears in each edition, highlights the innovative qualities of the plays and stresses the immense difficulties they pose due to their unconventional and varying theatrical nature. Taylor also wrote an introduction to a collection of three of Arden's plays published by Penguin in 1967,[98] in which he attempted to pinpoint the key to the difficulties "which audiences have found with all Arden's work: you never know where he stands in the play."[99] If in Osborne's case Taylor was one of several prominent, supportive mediators, in the case of Arden his account takes on the flavor of a campaign, geared to promote a playwright whose work is controversial. In each edition of *Anger and After* he explains, "we can stand a little uncertainty about which are our heroes and which are our villains, but where do we stand in a situation which seems to deny the very possibility of heroism or villainy?"[100] In the 1963 edition, Taylor contends that "there are signs that Arden is winning through." He perceives that the television broadcasts of Arden's plays in the early 1960s may lead to a "sort of break-through" and maintains that Sir Laurence Olivier's choice to produce *The Workhouse Donkey* "and the prospect of a West End revival of *Serjeant Musgrave's Dance* suggest that in the theatre also the tide is turning."[101] However, by 1969, Taylor acknowledges that while Arden's community and experimental theatre seem "to bring him much satisfaction, it is disappointing to those who eagerly await his long-delayed breakthrough to wider acceptance in the everyday professional theatre."[102] Yet Taylor retained in 1969 the closing of his account on Arden that had appeared in the earlier editions: "Sooner or later his definitive success with a wider public is assured."[103] The 1969 edition of *Anger and After* nonetheless concludes with the author's remarks on three "difficult" playwrights: John Arden, Harold Pinter, and Ann Jellicoe. Taylor writes that Arden is "a puzzlement; as spectacularly, prodigally gifted as any of our generation, he has somehow not yet, in spite of his reputation in enlightened quarters, managed quite to hit the taste of the public. . . . He has as yet offered no reason why a West End management should trust him except sheer talent, and that, unless the talent is running along reasonably familiar channels, is not quite enough for them."[104]

In the introduction to the 1965 *Encore* issue devoted to Arden's work, Simon Trussler, an editor of *Encore* since 1965, attempted to explain the incomprehension with which audiences and critics have tended to greet the dramatist's plays. He points to Arden's mistrust of abstract concepts and a consequent moral ambivalence in his writing as a possible source of this incomprehensibility. Where Taylor had referred to the "amorality" of Arden's dramas—rephrasing his 1962 reference in the 1963 edition—Trussler presented Arden as "a dramatist in search of a practical morality." Arden's plays, Trussler claimed, "have been episodes in this search: examination of ideas, people and attitudes, which have deliberately and honestly rejected an easy synthesis." Trussler also suggested that it was the dramatist's "highly sophisticated use of language, effecting degrees of stylization which are rewarding but demanding, and his supposed modifications of Brechtian devices, in the matter of construction as well as in that of gaining objectivity through a distancing of emotional response," that may have accounted for his "relative" failure to win a mass audience. He commented that "the act of cutting himself off from a metropolitan-dominated culture, both physically and increasingly in term of his art, has been of central importance to Arden's development; but it also has left him wide open to the uncomprehending hostility of metropolitan critics and audiences."[105]

Indeed, an essential factor in the development of Arden's career in the late 1960s and especially in the early 1970s was the shift in the playwright's own standpoint. Arden's change of perspective had been intimated in projects such as the eleven-hour Vietnam Carnival he staged with D'Arcy at New York University in 1967, when he was a visiting professor at the university, and the playwrights' work with the overtly socialist group Cast in 1968. Most revealing of Arden's state of mind at the time is his radio play *The Bagman, or The Impromptu of Muswell Hill*, written in the spring of 1969. It tackles the issue of the playwright's responsibility to society, displaying, albeit in a satirical and complex mode, Arden's reflections on his own career.

The Bagman, directed by Martin Esslin, then head of BBC drama, aired on BBC radio in March 1970. At the end of 1969 Arden had resigned the honorary position he had held since 1966 as chair of *Peace News*, a weekly pacifist paper. He spent the next year with his family in India. Arden added a preface to the published edition of *The Bagman* in 1971 in which he elaborated upon the impact of his Indian experience on his worldview in general and on his perception of the dramatist's role in particular.[106] On *The Bagman*, Arden wrote: "This play is in the nature of a dream. Some people think dreams foretell the future. This one in certain respects did."[107]

In her study on Arden, Frances Gray refutes Esslin's perception that *The Bagman* is "an exploration of the 'dilemma' of a liberal intellectual artist who feels himself unable to change the society he so accurately portrays." Gray contends that in 1969 "Arden's political thinking had already begun to change." She also remarks that Arden repeatedly rejected Esslin's view, both in the preface he added to the play and in his 1980 radio interview with Ronald Hayman.[108] Moreover, Gray maintains that it suffices to read the play, "or, curiously, to hear Esslin's own production to catch its tone clearly. It is a painfully honest and highly entertaining piece of self-satire."[109] Arden himself commented years later: "I was interpreted by some critics at the time as absolving the playwright from having anything to do in society. I don't believe that, and I didn't believe it then. The play is a satire, a self-satire; if I were writing it now I would try to make it clearer."[110] Interviewing Arden in 1991, George Gaston commented: "In *The Bagman* you returned to the radio, and this time with apparently a very personal play about a crisis of conscience. . . . The conclusion suggests your acceptance of an artist's role as a sympathetic but ultimately detached observer." Arden replied: "I don't know that the conclusion of that play is necessarily a real or directly personal conclusion. It is a conclusion of the character in the play, who is of course me but also not me. It's a fictional me, an Arden looked at sideways, and satirically. So I would caution about the conclusion being taken at face value. . . . I think that about the period when I wrote *The Bagman*, between 1969 and 1970, there was a development in my consciousness."[111]

Gray points to a sharp division in Arden's work, with the Indian experience serving "as the boundary." However, she suggests that Arden's activities (such as his involvement with political theatre) in this later phase of his career can be seen as drawing on debates and resources found in his early work.[112] Furthermore, Gray remarks, "after 1968 Arden was not alone in his political stance," referring to the change of the theatrical scene in the 1970s and the new dramatists—Howard Brenton, David Hare, Trevor Griffiths, David Edgar, and others. These second-wave dramatists manifested their commitment to socialism in their writing, she comments, unlike the dramatists associated with the first wave, who were socialists merely in outlook. She also refers to the plays written in the 1970s by established playwrights like Edward Bond that reflected a more consciously developed political analysis. "Arden and D'Arcy," she notes, "had their own impact upon the changes."[113]

Michael Anderson, tracing Arden's development as a dramatist, contends that the playwright's treatment of public themes in his dramas indicates one side of his commitment to society, while another side is represented by the many plays he wrote for particular occasions (for instance, *Left-Handed Liberty*), or for a particular group of people (for instance, *Harold Muggins Is a Martyr*, written for performance by amateurs at the left-wing Unity Theatre).[114] Anderson views Arden's autobiographical play *The Bagman* as an outcome of "a period of uncertainty if not of actual crisis," which the dramatist underwent along with "many other intellectuals of broadly liberal sympathies" toward the end of the 1960s. Anderson remarks that whereas early on in his career Arden had been perceived as an "uncommitted" writer—hence his refusal to preach—in time he "moved closer and closer to the revolutionary viewpoint of the radical left."[115]

Arden's shift regarding politics and theatre, to which he attested in interviews and prefaces following his visit to India, was apparent from his increasing involvement with community theatre and theatre of a political nature and manifested further in the plays he wrote with D'Arcy dealing with Irish politics. Although since 1960 the two had gone to Ireland every year, in 1971 they finally settled there in Corrandulla, County Galway, and as Arden explained in our interview, an increasing involvement in Irish life followed their move. Arden recalls that they became involved in the story of a woman in Oughterard who was being evicted from her cottage by an Englishman who owned the premises, and they decided to write a play based on this situation.[116] Called *The Ballygombeen Bequest,* it was first produced in the Falls Road, Belfast at a teachers' training college in 1972 and subsequently performed by the 7:84 Theatre Company at the Edinburgh Festival, at the Bush Theatre, London, and on tour. According to D'Arcy, when the 7:84 Theatre Company decided to present *The Ballygombeen Bequest,* company founder John McGrath and actor/director Gavin Richards were also very involved with events in Ireland. Although the playwrights stated that the play was fiction, when it opened in Edinburgh in 1972, D'Arcy recalls, performances would begin with this announcement: "The play is fiction but we all know who it's about . . . and here's his phone number."[117] Following the Edinburgh production Arden and D'Arcy were sued for libel. The case lasted five years and was settled out of court in 1977.[118]

Arden's agreement to collaborate with the Royal Shakespeare Company to produce his play *The Island of the Mighty* at the Aldwych in 1972 indicates that at the time he had not turned his back entirely on the established theatre. It was the conflict with the RSC management during and after the production of this play that was to culminate in Arden's break with the London theatre.

The Island of the Mighty, written between 1966 and 1969, is a revision of a trilogy commissioned by BBC2 in 1966. When a change in the policy of the Drama Department at the BBC kept the play out of production, Arden reworked a longer version of it for a theatre company in Wales. This version was not produced either. In 1972 the RSC decided to stage the play and asked Arden to produce a shorter version. Arden and D'Arcy rewrote the play after their year in India, drawing on their experience and observations in terms of ideological viewpoint and style of performance. The tragic story of the decline of a great king, which is set in the revised version against the background of peasant suffering, emphasizes the oppressive social system and the price paid by those who seek imperial power. Intended as a critique of King Arthur and his imperialist conduct, the

Royal Shakespeare Company
Direction
Peggy Ashcroft   Peter Brook   Peter Hall   Trevor Nunn
Trevor Nunn *Artistic Director*
Consultant Director
Peter Daubeny

THE ISLAND OF
THE MIGHTY

by John Arden with Margaretta D'Arcy

Aldwych Theatre

London WC2 01-836 6404

Licensees Theatres Consolidated Ltd.
Chairman D A Abrahams
Managing Director John Hallett
Programme 10p

Program cover of The Island of the Mighty, *Aldwych, Royal Shakespeare Company,*
December 5, 1972. © Royal Shakespeare Company.

presentation of the king-figure, according to the playwrights, demanded irony rather than pathos. The RSC production of the play missed the irony and further altered the intended style of performance, especially with regard to the music and setting. Although the management and the playwrights agreed in advance that Arden and D'Arcy were to watch the rehearsals in time to make any required changes, the playwrights' demands to change major aspects of the production were refused. Director David Jones claimed that there was not enough time for these changes and, fearing confusion on opening night, he was reluctant to allow a discussion between the playwrights and the actors. Since the actors themselves had voted against such a discussion, the play was performed as planned. When the conflict between the playwrights and the RSC management had not been resolved by opening night, the playwrights demonstrated in front of the Aldwych.

In my interview with Arden and D'Arcy, they explained their objections to the RSC production of *The Island of the Mighty* and recalled the events that followed their dispute with the management.

> D'ARCY: We had wanted it to be very much like either the Indian theatre or what was happening in Ireland, so you had musicians on stage, playing traditional music. Nobody was in full costume. They'd be coming in and out. . . . So you then have this movement constantly. . . . And they had wanted to make it into a Western, glossy play, because it was about Arthur.

> ARDEN: They wanted to make it into a patriotic British play, which it wasn't. . . . The actual acting was being directed in a way which brought up the role of King Arthur as a sympathetic character with whom the audience had to empathize, whereas instead, we wanted a critical look at him, in a much more kind of Brechtian performance. [. . .]

> ARDEN: Now the thing was, on seeing the rehearsals, we realized that there were areas in the play which needed cutting.

> D'ARCY: We couldn't make the cutting because the actors, the principal actors, were contracted to say so many lines.

> ARDEN: We wanted to do some reshaping of the play during the rehearsal, which, really, there was plenty of time to have done it, if—[. . .]

> D'ARCY: Because we were members of a union in Ireland; . . . our union was in Dublin, so we then had to take direction from the

British union, British Equity, if we were to maintain an official strike. British Equity said they were not going to maintain an official strike anymore, so we then had to go on unofficial strike. So that once Equity said it was an unofficial strike, it meant that the stagehands then could go in and so you might say that we were then, in fact, defeated. So we kept on with our unofficial strike outside. . . . We were not trying to stop the play, we were on strike because of working conditions, . . . but because it was an official strike, at the beginning, it meant that no one, technically, should cross the picket line, nobody working in the theatre could support us. So when Equity turned this into an unofficial strike, we then remained there until our contract was over, which was the first night. But we weren't trying to stop the show. We were just withdrawing our labor. I think that's very important.

ARDEN: We were standing outside the stage door with placards saying "Strike On Here." That's all we were doing. And getting very cold, because it was coming into winter.[119]

According to the press, at the end of the first week of the run actors from another theatre mounted the stage, demanding to stop the performance. When the audience voted for it to continue, the playwrights themselves burst into the auditorium, jumped onto the stage, and addressed the audience. Most famous is Arden's concluding exchange with the audience: "Look, are you actually saying to me that you wish me to leave the theatre?" And the audience roared in reply, "Yes!" "In that case," Arden announced, "I will leave this theatre and never write one word for you again." And he left.[120]

D'Arcy, recalling the support of Joan Littlewood, added, "All the best people supported us." She also recalled the press battle that ensued between the *Guardian*, presenting the playwrights' claims, and the *Times*, presenting the other side.[121] Some of the press coverage of the playwrights' dispute with the RSC management emphasized the authors' political viewpoint. However, when Arden was given an opportunity to explain his position in the *Guardian*, the emphasis shifted. In "Exit Stage: Left," Arden talked with reporter Raymond Gardner about *The Island of the Mighty* within the context of his work to date and directed his critique at the institutions: "These theatres are not supposed to provide challenging ideas." But primarily he spoke of his convictions and concerns as a dramatist. Gardner presented Arden as a playwright "committed to the theatre rather than to politics," as evidenced by his involvement with "community and organic theatre, in which the play may be constructed, or altered." Arden explained: "It is not a question of converting people by the plays but of simply advancing the bounds of theatre. It is converting people to the belief that theatre may have something to say to them." Arden pronounced his dislike of writing a play that would be a repetition of something he had done successfully before. His involvement with the political situation in Ireland had led him to write a completely new sort of play. "I've never regarded myself as anything but a writer," he said. "I have never seen myself as a director or political agitator but I've never been satisfied that the writer's role should simply involve sitting behind a typewriter. I've always wanted to be involved with more practical activities without having to initiate them and so my collaboration [with D'Arcy] enabled me to do a kind of writing which otherwise I would have never done."[122]

As Michael Anderson remarks: "Roughly speaking, the further Arden has moved to the left the more impatient he has become of the shortcomings of the established theatre."[123] Arden's change of viewpoint had evidently affected his interaction with the established theatre. It is equally apparent, however, that he was consistently uncompromising in his approach; he neither changed his dramatic work to suit the critics' or audiences' expectations, nor adhered to the demands of the mediating endeavor. Until the mid 1960s, although he pursued his own, singular mode of presenting his work, Arden had collaborated with established institutions and to this extent was a participant in the mediating endeavor. He was consequently provided with the backing of the theatrical establishment, the effect of which eventually out-balanced the difficulties posed by his challenging works. In the late 1960s and early 1970s Arden's path as a dramatist, motivated by his continuous search for new theatrical forms, gradually distanced him from the established theatre. After the conflict with the RSC management over the production of *The Island of the Mighty*, the breach between the playwright and the established theatre proved insurmountable, leading Arden to turn his back on the London theatre.

OTHER VOICES

Of all his generation (he was born in 1930) he [Arden] has come nearest to greatness while staying furthest from popular recognition. —John Barber, 1977

On July 3, 1978, six years after Arden's break with the London theatre, Radio 4 broadcast his play *Pearl*, produced and directed by Alfred Bradley. A notice in the *Guardian* announced the play and referred to the events in 1972 when Arden and D'Arcy "withdrew their labour" and picketed the RSC's Aldwych production of *The Island of the Mighty*.[124] This was the inspiration for *Pearl*, "a play about the writer's relationship with theatrical management." Subtitled "A Play about a Play within the Play,"[125] *Pearl* is set in the late 1630s just before the English Civil War. It concerns a disaffected dramatist, Tom Backhouse, who, under the influence of an actress, Pearl, attempts to bring about change in a deeply troubled time by staging a revolutionary play. The performance of the play is wrecked, however; both Backhouse and Pearl are assaulted. He is grotesquely deformed and she becomes a blind beggar, and the theatres are subsequently to be closed—the Puritans in fact closed all the theatres in 1642.[126] Arden, quoted in the notice, said: "That the situation in the play does put up strong points of similarity with the present day is no accident. The theatre generally is still a Cavalier perquisite."

A film by Andrew Shell portraying the recording of *Pearl* in the BBC's Manchester Studios was broadcast on the South Bank Show on July 1, 1978, two days before the play aired on the radio. A brief notice in the *Times* advertised the TV broadcast: "John Arden. A profile of one of our major playwrights as the cameras follow the production of his forthcoming new radio play, *Pearl*. . . . Melvyn Bragg talks to him about his work, and the film explains the making of a radio play."[127] Michael Billington in the *Guardian* wrote a highly favorable preview of *Pearl*, titled "Pearl of Great Praise."[128] Noting the play's autobiographical components—the dramatist's professional difficulties and private convictions—he claimed that "above all the play is rooted in the belief that drama should address itself to big issues. It seethes with a fine contempt for those who demand nothing from their poets," an interesting judgment in light of critical views voiced during Arden's early career. "What the play clearly establishes however (not that some of us ever doubted it) is that Arden is a major dramatist. He has the gift of using the past to illuminate the present. He instinctively likes moral complexities." Implicitly acknowledging the pitfall-strewn course of the playwright's career, Billington commented: "Perhaps the real importance of *Pearl* is that it shows Arden can work well in an atmosphere of mutual trust and that he has the capacity to write plays that are accessible to a large audience . . . and which also radiate intelligence."[129] Billington's conclusion seems like an attempt to mitigate the consequences of the row surrounding the RSC production of *The Island of the Mighty*. "Is there any chance that our major theatre companies," he asked, "following Bradley's example, will now have the courage to commission a new work from this unfashionable, hugely talented dramatist? And equally important, is Arden, this neglected Titan, still prepared to occasionally go it alone?"[130]

The television broadcast as well as the previews contributed to the favorable reception of Arden's play, which included high praise by the critics. Gillian Reynolds's radio review in the *Daily Telegraph*, titled "Best of British Drama"[131] was typical: "John Arden's *Pearl* poured into the ear a two-hour tumult of character, action and ideas, infused with irony, enriched with intellect, performed with passion. It was an affirmation of all that is rich and strong in the British dramatic tradition and a celebration of the radio's role in keeping that tradition alive." In his conclusion, Reynolds commented that "the argument takes such strange root in the mind is due to Arden's vivid and poetic gift. He keeps unlocking doors between history and possibility."[132] *Pearl* won the Giles Cooper Award as one of the best radio plays of the year.

The case of *Pearl* further confirms the effective result of Arden's collaboration with powerful mediating forces. The greatest London success of an Arden production with critics and audience alike, *Armstrong's Last Goodnight* at the Old Vic in 1965, can be attributed to a large extent to the skillfully devised mediating campaign of an established institution.

As far as mediation is concerned, in the later phase of his career Arden persistently adhered to his singular route; his author's note appears in published collections of his stage and radio plays and his and D'Arcy's notes in published collections of plays written in collaboration. In 1977 Arden published a collection of essays, *To Present the Pretence*, in which he describes and comments on various theatrical forms and experiments, such as the eleven-hour Vietnam Carnival he had staged with D'Arcy at New York University (in the essay "Roll up Roll up to the Carnival of War!") or the traditional dancing that he and D'Arcy had watched when they visited India (in the essay titled, "The Chhau Dancers of Purulia"), while in the essay titled "Playwrights and Play-Writers," Arden deals with the playwright's role. He expresses his critique of the existing theatrical system and centers in particular on the comparatively modern phenomenon of the "emasculating elevation of the Director above the Playwright and above the Actor."[133] Referring to Shakespeare's time, Arden maintains that dramatists should become essential and permanent members of acting companies, thereby enabling them to be in control of their work.

Arden's path as a dramatist in the late 1970s is exemplified by two works, *The Non-Stop Connolly Show: A Dramatic Cycle of Continuous Struggle in Six Parts*, and *Vandaleur's Folly*, both written by Arden and D'Arcy. Based on the life of Jim Connolly, the Irish revolutionist, *The Non-Stop Connolly Show* was performed complete in six parts, lasting twenty-six hours, at the Liberty Hall in Dublin over Easter in 1975, in celebration of the anniversary of the 1916 rising. Parts of the cycle were performed later on tour and the playwrights staged a production of readings with music and songs for a limited period of consecutive one-hour lunchtimes by Inter-Action at the Almost Free Theatre in London in May 1976. *Vandaleur's Folly*, whose theme was also Irish history, was performed on tour in 1978 by the 7:84 Company. Toward the end of the 1970s, Arden stopped writing stage-plays, although he continued to write plays for the radio and later shifted to writing novels.

LATER VOICES

Since the 1970s, agents from the critical and academic domains have invaded the territory of Arden's dramatic work. Thus, although Arden has withdrawn from theatre altogether, he is still present as a dramatist in the vast number of studies produced; perversely the continuous critical controversy associated with his dramatic work has maintained the recognition of his unique contribution to theatre and his reputation as a dramatist. Studies by Trussler, Hunt, Glenda Leeming, and Gray that center on Arden's work alone; studies that include his work as one of the subjects of inquiry such as those by Anderson and Julian Hilton; and studies by Colin Chambers and Mike Prior that concentrate on the works created in collaboration with D'Arcy, all begin with the controversy associated with his dramatic work. The studies' narratives on Arden represent an ongoing attempt to categorize his work, or to pin down his image as a dramatist. Studies that tackle the issue of Arden's political orientation typify this effort.

Arden's early (moral and social) plays were attacked by critics for their lack of explicit commitment ("he takes no sides"), while his later plays, most of which were written in collaboration with D'Arcy, were criticized for being overly committed ("sacrificed artistry to activism"). Michael Cohen's point of departure in "The Politics of the Earlier Arden" is the debate over whether the dramatist had in fact undergone a radical change—described by one critic as "from liberal to Marxist," and by yet another as "from detachment to anger"—or whether his political position had been clear all along, as Hunt had claimed. Cohen's article was published five years after Catherine Itzin's instructive study, *Stages in the Revolution*, which declares: "John Arden was always a political playwright in the broadest sense of the word." She notes that "in the fifties and early sixties he described himself as a pacifist," whereas "by the late sixties Arden had . . . become a revolutionary socialist." Itzin refutes the perception of some critics at the time that Arden's radical change of attitude was like "a Jekyll and Hyde transformation." Rather, "it was in retrospect the logical—arguably inevitable—conclusion to his political concerns and commitments." Arden's stance after 1968, manifest in "direct confrontation with conventional theatre management, and political action and participation," had originated "in what is called community theatre," Itzin claims, and it is at this time and in this area that his collaboration with D'Arcy began. Itzin believes that in their work with non-theatre audiences in non-theatre venues during the early sixties, Arden and D'Arcy "were laying foundations for the alternative movement that mushroomed in Britain between 1968 and 1978."[134] She traces Arden's political concerns to the beginning of his career as a dramatist and claims that all his early plays "were quite blatantly *about* politics and political matters, often sparked off by political events, historical and contemporary."[135] Arden's growing "politicisation," according to Itzin, was caused by events in the public arena during the late sixties and, in the private sphere, was affected by Arden's and D'Arcy's experience in New York, their work with CAST, and their visit to India. Itzin remarks that the course of action taken by the two during their dispute with the RSC, at the time an unheard of phenomenon, was by 1979 "no longer regarded as ludicrous,"[136] due to the efforts of the Theatre Writers Group. Itzin's argument, which advances a view of Arden as a political playwright throughout his career, reflects her attempt to present a coherent profile of the dramatist.

Yet another instructive study, *The Politics of Performance* by Baz Kershaw, published in 1992, also addresses Arden's ideological standpoint. Kershaw argues against the critique of Arden's early plays as displaying a "critical detachment," voiced by such as Taylor (1978), and Hayman (1979). Kershaw's study deals with alternative and community theatre, in particular British. In tracing its development, he centers on representative and influential practices since the 1960s beginning with the community

dramas of John Arden and Margaretta D'Arcy. He remarks that most theatre critics and historians have ignored Arden and D'Arcy's 1960s projects
and "even historians of alternative theatre have usually overlooked the
importance of Arden and D'Arcy's community dramas."[137] He pays tribute to their contributions, however.

Itzin's and Kershaw's readings of Arden's, and of Arden and D'Arcy's,
theatrical work as political are especially significant considering that Arden's later work was neither associated with nor endorsed by any particular political movement. D'Arcy acknowledged this point in our 2001 interview: "You have to get patrons if you're doing political stuff, you need
to get taken up by a political movement."[138] That the playwrights had no
such patrons is hardly surprising. Arden did not establish a long-term collaboration with any particular company[139] or director, which might have
proven helpful in his case, as it did in the cases of Osborne vis-à-vis Tony
Richardson and Wesker vis-à-vis John Dexter.[140] In this sense, Arden's
most beneficial collaboration had been with *Encore* magazine, which not
only continuously supported his dramatic work but also provided him
with the opportunity to express his convictions as a playwright. Although
Encore was discontinued in 1965, the *New Theatre Quarterly*, edited by
Simon Trussler, one of *Encore*'s editors, and the late Clive Barker, resembles *Encore* in many respects and has continued to pay special tribute to
Arden's theatrical works and to works by Arden and D'Arcy.[141]

Arden's presence in the critical and academic domains is manifest in
another group of studies, each centering on a different aspect of his dramas. These studies' vast and particularly heterogeneous range of subjects
and perspectives—for example, the function of song in his dramas, or
Arden and the Absurd—corresponds with Arden's multifaceted dramatic
work. Both this proliferation of studies and the reviewers' difficulties with
Arden's early work derive from the playwright's wide range of subjects
and styles. Another example of the reassessment of Arden and D'Arcy's
plays is a 1955 case book of essays pointing to their influence on succeeding dramatists.[142] Susan Bennett, for instance, suggests reading Arden's
Armstrong's Last Goodnight "as an artifact which predicts future developments on the British stage." She points out that mainstream theatre by
the late sixties had begun to accommodate a more Brechtian theatre—
evidenced by Howard Brenton's 1976 *Weapons of Happiness* commissioned
as the first new play for the National Theatre—and claims that Arden's
early plays facilitated the inclusion of more politically aware drama in
mainstream repertoire. Also owing much to Arden's bridge between

Brechtian practice and mainstream English stage are such large-scale epics as David Edgar's *Nicholas Nickleby*, produced in 1980.[143]

If later reassessments of Arden's work seem incompatible with some of the early critical judgments of his plays, a similar shift is manifest in the mediatory channel of the press, exemplified by two press articles published a decade apart. "Out of the Sink into the Shadows: From Angry Man to Forgotten Man—The Reclusive Playwright," by Nick Smurthwait, appeared in the *Sunday Telegraph* in 1993, preceding the Royal Court revival of *Live Like Pigs*. The article primarily traced the troublesome reception of Arden's plays, by critics and audience alike, throughout his career. Referring to the scandal surrounding the RSC production of *Island of the Mighty*, Smurthwait stressed that "even in the highly politicised atmosphere in the early 1970s, Arden and D'Arcy cut a formidable couple. Both were deeply intense and scornful of anything with any commercial leanings." Smurthwait also mentioned the "speculation that the move to Ireland had done terrible things to Arden's creative capacities" and quoted Neville Blond, then chair of the ESC, to Devine, following the first production of *Live Like Pigs*: "Not another Arden, George."

Ten years later, in 2004, "Britain's Brecht," written by Nicholas Wroe, appeared in the *Guardian*. This broad profile of Arden, its tone different from Smurthwait's article, quoted Raymond Williams's assessment of *Serjeant Musgrave's Dance* in 1968: "John Arden is the most genuinely innovative of the generation of young English dramatists of the fifties." Wroe remarked, however, that Arden's career "was not progressing along standard lines." By the time of the dispute with the RSC in 1972, "Arden was geographically as well as culturally and politically distanced, having moved to Ireland and almost uniquely for an English writer at the time, taken up Irish issues in his work." The profile acknowledged the playwright's astonishing productivity, and the innovative and challenging nature of all his work, and cited laudatory reviews of Arden's three novels and collection of short stories, *Stealing Steps*, published in 2003. In his conclusion Wroe returned to *Musgrave*, then recently revived, which he found relevant even four decades after it first appeared.

Although this book gives mediators the first say on a playwright, in this case the playwright's own words serve as a concluding note: "The thing is that I'm writing fiction. Academics are trying not to. Of course they're constructing. Because if you write a book about playwrights you are actually inventing a kind of person that you would like that playwright to be" (Arden interview).

Harold Pinter

Who Controls the Playwright's Image?

Mel Gussow: Who's Harold Pinter?

Harold Pinter: He is not me. He's someone else's creation.

—Mel Gussow[1]

Pinteresque: Of, pertaining to, or characteristic of the British playwright Harold Pinter or his works. Marked especially by halting dialogue, uncertainty of identity, and air of menace.

—Oxford English Dictionary

He was Pinter from the beginning. As a nameless dramatist once said: I feel sorry for Harold. Other people can choose between comedy and tragedy, Pinter always has to write a Pinter play.

—Peter Hall on Pinter at 70[2]

One of the many awards bestowed on Harold Pinter was for his play *Betrayal*, which won the 1979 Play of the Year award from the Society of West End Theatre. At the ceremony the playwright began his acceptance speech by saying, "I am very surprised. No more, I suppose, than Michael Billington."[3] The audience, startled at first, laughed. Michael Billington—a great advocate of the dramatist and eventually his biographer—had written a harsh review of *Betrayal* in 1978. Pinter's barb on such a public occasion was no accident. He has maintained throughout his career direct and indirect dialogue with the critics of his work.

Of all the forces that mediate between a playwright and the public, theatre reviewers may be of cardinal importance. Along with journalists and interviewers, they act as external mediators—employing channels such as television, radio, and print media to form, cultivate, and modify a playwright's image as dramatist. Theatre reviewers, who present the first critical judgment on individual productions of a dramatist's plays, constitute a major factor in shaping the perception of that playwright's dramatic style and lay the groundwork for the critical assessments that follow, including academic studies, which further influence the position of the playwright in cultural or historical memory.

The reviewers' mediation of Harold Pinter's plays through the different stages of his career present an intriguing phenomenon. Pinter's early plays, unlike those of John Osborne and John Arden, were not associated with a particular theatre company or director. Although several directors and producers helped promote Pinter—for example, Michael Codron, who produced Pinter's first play in London—the theatre reviewers constituted the most significant force in mediating the dramatist's early plays, an influence they tried to maintain as Pinter grew more secure in the theatrical field, even to the point of downplaying the canonical standing he would acquire later.

The very terrain of Pinter criticism is a contested subject in research circles devoted to the playwright, exemplified by two scholarly works that deal with Pinter's critical reception: Austin Quigley's 1975 study *The Pinter Problem,* in which the diversity and, for Quigley, the unsatisfactory nature of critical attempts to elucidate the enigmatic effect of Pinter's plays serve as a point of departure; and Susan Hollis Merritt's *Pinter in Play: Critical Strategies and the Plays of Harold Pinter* (1990), which maps the critical approaches to Pinter's work from a reader-response perspective.

Pinter is well known for his own pronouncements regarding his theatrical practice, as in: "I'd say that what goes on in my plays is realistic, but what I'm doing is not realism,"[4] or, "I suggest there can be no hard distinctions between what is real and what is unreal, nor between what is true and what is false. A thing is not necessarily either true or false; it can be both true and false."[5] While seeming to collaborate in providing a key to his plays, such statements themselves comprise contradictions and therefore elicit questions rather than supply answers. Although such statements convey Pinter's critique of, and objection to, the tendencies of critical discourse to classify and categorize, Pinter critics and scholars have co-opted them to confirm one or another interpretation of his dramatic work or commentary on it.

Such statements both exemplify Pinter's pronounced views on his work during the early stage of his career and reflect the interactions he established with critics of his plays. Typically, in the first stage of such an interaction, Pinter responded to criticism about his work in an interview or a talk. This response elicited a chain of further critical interpretations that were subsequently incorporated into the critical discourse.[6] To this extent, Pinter's career demonstrates an ongoing bi-directional interaction between a playwright and the critics of his work—in particular theatre reviewers, journalists, and academics—that entails a continuous dialogue, albeit between the lines. This dialogue, in turn, contributes to the formation, cultivation, and modification of Pinter's (or any playwright's) constructed image. Pinter's tendency to make implicit or enigmatic pronouncements that modulated into direct or explicit responses to critics, journalists, and interviewers, together with his later tendency to shift between dramatic modes, suggests an overarching framework within which the interaction between the critics and the playwright can help explain the twists and turns of Pinter's writing career.

THE FORMING OF A PLAYWRIGHT CONSTRUCT

Theatre reviewers, acting as external mediators, provide initial legitimacy for playwrights not yet accepted into the theatrical canon.[7] As demonstrated in the case of John Arden, throughout the process of a playwright's acceptance reviewers seek to meet two major conditions: initially, they need to define and locate the new dramatist within the overall context of the theatre tradition; and, once this affiliation has been achieved, they promote, or market, the new playwright's particular means of theatrical expression. Since the new playwright is usually affiliated with an accepted theatrical school or dramatic style, each addition not only influences canon formation and expansion of canon borders, but also plays a role in the definition of theatrical schools and historical sequences.[8]

The process of acceptance thus entails two oppositional, though complementary, critical tendencies: the presentation of the recognizable and the introduction of the original. The construct devised on the basis of a playwright's work is the by-product of the amalgamation of these two critical tendencies. Its gradual consolidation over the process of the playwright's admission into the canon provides the reviewers with the means to locate the newcomer within it and serves in their enhancement of a playwright's prestige or cultural capital.

Although the construct is derived primarily from the playwright's dramatic works, the personalities and attitudes of the dramatists may be subject to mediation in their own right. Any information on the playwrights, including their convictions and earlier views of their work, can be incorporated into their emergent construct and used selectively to further market their plays and cultivate their reputation by means of media coverage or in reviews of their subsequent works. The dramatists themselves inevitably arouse growing curiosity once they have acquired an established standing.

The emergence of the construct is an integral part of a playwright's admission into the theatrical canon, yet the specific components of the construct and the particular process of its formation differ in each case. The construct will be of definitive importance in the later stages of a playwright's career, deployed and modified by scholars dealing with the playwright's oeuvre. If the construct facilitates the reviewers in the prompt mediation of the dramatist's new plays, the scholarly studies that follow use it as a point of departure and a way to locate the playwright within the broader context of historical or cultural memory.

The career of Harold Pinter offers an especially instructive case for illustrating the evolving stages of a playwright's construct, shaped by the various interactions emerging between the dramatist and the mediators of his work through different phases of his career. Pinter is a playwright who assumes an active role in determining his own dramatic image, either by once again writing a play that seems incompatible with his previous works, thereby appearing to challenge his constructed image,[9] or by participating in the mediating processes and thereby negotiating the criteria by which he might appear to be judged.

CONSOLIDATION OF THE "PINTER" CONSTRUCT

The critical reception of Harold Pinter's first performed play in London, *The Birthday Party*, has become somewhat mythical in light of his eventual theatrical success. Directed by Peter Wood and performed on May 19, 1958, at the Lyric Theatre, Hammersmith, the play was pronounced by reviewers obscure, delirious, oblique, and puzzling and was dismissed as a theatrical failure.[10] The majority of reviewers attacked the play and derided it to such an extent that it was taken off following the Saturday performance, after only a week's run.[11] Harold Hobson's review in praise of the play,[12] published on Sunday, was thus too late to save the fate of the production. A number of other critics also expressed favorable views but these, published several months later in *Encore* magazine, did not affect the decision to take the play off.[13] For instance, Irving Wardle's article, "Comedy of Menace," published in the September-October (1958) issue, linked four new "promising" playwrights: Pinter, Nigel Dennis, N. F. Simpson, and David Campton. This influential article contributed to the perception of Pinter in the years to come as the "Master of Menace."

The *Encore* publishing house in fact published the first edition of Pinter's play *The Birthday Party* in 1959.

The critical view shifted for the next three stage productions of Pinter's works—the sketches "Trouble in the Works" and "The Black and White" in July 1959[14] and "Last to Go," "Request Stop," and "Special Offer" in September 1959[15]—as well as for the double-bill comprising *The Dumb Waiter* and *The Room*, directed by the playwright in January 1960.[16] Pinter's puzzling dramatic style, perceived previously as the major flaw of *The Birthday Party*, was now attributed to his originality.[17] In reviews of *The Caretaker* in April 1960,[18] the next stage production of a Pinter play in London, the playwright's enigmatic theatrical style was presented as his drama's main source of attraction.[19] Robert Muller, for example, praised Pinter for his unique ability not only "to create *a world of his own, an entirely personal world*," but also to compel "a desire in his public to penetrate it."[20] Turning the flaw into an attraction, Muller added, Pinter "effortlessly . . . produces atmosphere at once puzzling, dramatic, and charged with fascination."[21]

The initial critical rejection of *The Birthday Party* reflected the reviewers' difficulty in identifying its dramatic style or in associating this with any established dramatic model. Although they pointed out various possible influences, the reviewers could not locate the play specifically, in terms of affiliation, within the framework of British or European theatrical traditions.[22] In their reviews of *The Caretaker*, however, the critics pointed to certain influences, especially Beckett's, and posited a particular affiliation.[23] Pinter's theatrical style, nonetheless, was presented as unique precisely by virtue of its enigmatic nature.[24] A few reviewers now went as far as presenting Pinter's drama as a major contribution to the development of British drama,[25] an ironic reversal of their initial rejection of local talent. Once Pinter's drama was affiliated with accepted theatrical models, it became a part of an ongoing historical sequence. Yet his theatrical language was familiarized only up to a point. Pinter was a chapter in a theatrical tradition, but the solution to the particular enigma he poses was withheld in order to ensure his greatness. Thus, the inexplicable quality of his dramas, seen formerly by reviewers as a major flaw, served to enhance his original contribution and eventually became his trademark.

The Caretaker received the *Evening Standard* Drama Award for the best play of 1960. In March 1961 it was transferred to the Duchess Theatre, and *Plays and Players* pronounced Harold Pinter the Personality of the Month and "perhaps the most significant and powerful of our new dramatists." Referring to the hostile critical reception of *The Caretaker* in Paris, the notice concluded: "In London, however, Pinter remains the darling of the critics."[26]

Pinter's plays were broadcast on the radio and television during the early phase of his career, media exposure that contributed to his promotion and enhanced his reputation. His play *A Slight Ache* was broadcast on BBC radio's Third Program on July 29, 1959; *A Night Out*, in which he himself acted, was broadcast on the same program on March 1, 1960 and on ABC television on April 24, 1960. *The Birthday Party* was broadcast on television (Associated Rediffusion, March 22, 1960), as was *Night School* (Associated Rediffusion, July 21, 1960). Subsequently, *The Dwarfs* was broadcast on the radio (BBC Third Program, December 2, 1960) and *The Collection* on television (Associated Rediffusion, May 11, 1961).

In 1963, John Russell Taylor contended that the commercial success of *The Caretaker* in 1960, as compared with the commercial failure of *The Birthday Party* in 1958, "was almost entirely the work of television."[27] Ronald Hayman, accounting for the larger audience and longer run of *The Caretaker* as compared with *The Birthday Party*, in 1973 emphasized the role of Michael Codron, the producer of both plays. Hayman refers to other contributive factors: Hobson's review, the BBC commission of Pinter's plays for radio and television, a prestigious amateur revival of *The Birthday Party* at the Tower Theatre, a number of West End reviews with Pinter sketches in them that were also produced by Codron, and articles and conversations. Hayman asserts nonetheless that because "the initiatives which established Pinter's reputation were Codron's, he, more than anyone else, created an audience for him."[28] Richard Eyre and Nicholas Wright describe and assess the reception of Pinter's early plays in their 2000 study *Changing Stages*,[29] commenting that "what was unusual was that the flop of *The Birthday Party* was immediately seen, not as a failure of the play but as a failure of the system. The liberal establishment in the shape of BBC Radio and commercial television . . . rushed to put things right." Eyre and Wright dismiss the view that the critics were to blame for the failure of *The Birthday Party* in 1958. At the same time, they insist that "if the play had still been on," Harold Hobson's review—"one of the greatest raves that he ever wrote"—"would have ensured packed houses and a West End transfer." Eyre and Wright further argue that when *The Caretaker* opened it was clear "that there wasn't just an appetite for Pinter's plays: there was a cavernous public need."[30]

The broadcasts of some of Pinter's early radio plays coincided, more or less, with the BBC broadcasts of Samuel Beckett's work between 1957 and 1964.[31] In view of Beckett's stature by that time, the association of Pinter's plays with Beckett's possibly added an important new form of promotion. Further, Methuen published Pinter's plays to date in 1960 and 1961, expanding the orbit of his reception. His growing acclaim outside Britain also enhanced his reputation at home.

Interviews with John Sherwood and with Kenneth Tynan that were broadcast on BBC Radio in 1960 increased Pinter's visibility.[32] In fact, Pinter's reluctance to engage in conversation about his work during the early stage of his career became in itself a much publicized phenomenon.[33] In these two interviews, in the 1961 conversation with Richard Findlater, and in the famous interview with Lawrence Bensky in 1966,[34] the playwright himself appeared to contribute to the "enigmatic" image associated with his work. Pinter's participation in the mediating process of his work, at this early stage of his career, thus took a dual tack of collaboration and evasion.

Noteworthy, in this context, is an unsigned note in the program brochure of the 1960 production of *The Room* and *The Dumb Waiter*. The note offers a plot outline (open to various options) and presents statements relating to issues such as the intangible nature of truth in general, and truth as represented on stage.[35] A letter Pinter wrote to the editor of *The Play's the Thing* in 1958, responding to questions about his writings, included several phrases similar to those appearing in the unsigned note. This letter, as well as Pinter's well-known talk "Writing for the Theatre," delivered at the Seventh National Student Drama Festival in Bristol in 1962, leave no doubt as to the identity of the writer of the unsigned note.[36] It is reasonable to assume that in view of the unfavorable reception of Pinter's first produced play in London and the reviewers' bafflement, the playwright had ventured a mediating tactic to win the audience over to his side. In essence, he chose to present his dramas on his own terms, setting forth the views in the light of which he believed his plays should be judged. In fact, Pinter's own mediating intervention would become a reference point in critical studies of his work, notably Martin Esslin's *The Peopled Wound*.[37] Pinter's Bristol talk is a discrete instance that reflects, in a more explicit and elaborate form, the playwright's mode of participation in the mediating endeavors. Pinter did not supply explanations,[38] but rather presented the inexplicable quality of his works as rooted in his ideology and perception of life.[39]

"Here for the first time is Pinter on 'Pinter between the Lines'," reads the introduction to the talk, printed in the *Sunday Times*,[40] presenting the dramatist as "Britain's most controversial playwright," who prefers "to remain silent between his plays." Characteristically, in his seeming willingness to collaborate, Pinter set out to manipulate his audiences, and his mediators into the bargain. Through expressing his view of language, he proposed to alter the norms by which language spoken onstage is judged. He thus manipulated his implied judges into valuing the language spoken in his plays for its ambiguous quality, rather than perceiving it as deviant and puzzling. Pinter's implicit proposal to change the contract between audience and playwright was an active step designed to influence and shape the reception of his plays. Centering on the issue of language in general, and on the dialogue in his plays in particular, Pinter called attention to the major role of dialogue in these plays while substituting the term "ambiguous" for the less valorous "puzzling." "Ambiguous," of course, suggests a far more positive evaluation of the dialogue. Pinter concluded his talk by quoting Samuel Beckett's statements at the beginning of his novel *The Unnamable*.

In 1962 *The Collection*, broadcast on television a year earlier, was performed at the Aldwych Theatre, codirected by the playwright and Peter Hall.[41] Pinter directed the next stage production of his plays, the double-bill comprising *The Lover* and *The Dwarfs* on September 18, 1963, at the Arts Theatre Club, London. Both plays had originated in other media, *The Dwarfs* on the radio and *The Lover* on television. Most reviews of this double-bill reflected the impact of the views Pinter expressed in his talk, printed in the *Sunday Times*. The issue of dialogue, for instance, occupied many reviewers, presumably partly as a result of Pinter's particular attention to this subject when speaking of his own work. The drama critic of the *Times*, who described the language in both plays, remarked of *The Lover*: "The dialogue is beautifully spare and concrete, making every point with the minimum exertion."[42] This critic's perception that "what connects the two plays is an incurable obsession with the elusiveness of reality," appears to rely directly on Pinter's own expressed view that "there can be no hard distinction between what is real and what is unreal."[43] Bernard Levin, in his *Daily Mail* column, referred directly to Pinter's talk and mentioned the playwright's objection to the perception of his plays as abstract.[44] Most reviews contained the reviewers' accumulated impressions of Pinter's previous plays; several described the plays, or the style of direction, using such words as "Pinterismus," or "Pinteresquely."

W. A. Darlington's review offered an especially wide, and wild, range of Pinter diversions. Titled "Pinter at His Most Pinteresque," it described the plays as "pinting," "pintation," "pintic," and "impintist," and the directing style as "pinteresquely."[45]

During 1963 and 1964 Pinter's television dramas and screenplays won both international and British prizes.[46] These prizes, which clearly reflected the growing recognition of Pinter's unique contribution as dramatist, screenwriter, and director, in turn cultivated his reputation.

A revival of *The Birthday Party* on June 18, 1964, directed by the playwright, was performed six years after the play's first London production. Its favorable reception demonstrated the reviewers' diminished tendency to compare the play to accepted theatrical models. The notices particularly praised Pinter's "gift for dialogue."[47] His work, recognized at this point as an original contribution to British drama, was presented to the public under the label "Pinteresque."[48] This label can be perceived as the final transformation of the epithet "puzzling" previously attached to Pinter's dramatic work,[49] which would hereafter be promoted under a "Pinter" label. This label, in itself, was to function as sufficient clarification of supposedly incoherent elements, familiarizing the uninitiated public with this playwright's unique theatrical expression, whose very unfamiliarity had led to its initial rejection.

Herman Schroll perceives the critics' employment of "Pinteresque" to be an outcome of their inability to find a ready-made label for the playwright's works. Although Schroll acknowledges that the reviewers used this label only after Pinter was already accepted by the critical community, he fails to see its connection to the playwright's critical acceptance. Furthermore, Schroll views the label as a hindrance to the playwright's career rather than as a critical strategy that served the reviewers in their enhancement of his prestige.[50]

Pinter's standing was apparent by 1965, when his next full-length play, *The Homecoming*, directed by Peter Hall, was performed by the Royal Shakespeare Company at Aldwych on June 3, 1965. The first page of the program note for this production features a large photo of Pinter with Peter Hall. In "Five Desperate Years of Harold Pinter," Barry Norman considers that *The Homecoming* marked "Pinter's return." Although the playwright had collected awards "with almost monotonous regularity over the past few years," in Norman's opinion *The Homecoming* was his "first major piece of original writing, for more than five years, since *The Caretaker*."[51]

In their reviews of *The Homecoming,* critics drew upon the critical repertoire established in earlier reviews of Pinter's plays, either by choosing to treat the Pinteresque aspects of the play[52] or by explicitly referring to the familiarity of aspects or attributes that had been commented upon earlier.[53] Although the reviews of *The Homecoming* were not wholly favorable, the recurrent references to earlier, critical perceptions of Pinter's dramas indicate that he had acquired a critical existence."[54] At this point, which marks the completion of the dramatist's admission into the theatrical canon, a well-defined "Pinter" construct had come into being. It was based on the augmented critical repertoire associated with the playwright's work and stored for potential future use. This critical construct evolved from the package of attributes that had emanated from the early, critical perceptions of Pinter's plays in the phase leading up to his acceptance.

The construct comprised attributes that were either stamped explicitly or associated implicitly with the label Pinteresque. The reviewers' frequent use of the term reflected an implicit critical agreement as to the distinctive attributes of Pinter's dramatic work.[55] Moreover, the construct implied the reviewers' recognition of new dramatic norms that had come to be associated with Pinter's work. The term Pinteresque thus functioned not only as shorthand for the agreed dramatic attributes, but also as a signifier of new dramatic norms that both drew on and expanded the existing repertoire of theatrical modes.[56] Although Pinter's work was still perceived as enigmatic, its presentation as such by the critics was now descriptive in nature rather than indicative of its abnormality. Pinter's particular means of theatrical expression, now at the critics' disposal, would subsequently be presented as one more dramatic paradigm facilitating the reviewers' acceptance of new playwrights.[57]

During the next two years critical acclaim continued in the form of various awards. In 1966 Pinter was appointed Commander of the Order of the British Empire and in 1967 *The Homecoming* received the New York Drama Critics Award.

Pinter's *Silence* and *Landscape,* also directed by Peter Hall, were performed by the Royal Shakespeare Company at Aldwych on July 2, 1969. Dame Peggy Ashcroft played Beth in *Landscape* when it was first broadcast on BBC radio, April 25, 1968, and subsequently in the stage version. Frances Cuka played Ellen in *Silence.* The radio production of *Landscape* was itself a focus of critical attention in an article by Kathleen Tynan, "In Search of Harold Pinter," published the following day. Tynan asked Pinter about the lord chamberlain's request that he cut four words from

ALDWYCH THEATRE

LONDON WC2 TEMPLE BAR 6404

ROYAL SHAKESPEARE COMPANY in

THE HOMECOMING

by HAROLD PINTER

programme one shilling

Program cover of The Homecoming, *Aldwych, Royal Shakespeare Company, June 3, 1965. © Royal Shakespeare Company.*

Landscape, a demand that Pinter had refused.[58] In the main however, the article centered on Pinter's themes and theatrical devices, his views on his work, and his convictions in general. Pinter adhered to his usual intricate mode of response to critical perceptions (and misperceptions) of his plays and amply demonstrated both collaboration and evasion. *Landscape*, for example, is "simply, as it stands, about a woman around 50. And she is talking. That's all I bloody well know. I don't know where she is. Certainly it's not a room. So the characters can't open a door and come in, but I think they're there." To interviewer's comment "about the accusation that his work is full of gamesmanship," the playwright explained: "What takes place is a mode of expression; a chosen device. It's the way the characters face each other under the game that interests me."[59]

Harold Hobson bestowed high praise on *Silence* and *Landscape*. Discussing the striking similarities between these two "memory" plays, Hobson commented: "The audience has to piece together into some sort of shifting coherence the fragmented details of the partly recollected past." He highlighted their singular depiction of "ordinary matters," a talent "Mr. Pinter has been famous for ever since *The Caretaker*," Hobson asserted. He also praised Peter Hall's "faultless production" and the performance of the cast in general, particularly Dame Ashcroft's total immersion in the role of Beth. John Bury's "masterly settings" for both plays were also singled out for praise.[60] In fact, most reviewers expressed highly favorable views of the plays and of the production in general, praising the "exquisite" performance by the cast. Several referred to the censor's request that Pinter amend *Landscape* "on account of a few earthy words," which the playwright had refused to do, and the play was broadcast on the radio. One of the few hostile reviews, in the *Evening Standard*, accused the Royal Shakespeare Company of getting involved "in the greatest catastrophe of Harold Pinter's career," demanding: "How did Peggy Ashcroft, Peter Hall, the director, and John Bury the designer, so lose their professional judgment as to put the plays on?[61]

This attack apparently did not deter the RSC from producing Pinter's play *Old Times* in 1971. During the years between the three RSC productions of his plays, Pinter wrote radio plays, television dramas, and screenplays, in addition to a one-act stage play and revivals of his earlier plays. He also acted in and directed several of his own plays, as well as directing plays written by others, notably James Joyce's *Exiles* at the Mermaid in 1970—the first successful production of this play.[62] There was wide press coverage of his various theatrical activities, and in 1970 Pinter was awarded the German Shakespeare Prize.

Harold Hobson found *Old Times* "the most daring play Pinter has written." He wrote: "Pinter does not tell the story at all, though he might allow you to guess it. He tells you what, when the play has ended, had not happened. Yet perhaps it will happen." Hobson praised "Hall's infinitely subtle production"; the "irresistible grace" of Dorothy Tutin's performance in the role of Kate; the "provocative, enigmatic smile which makes the Mona Lisa look like a girl on a sponsored walk," which he saw in Vivien Merchant (as Anna); and Colin Blakely's performance as Deeley, which put him "in the top rank of actors."[63] The prominence of the director and cast clearly indicate the playwright's standing at that time.

In 1973 Pinter was appointed associate director of the National Theatre, a post he would hold for ten years. In 1975 his play *No Man's Land* was staged at the National Theatre. Peter Hall directed it, John Bury designed the set, and Sir John Gielgud and Sir Ralph Richardson, both stars who had acquired their reputations in Shakespearean roles, played the leads. Nearly all the reviews praised their performances and commented on their reputations, and their appearance in the production sealed the incorporation of Pinter's work into the British theatrical tradition. Michael Billington judged Pinter, in fact, as the bearer of that tradition, the playwright who continued the legacy of English comedy from *Twelfth Night,* who was "very aware of the English comic tradition, both on the literary and music-hall level." Billington elaborated on "the way Pinter's play both exploits and explores the peculiar English comic style" and concluded his review: "*No Man's Land* is, in fact, everyman's land."[64] The incorporation of Pinter's work into theatrical tradition paralleled the impression of the majority of reviewers that *No Man's Land* was highly Pinteresque. Most critics mapped this play as "Pinterland," finding that it crystallized distinctively Pinter themes and traits.[65] Billington described it as "a masterly summation of all the themes that have long obsessed Pinter."[66] Milton Shulman suggested that it was "the quintessential recipe for a Pinter play," mostly "obscure and elusive" but indicative of "Pinter's remarkable ear."[67] Wardle, who thought the title "could be applied to most of [Pinter's] recent work," declared: "*No Man's Land* remains palpably the work of our best living playwright in its command of language and its power to erect a coherent structure in a twilight zone of confusion and dismay."[68] John Barber, in his more reserved review, "Richardson and

No Man's Land

Harold Pinter

Program cover of No Man's Land, *Old Vic, April 23, 1975. © Royal National Theatre.*

Gielgud in Fine Partnership," proclaimed the play "yet another variation on the theme of privacy invaded."[69] J. C. Trewin suggested that Pinter seemed "to be journeying once more through a world of his own, leagues beyond our life,"[70] attributing the powerful effect of the play to Hall's production and to the immense virtuosity of the performances of both Gielgud and Richardson, while doubting the quality of the play itself. Nicholas de Jongh chose to address the variety of interpretations of Pinter's work and the differing influences to which the work was allegedly susceptible.[71] "Pinter," de Jongh ironically remarked, "has sensibly said little about his methods and intentions and left Martin Esslin to interpret every sentence and wring the last significances from his work."

De Jongh's remark reflected, between the lines as it were, the struggle for control over the emergent Pinter canon among the mediators of his work. The process of canonization of a playwright would appear to set in motion an ongoing rivalry among the mediating forces invested in his career as to whose authority shall reign. Over the early course of his career Pinter was at the apparent mercy of the reviewers. Their recognition of his dramatic contribution was manifested in the emergent "Pinter" construct. His continuous collaboration with the prominent director Peter Hall, especially from the mid-1960s onward, and the association of his dramatic work with distinguished casts and with institutions such as the Royal Shakespeare Company and thereafter the National Theatre were subsequent markers of the theatrical establishment's support. Pinter's prestige was also cultivated by the publication of numerous studies dealing with his oeuvre. As early as 1962 John Russell Taylor accorded Pinter's work elaborate treatment in the first edition of his influential study *Anger and After*. Martin Esslin's influential *Theatre of the Absurd* (1961)—especially his 1980 third revised edition[72]—and his monograph on Pinter (1970) emphasize the playwright's importance.[73] Although Esslin had established himself as the authority on Pinter's work, he faced competition for the "Pinter" territory from Austin Quigley, among others.[74] Quigley's 1975 study on Pinter marked a turn in scholarly views of the playwright's oeuvre. The emerging corpus of studies generated yet more publications, thereby expanding the Pinter publishing phenomenon. If the extent of Pinter scholarship itself indicates the playwright's stature, the importance of academic studies on Pinter's oeuvre also lies in their impact on the ongoing mediation process of his plays. Of particular consequence is the playwright's own position toward critical views of his work, manifested explicitly in his direct responses and implicitly in his ongoing writings and productions. At the time of the first production of *No Man's Land*, the rivalry among theatre reviewers and academics over control of the "Pinter construct," still an undercurrent, was as yet unmarked by the playwright's own intervention.

MIDCAREER: THE CONSTRUCT CHALLENGED

Most critics apparently are not able to view a play as it is by itself, distinctly and simply. They must relate it to what they saw last week or last year; usually this relation is tenuous, cock-eyed, unjust to both works. The critic is afraid to either sink or swim when he sees a play; he must grasp the lifeboat of a category.
—Pinter in interview with Harry Thompson, 1961

The forming of a dramatist's construct not only serves the reviewers in the process of admitting a new playwright into the theatrical canon, but also reinforces their function and authority in the theatrical field. However, their active involvement with a playwright's career does not terminate once the latter has been admitted into the canon and eventually become established. Reacting to the productions of new plays by an established playwright, the reviewers' objectives change and therefore so does their function; throughout the middle stages of a playwright's dramatic career, reviewers seek to ensure that playwright's central position in the theatrical canon. Typically, this means affirming the playwright's previously constructed image.[75] The established playwright thus seems to acquire a critical existence that belongs to the critics who created him as a critical construct.

An established playwright may write a play apparently incompatible with his previous works, seemingly challenging his constructed image and hence the critical criteria by which he was previously judged. Whether or not the play is objectively incompatible with the playwright's previous work is irrelevant here. What is significant is that many critics consider it to be so. At stake is their authority and function and yet they must react promptly to devise a mediating mode that best serves the new play. The following five modes of operation are potentially available to them:

1. *Freeing the playwright*: The reviewers, adhering to their function as creators of the playwright's construct, embrace the deviant play. However, they thereby invalidate their previous critical judgments with regard to the playwright's affiliation and endanger their authority as a constitutive force in the theatrical field.

2. *Revising the construct*: The reviewers devise a new construct
   that suits the deviant play, relocating the playwright's position
   accordingly. This accommodation, however, would involve a
   series of changes regarding the playwright's affiliation, requiring
   a longer period of adjustment. Forced to react promptly, the
   reviewers cannot, in fact, present a substitute construct when first
   encountering the deviant play.
3. *Maintaining the existing construct*: The reviewers ignore the play's
   deviant nature. They present the new play as an uninterrupted
   development in the playwright's poetics, subordinating it to their
   previous critical judgments.
4. *Denouncing the deviant play*: In the absence of a ready-made
   alternative and unwilling to endanger their authority, the
   reviewers use their powers to present the play as lacking the
   quality of the playwright's previous dramatic works.
5. *Adopting a dual approach:* The reviewers embark on a critical
   mode that seeks to achieve a double function: the selective
   acknowledgment of the novelty of the new play and the
   simultaneous upholding of previous critical judgments.

In fact, theatre reviewers tend to respond cautiously to what appears to
be a deviant play of an established playwright. Forced to react promptly,
they employ different emergency modes rather than legitimize the playwright's unpredictable move from the start, apparently seeking to reaffirm and guard the existing critical repertoire associated with the playwright in question.

PINTER'S *BETRAYAL*

Pinter's play *Betrayal* was his first deviant dramatic work. Its first
London production was directed by Sir Peter Hall (knighted in 1977) and
performed at the National Theatre on November 15, 1978.[76] In his com-
pilation on Pinter, Malcolm page writes that: "*Pinter has gone straight.
He tells the story of a wife's affair with her husband's best friend. We are
given all the facts we need to comprehend the plot and the behavior of
the three characters; nothing gratuitous, mysterious, or menacing occurs
offstage.* . . . Moreover, the speech, middle-class for once, has become
more stylized and elegant although just as actually heard. . . . The story of
their threesome begins at the end . . . and ends at the beginning."[77]

In their reviews of the production most critics implicitly acknowledged that *Betrayal* did not correspond to the "Pinter" construct. Their
responses displayed the particular modes they had endorsed, in regard to
the five options suggested earlier. The majority tended to adopt the fourth
option, presenting this play as lacking the quality of the playwright's previous dramatic works. In light of the reviewers' puzzlement—a leitmotif
that ran throughout Pinter's critical reception—several of the unfavorable reviews of *Betrayal* are somewhat amusing. These reviewers primarily complained of the clichéd nature of the play.

Michael Billington, for example, felt betrayed: "What distresses me is
the pitifully thin strip of human experience it explores and its obsession
with the tiny ripples on the stagnant pond of bourgeois-affluent life. . . .
Pinter has *betrayed* his immense talent by serving up this kind of high-
class soap-opera (laced with suitable cultural brand-names, like Venice,
Torcello, and Yeats) instead of a *real* play."[78] Billington's response is instructive of critical conduct not only in light of the eventual success and
popularity of *Betrayal*—the play was revived numerous times on stage
and was made into a successful film—but also because he was an early
proponent of Pinter's plays and later his biographer, and he would defend the dramatist in the turns to follow. Indeed, in his review of the 1991
production, directed by David Leveaux, Billington expressed his "second
thoughts on Pinter's *Betrayal*," finding it "a much better play."[79]

Other reviews of *Betrayal* also demonstrated the critics' disappointment in the face of Pinter's deviant play and disclosed their reluctance to
give up the "Pinter" construct. Wardle's review, "Pinter, Master of Ambiguity, Offers a Blank Statement of the Obvious," described the Pinteresque ambience of the first scene: "A man and a woman meet in a bar
and start exchanging loaded small-talk about mutual acquaintances. . . .
Perhaps they were once lovers, or were once married; or perhaps . . . .
at which point, Pinter halts the game and explains everything." Wardle, possibly reconstructing his own surprise, goes on: "In other words,
Pinter, the master of ambiguity, has laid out the facts as explicitly as a
police witness: and the stark contrast with all his previous work does
not end here." Although Wardle praised Hall's production as well as
the cast's performance, he stated conclusively: "The dramatic tempera-
ture instantly rises: but not far, and not for long."[80] The drama critic of
the *Sunday Times* was more explicit. He started by mourning "our expectation," described *Betrayal* as "altogether free of those elements we
have come to call 'Pinteresque,'" pronounced his dislike of the play, and

10p

Betrayal

NEW PLAY BY HAROLD PINTER

NT
NATIONAL
THEATRE

Program cover of Betrayal, *National Theatre, November 15, 1978.*
© *Royal National Theatre.*

declared bluntly: "*Betrayal*, the work of a man who has lost an empire and not yet found a role, is in its content empty, and on its surface dull."[81] Yet another reviewer, Sheridan Morley, who perceived the play as a "not very strong one" and too predictable, warned that "anyone expecting any of the ambiguity or menace of the earlier Pinters is in for a sharp disappointment."[82] Robert Cushman's review exemplifies the third option—an attempt to maintain the existing construct. Cushman perceived *Betrayal* as compatible with the "Pinter" construct to the extent that it manifested the playwright's attempt to challenge critics and audience alike: "*Betrayal* might fittingly be re-titled Pinter's Revenge. I have been accused, he seems to be saying, of withholding the details of my characters' past lives. This time I will give them to you. Much good may it do you." Cushman took the opportunity to mock the playwright's scholars: "We are in Robert's house so his territory is being violated: Pinter scholars please note." He went on to suggest that the play "tricks" the audience and critics alike on various levels: first, the playwright does not reveal as much as it may seem ("it is a good joke, though whether on us or him I am not sure"); and second, "the structure of the play is literally a betrayal, and figuratively as well since it is treasonous to what have been assumed, perhaps too glibly, to be Mr. Pinter's dramatic principles."[83]

Betrayal, which had caught the critics by surprise, to an extent prepared the grounds for Pinter's next deviant play, performed four years later. But *A Kind of Alaska* posed a tougher challenge, for it demanded a new construct.

PINTER'S *ALASKA*

Pinter's mid-career play, *A Kind of Alaska*, in which the playwright explicitly challenged his constructed image, marked a key phase in the dialogue established between Pinter and the mediators of his work.[84] *A Kind of Alaska*, also directed by Peter Hall, was performed at the National Theatre on October 14, 1982, in a triple-bill production, entitled *Other Places*, along with *Family Voices* and *Victoria Station*. In the play Deborah, who falls victim to a form of sleeping sickness, is awakened after twenty-nine years by a drug injected by the doctor who has taken care of her all these years and who has married her sister. The play centers on Deborah's awakening. Significantly Pinter acknowledges Oliver Sacks's 1973 book *Awakenings* as the literary source for his play, thereby supplying a context within which one can, or should, grasp the unusual situation depicted.

Program cover of Other Places, *National Theatre, October 14, 1982.*
© Royal National Theatre.

A Kind of Alaska again surprised the critics. Most reviews of the first production reflected their notion that Pinter had changed direction. The reviewers nonetheless modified their critical repertoire only to a point, tending rather to rely on the repertoire they had previously constructed. That is, they chose the fifth option, the dual approach. They seemed eager to draw attention to a possible transformation of the enigmatic playwright in view of his most recent play, while avoiding specification of the theatrical components that had elicited such critical judgment.

The critics' puzzlement regarding Pinter's poetics, which had dictated their strategy throughout the process of his acceptance, appeared to vanish utterly in the face of *A Kind of Alaska*. In marked contrast to the disappointment of most reviewers when they encountered the too obvious *Betrayal*, most of them expressed their great relief that Pinter-land had ceased to be obscure. John Barber remarked, for example, that Pinter "was never less obscure than here, or more profoundly eloquent about the fragile joy of being alive."[85] Most reviews were highly favorable. Many critics found Pinter, in light of *A Kind of Alaska*, an engaged playwright whose play offered human concerns. After *Alaska* Pinter was no longer presented as a playwright who portrays "an entirely personal world," but as one who operates in the orbit of a popular book based on medical phenomena (Oliver Sacks's *Awakenings*) that had aroused wide public interest—Pinter's explicit reference to the source of his play had left an imprint. "*A Kind of Alaska*," wrote Robert Cushman, "is a departure for Mr. Pinter as *Footfalls* was for Samuel Beckett. Once again, we are presented with a character in a world of her own, but we are given medical evidence for her condition documented in the programme."[86] The reviewers were nonetheless at a loss: the previous "Pinter" construct was not in accord with the playwright's new work, but they did not have a ready-made alternative. They therefore employed an emergency mode, acknowledging selectively the novelty of the play, highlighting the reference to Oliver Sacks as the play's major anomalous feature, while they avoided direct consideration of the other, more radically different dramatic attributes, such as the particular nature of the awakening of the protagonist.

Striking evidence for the reviewers' endorsement of an emergency mode appears in their selective treatment of the literary source. None of the reviewers, with the exception of Benedict Nightingale,[87] mentioned the case of Rose R. from Sacks's book as the most probable one upon which the play is based.[88] Moreover, none of the reviews, including Nightingale's, referred to Pinter's decision to base his play on this particular case history rather than on any of the other of Sacks's cases, male or female. While repeatedly acknowledging Sacks as Pinter's source, none of the reviewers mentioned or discussed Pinter's changes to the source data, which are quite significant. Unlike Deborah, the awakened woman in the play, who was sixteen years old when she fell victim to the sleeping-sickness, Rose R. was twenty-one. Deborah's awakening occurs after twenty-nine years when she is forty-five, whereas Rose R. awakened after forty-three years when she had reached the age of sixty-four. Deborah, then, has been asleep throughout the years of her maturation, unlike Rose R. Further, in contrast to the passive conduct of the princess in the Sleeping Beauty fairy tale, Deborah's attempt, upon awakening, to confront the implications of her situation, suggests feminist sympathies on Pinter's part. A commentary on Pinter's decision to base the play on the case history of Rose R., as well as a discussion of his different fictional data, might have compelled the reviewers to consider new issues, such as the possible influence of a feminist approach, which were foreign to the critical repertoire associated with Pinter's plays.

The reviewers' promotion of the play, which did not entail a direct treatment of its novelty, may represent a form of defense. It consisted of two different although interlinked strategies: *comparison* and *forecasting*, modified applications of the two major strategies typically employed by reviewers throughout the first phase of a playwright's process of acceptance.[89] The comparison strategy is employed with a view toward creating a familiar context for the new dramatist. At this stage—Pinter's mid-career—this strategy underwent modification in accordance with the reviewers' altered needs. Comparing *Alaska* to Pinter's earlier works, the reviewers referred primarily to the absence of the familiar Pinter-esque attributes. The strategy thus served simultaneously as a retrospective affirmation of earlier critical assertions and as a confirmation of the reviewers' continuing role as the authoritative force in determining the playwright's construct.

The second strategy, forecasting, presents a play by a new playwright as containing the promise of a major, original contribution, thus facilitating the dramatist's admission into the canon. The later modification of forecasting marks a new play by a now established playwright as a turning point in his theatrical expression. The emphasis thus shifts from the particularities of the play to the broader issue of future changes in the playwright's poetics. Presenting a change in the playwright's poetics assists reviewers to further enhance the prestige of an established playwright, and so to reinforce his canonical position. The reviewers' use of this second strategy in regard to Pinter, like their use of the first one, reaffirmed their authoritative position in the theatrical field. The following examples demonstrate the use of these two strategies.

In his review of *Other Places,* Wardle differentiated among the three plays in the production. The first two show Pinter "re-exploring familiar territory: the third, *A Kind of Alaska,* shows him *breaking into new ground. Most unusually for this author, the play comes with an explanatory programme note citing a literary source*: Oliver Sacks' *Awakenings.*"[90] Nightingale began his review by referring to Pinter's reputation, contending that *A Kind of Alaska* demanded the most attention, since "*for the first time in his stage career, Pinter acknowledges a source.*"[91] Sheridan Morley commented that the other two plays included in *Other Places* "are really only a curtain-raiser for the last, *A Kind of Alaska,* which instead of harking back to past triumphs suggests that *Pinter is in fact now moving forward into some altogether new direction. In the first place, and extremely unusually for him, the play is derived from a book, and a book of medical fact.*"[92]

All other reviews of the first London production of *A Kind of Alaska* also cited Oliver Sacks's book and the medical phenomena on which his cases are based.[93] In view of the favorable critical reception of *Alaska* it appears that it was provision of the medical data that helped the reviewers fill in the Pinter gaps, endowing the unusual situation with coherence. At the same time, Deborah's enigmatic world as depicted in *Alaska* enabled the reviewers to present this play as corresponding with the playwright's already devised construct, that is, in line with the enigmatic dramatic world associated with Pinter's earlier works.

The reviews of the first production of *Alaska* show that the reviewers had adjusted the existing repertoire to meet their altered needs, rather than expanding it. Their discourse, apparently restricted to a limited repertoire, made the means at their disposal incongruous with the requirements of the challenge: a direct critical consideration of the playwright's unpredictable poetic move. The reviewers hence devised a form of modification that drew on earlier critical constructions of Pinter, thereby disguising the repertoire's restricted nature and simultaneously ensuring their own authority. They modulated the comparison and forecasting strategies accordingly and they presented the playwright's move into new territory in light of the previously defined territory and attributed this move, reflected at the time in a single play, to a more general poetic change designating new ground that was critically acknowledged and defined in advance. In other words, the reviewers reclaimed the playwright's unpredictable move as further corroboration of their own powers in the field.

If the reviews of *Alaska* exemplify critics' dual approach, several academic studies of the play demonstrate alternative options that clarify, by comparison, the constraints on the reviewers' discourse and the principles underlying it. It is true that, in the later stages of a playwright's career, theatre reviewers can be perceived as acquiring a historical perspective similar to that of academic scholars. Nevertheless, the major factors that affect the response of theatre reviewers to a playwright's unexpected move are still derived from their particular function—the prompt mediation of new plays—and restricted to the means at their disposal, as well as derived from their attempt to maintain control of the dramatist's construct.

Academic studies demonstrate a different sort of critical constraint. In accordance with their respective ideological or critical orientations, scholars often strive to root their retrospective readings of a play within the context of theories or ideologies current at the time of their repeated interrogation. Such studies serve a mediating function by presenting new and divergent readings of the play that tend to integrate or apply more current ideologies in their approach to the playwright's poetics.[94] Early 1990s readings of *Alaska* by Katherine Burkman, Moonyoung Ham, and Ann Hall are examples that are for the most part feminist in their methodology and ideological commitments. These readings revolve around the centrality of the female figure, Deborah. The articles by Burkman and Ham were first presented at an international Pinter festival at Ohio State University, celebrating Pinter's 60th birthday in 1987. Both were subsequently published in a collection titled *Pinter At Sixty*,[95] comprising talks given at this conference. Separately and together, the festival and the publication of the collection served a mediatory function: they reflected Pinter's acquired status and, in turn, further cultivated it.

According to all three scholars, Pinter's main interest in *Alaska* lies in the process through which Deborah comes to recognize herself as a grown woman.[96] This emphasis throws into relief the absence of comparable themes in the critical reviews of *Alaska*, given its incompatibility with the reviewers' repertoire for Pinter's plays. The three scholars seem to confront the playwright's new territory head on, unlike the reviewers, who tended to approach the play's novelty only indirectly. In contrast to the reviews, whose promotion of the playwright's deviant play relied primarily on earlier critical constructions of Pinter, the academic studies exemplify the second operational option: opening up and extending the Pinter repertoire. These studies derive their powers from the alternative view they suggest of Pinter's drama.[97]

A critical study by Guido Almansi and Simon Henderson, published in 1983, exemplifies yet another operational option. Comparing the option endorsed by Almansi and Henderson to that employed by the reviewers is especially instructive since, unlike the three other studies referred to, which were published several years after the first London production of *Alaska*, this study was published only a year after the production. In presenting *A Kind of Alaska* as the playwright's move into unfamiliar and unexplored territory, these authors appear to employ the first option: that of liberating the rebellious playwright. They contend that "*Pinter, like his characters, is a master of mimicry, a Houdini of the text. . . .* Pinter cannot be pinned down to any view expressed by a character or extracted from his plays by a critic's dental pliers. . . . Though his words linger around the venue of many a scandalous verbal outrage, *Harold Pinter is not there.*"[98] On closer inspection, the critical mode that Almansi and Henderson adopt reinforces their overview of Pinter's work. They attempt to chart the playwright's footprints via his various plays. They suggest viewing his plays as modeled on various forms of games. Their conclusion is consistent with their game model, in terms of which Pinter is seen as triumphing over the critics in a kind of hide-and-seek. It is striking that the four academic studies of *Alaska* illustrate precisely those optional modes—revising the construct and freeing the playwright—that the reviewers in their attempts to assimilate a deviant play so assiduously avoided.

TOWARD THE EXPLICITLY POLITICAL: A BATTLE OF FORCES

After *Alaska*, Pinter appeared to confirm the reviewers' predictions, at least concerning a change in his dramatic objectives. His next sequence of plays was overtly political, presenting critics with a new challenge. Pinter's review sketch *Precisely* was first performed by the playwright in London on December 18, 1983;[99] a new play, *One for the Road,* followed on March 13, 1984.[100] The playwright performed in *Precisely* and directed *One for the Road*. In *Precisely,* two men converse about the number of people who might be expected to die in a nuclear war and agree that whereas twenty million dead sounds reasonable, those who argue that the figure could reach thirty or even forty million are practicing public deception. *One for the Road* concerns the interrogation of a family—a couple and their son.

Both the man and the woman are subjected to physical torture, and the little boy is murdered following his interrogation, but neither the torture nor the murder is presented on stage.

The reviews of *One for the Road* were cautious, reflecting the reviewers' vacillation between the familiar "Pinter" construct and the playwright's new, overtly political dramatic work. Most reviewers articulated the playwright's shift but refrained from passing judgment on the new and different play. Ned Chaillet, for example, claimed: "Harold Pinter is the most eminent of living English playwrights. *Until recently there were a few certainties about his ambiguous work.*" But Chaillet saw the playwright's newest premiere as "*clearly demonstrating a new explicitly political stance*," explaining that "Mr. Pinter has been actively political . . . , but *never till now has his horror found its way into drama.*"[101] Referring to Pinter's "shift," Rosalind Carne pointed out that "*the old concerns remain*" but that, unusually for Pinter, there is "*no space for ambiguity about the moral slant of the play.*"[102] Michael Coveney cited in his review the playwright's own explanation, perhaps to avoid dealing with the play's explicitly political concerns: "Pinter himself acknowledged that it becomes increasingly impossible not to contemplate the political ugliness of the world." Coveney maintained that "*in characteristically elliptical style*, Pinter marks out the distance between people. For the first time in a play of his, however, the state, the regime or whatever, is a factor."[103] Eric Shorter, exploiting the ready-made critical repertoire, traced a familiar Pinter by assessing the play as "*another of Mr. Pinter's well known power games*,"[104] while Christopher Hudson found that *One for the Road* "is not suggestive: it is declamatory."[105]

In its first revival, in 1985, *A Kind of Alaska* took place at the Duchess theatre.[106] The critical responses to the revival of *Alaska* differed significantly from the surprised reactions to its first production. Not only were the reviewers already familiar with the play, but they also now had a new context within which to view it, namely, Pinter's dramatic move toward an explicitly political drama. Despite acknowledging and proclaiming the playwright's shift, the reviewers went only so far as to designate the general direction of the move in light of Pinter's previously devised construct.

In "A New Map of Pinterland," Billington stated: "The production offers fascinating evidence of Pinter's move from being a dramatist of *steely ambiguity* to one of *human compassion and political concern*," but that "the weakest piece is *One for the Road*, . . . which marks *a decisive shift for Pinter from mysterious obliquity to political rage*." Furthermore, he stressed: "What makes the evening significant is *Pinter's own move into other theatrical places*. But, now that he has mapped out new territory, I just wish he would extend his discoveries into a full-length play."[107] Wardle traced familiar Pinter elements in *Alaska* and *One for the Road*, contending that both "show Pinter himself *on the move to other places* and, *for the first time, taking his material direct from the world of public reality*: *Alaska* deriving from Oliver Sacks' case-histories, *Awakenings*, and *One for the Road* marking *his self-proclaimed debut as a political writer*." Like Billington, Wardle emphasized the playwright's shift, "One fascination [the two plays] offer is that of watching "*a talent that thrives on ambiguity and mystery coming to grips with highly specific material*."[108] Both reviews reflected the critics' caution in openly affirming Pinter's shift into overtly political drama, and both tended to describe rather than to promote the playwright's move. But whereas Billington found *One for the Road* "the weakest," Wardle insisted that "for all their new subject matter, both plays spring most to life as interrogation drama—the form with which Pinter first arrived in *The Birthday Party*." In both reviews Pinter was presented anew ("taking his material direct from the world of public reality" instead of "creat[ing] a world of his own"),[109] while also reflecting these reviewers' reluctance to engage in full-scale revision of the "Pinter" construct, and hence their hesitation to legitimize a new image.

John Peter's review offered yet another perception of Pinter's new drama: "When *One for the Road* opened last year it was suggested that Pinter had somehow discovered the outside world; that the dramatist of private claustrophobia suddenly woke up to the reality of real power, terror and torture. This naïve view wouldn't survive a good production (or close reading) of *The Caretaker*, *The Homecoming*, or even *Old Times*. All these plays simply ripple and heave with the language of sinuous intimidation; Pinter has always understood the devious ways and the almost erotic cruelties of people whose indispensable pleasure is the fear and pain of others."[110] According to Peter's perception the playwright's most recent plays could be seen as a continuation of his earlier ones, showing a natural development rather than a shift in his dramatic direction.

A transformation in the critics' attitudes occurred simultaneously with a shift in the playwright's own position toward the mediation endeavor. If during the early stage of his career Pinter's role in the mediation of his work had consisted of collaboration and evasion, he turned rebellious in *Betrayal* and challenged his constructed image in *Alaska*. In this phase, however, beginning with *One for the Road*, his position became one of collaboration to the extent that now, when interviewed, Pinter supplied his interlocutors with explanations, stated his intentions and, moreover, acknowledged his dramatic move toward an explicit political stance as well as clarified the motivations underlying it.

The republication of *One for the Road* in 1985[111] reflects this new collaborative dynamic. This edition includes an introduction entitled "A Play and Its Politics," a conversation between Pinter and Nicholas Hern, and a brief account by Pinter of the background of the play, in which he describes his visit to Turkey with Arthur Miller on behalf of International PEN in 1985. In the conversation with Hern, Pinter describes *One for the Road* as a move toward a more explicit politics of commitment: "The facts that *One for the Road* refers to are facts that I wish the audience to know about, to recognize. Whereas I didn't have the same objective at all in the early days."[112] Pinter does not present this commitment as emerging from a vacuum. He explains that he has always viewed politicians, political structures, and political acts with what he describes as "detached contempt." He further explains that for more than twenty years he had felt political engagement to be futile, but his growing concern with the issues of nuclear power, violence, and the "official torture, subscribed to by so many governments," now prompted him to take a political stance.[113]

These explanations suggest that Pinter, apparently aware of the discomfort elicited by the overtly political nature of his newly performed works and of the shift registered by the reviewers, had inflected this perceived shift with his own motivations to mediate his new image to critics and audience alike. Moreover, assuming a collaborative position in mediating his drama at this point in time corresponded with and was in service of his pronounced, changed objectives, further demonstrated by his continuing to write political drama. His next play, *Mountain Language*, performed at the National Theatre on October 20, 1988, and directed by the playwright, portrays the visit of a group of women to a prison camp where their relatives are incarcerated. The women are informed by the officers that they are not allowed to speak their own "mountain language," which is banned. The play centers on two of these women, who undergo a shocking experience when they meet their loved ones. It is a record of trauma (both the collective and the individual/personal) that carries a strong political message.[114]

Pinter's reputation as a playwright was by now widely and internationally recognized. Although he was criticized by the press for his outright political protestations and for his increasingly political activities,

Program cover of Mountain Language, *National Theatre, October 20, 1988.*
© Royal National Theatre.

theatrical institutes such as the National Theatre continued to provide him with a stage—and in *Mountain Language,* one that showcased a distinguished cast of actors—Michael Gambon, Eileen Atkins, and Miranda Richardson in the lead roles. The majority of the critics, however, ignored the playwright's involvement in mediating his new image and continued their battle against his political drama. They attacked the play, the playwright, and the distinguished theatrical establishment for backing him. Most reviews, excluding Billington's, which praised *Mountain Language,*[115] ranged from reserved comment to harsh attack. The reviewers complained about, and in many cases ridiculed, the play's twenty-minute length after Pinter's "long silence"—four years since his last new play and ten years since his last full-length play. They found the distinguished location, the National Theatre, and the cast incompatible with the "shallow" and "unoriginal" dimensions of this long-awaited offering.

The struggle for control among mediators of this playwright's work, earlier on manifested in the undercurrent of rivalry between theatre reviewers and academics, now became an overt attack on the coalition of the playwright and the established theatrical institutes. If earlier the rivalry centered on the association with a canonical playwright, the battle now revolved around the legitimization of his dramatic move toward explicitly political drama and implied a reconsideration of the construct attached to his work, which appears to—but may not—fall under the authority of theatre critics. Moreover, the playwright's new plays, which were incompatible with the construct as devised, also called into question the canonical position to which he had been assigned. It is thus logical that reviewers would tend to devalue his divergent work. The overall critical responses demonstrated, in varying degrees, the reviewers' disappointment with and harsh criticism of the "Emperor"— a frequent ironic reference to Harold Pinter, perhaps because of his "new clothes," whose eagerly awaited dramatic work, they claimed, matched neither the quality of his earlier works, nor the expectations attaching to "Britain's leading playwright."[116]

Several articles on Pinter published during this stage of his career reflect the tendencies underlying the critics' views. The mediating function as practiced by interviewers and journalists differs from that of the reviewers in that interviewers provide a stage for the playwrights themselves that often serves as an opportunity to promote their recent or forthcoming work. Whereas reviewers must react promptly to productions of a playwright's new dramas, journalists writing about theatre, who at times also function as theatre critics, acquire a certain critical distance in terms of time and perspective. Press articles thus fall between reviews on the one hand, and academic studies on the other, in terms of both critical distance and the scope of their coverage. Journalists often sum up a playwright's career at specific or significant points in time and simultaneously reflect the prevailing critical views.

Polly Toynbee's "Master of Strident Silences," an overview of Pinter's relationships with the press, is especially relevant here.[117]Alluding to a critic's statement that "it's all a case of the 'Emperor's clothes,'" this journalist asked, "But where's the Emperor? Are the clothes draped around an empty space at the core?" Of the playwright's early years she wrote: "Pinter was always enigmatic. He wouldn't say. The silences, the unspoken menace, the evasions and the ambiguities of the plays were left there for literary critics to attempt to decode on their own. . . . Wouldn't he give us a clue? Pinter gave no clue." Of the playwright's attitude in the "new phase" of his career: "Pinter these days is not gnomic, obscure or ambiguous. He makes himself pretty plain." Of Pinter's "political phase" and the tensions it generated, Toynbee remarked on the claims that "Pinter's 'politics' destroyed his writing," that his "politics moved in to mask the chasm where his writing used to be," and that "all Pinter's bristling political rage and fury might have something to do with the frustration at a writer's block that has lasted so long." She sums up: "If Pinter no longer writes plays, he continues as the best scriptwriter. . . . It is, as they say, too early to tell whether his most famous early plays . . . will enter the canon of continually performed classics. . . . But even if they were to become eventually unperformable, they will remain as exceptionally important literary monuments." Toynbee's article airs the reviewers' notions that Pinter's supposed "low productivity" and the nature of his recent dramatic work call into question his canonical status. But these doubts bear primarily on his overtly political corpus, though they may have an impact on his earlier work as well. In light of the reviewers' striving to ensure the canonical position of an established playwright through the mid-late stages of his career—a canonicity to which they have contributed—Toynbee's view represents a transformation in process.

Pinter's sixtieth birthday in October 1990 gave journalists the opportunity to air overviews of his career. The controversy around his dramatic work throughout the 1980s was a major theme. John Peter's "Harold Pinter: The Poet of No-Man's-Land" in the *Sunday Times*, for example, discussed the career of "Britain's leading dramatist,"[118] who, according to Peter, has maintained his distance from journalists by diminishing his public presence and giving only a few interviews throughout his career. Addressing Pinter's growing engagement with politics, Peter refuted the view that suspected the playwright of insincerity and that ridiculed his "late awakening." Peter claimed instead that "Pinter's involvement in politics is rooted in sincere convictions, and that it resulted in two short plays which have far more to do with his earlier work than most people realise." Comparing *One for the Road* and *Mountain Language* to the earlier *Birthday Party* and *No Man's Land,* he pointed out that later plays reflect a shift in dramatic subject matter rather than a change in the playwright's sensitivity and flexibility: "What we see here is an artist of the first rank bearing witness to the nightmare reality of his time. . . . He does not live in a no man's land which never moves, which never changes, which never grows older, but which remains forever, icy and silent. No he does not." In quoting the famous lines from *No Man's Land,*[119] Peter assumed the readers' familiarity with the play. He thus drew on Pinter's canonicity—assuming the lines of his best-known plays were familiar to the public—to promote his recent work, thereby further cultivating the playwright's reputation. To this extent, Peter's article explicitly counters the tendency reflected in Toynbee's article.

Rhoda Koenig, in "Past Master of the Pregnant Silence," was less sympathetic than Peter. She alluded to Pinter's private life, such as his scandalous divorce from Vivien Merchant and his life with Antonia Fraser; addressed his "writing block"; described his political drama as "didactic and stiff"; and scoffed at explanations proffered for its emergence— namely, that "political guilt [is] strangling Pinter's theatrical self-expression" or that "he is embracing political protest as way of acting out his frustration."[120] She judged Pinter's political conviction, as manifested in his political dramas, as insincere.

Pinter answered the critics of his political dramas in two new dramatic works, *The New World Order* on July 19, 1991,[121] and, on October 31 of the same year, *Party Time,*[122] both of which he also directed. *The New World Order,* like *One for the Road* and *Mountain Language,* deals directly with the abuse of power by interrogation, torture, and various sanctions and prohibitions. In all three plays the victims' crimes are not specified but referred to in a vague, indirect way. *The New World Order* presents a victim's anguished wait for his victimizers' actions. Although the playwright does not specify a particular time, location, or political situation for *One for the Road, Mountain Language,* or *The New World Order,* the three plays directly protest the abuse of power legitimized by a political regime. *Party Time,* also a political statement, deals with the phenomenon of public denial and critiques the attempt to keep the threat outside while keeping the party going inside.[123]

The New World Order was performed at the 1991 London International Festival of Theatre (LIFT), which offered, in association with the Royal Court and the National Theatre Studio, a season of political plays at the Theatre Upstairs under the title "Cross References." Although the plays chosen had been commissioned to last thirty minutes at most, Pinter's *The New World Order,* which lasts less than ten minutes, elicited a host of poisonous responses. "Harold Pinter," wrote Annalena McAfee, "*The Incredible Shrinking Playwright,* faces controversy over his latest bonsai drama."[124] Charles Spencer found him "*in danger of becoming one of the great comic figures of British public life.*" Spencer granted the playwright his "past achievement" but judged his conduct "unfit" in light of his diminishing progress: "Though his muse seems to have deserted him long ago, . . . he is clearly reluctant to quit the stage he dominated for so long—despite the fact that *he has almost nothing to say.*" Spencer attacked *Mountain Language* and pronounced of *The New World Order:* "The piece isn't just a sad symptom of a talent in decline, it is paranoid as well."[125] Like Spencer, most reviewers took Pinter's reputation as their major target of attack. "*So high is Harold Pinter's reputation, and so low his dramatic productivity,*" claimed Benedict Nightingale, "that his slightest squiggle seems of special interest these days. He would only have to breathe on his shaving mirror, and scrawl a few syllables with his finger on the disappearing steam, for a hundred Eng. Lit professors to jet in with cameras, glass cutting equipment and preservatives."[126] Indeed, Nightingale's cynical remark was an explicit manifestation of the growing resistance of theatre reviewers to academics, reflecting the undergoing battle of mediating forces. While the reviewers accused theatre institutes such as the National Theatre of succumbing to Pinter's stature, maintaining and further cultivating his reputation in spite of his declining talent, they blamed academics for their loss of judgment. The issue implicitly raised was: Whose judgment can be trusted? Posing the question in these terms suggests another turn in the struggle for control.

Pinter's play *Party Time* was first performed in a double-bill with *Mountain Language,* directed by the playwright at the Almeida Theatre in 1991. The Almeida Theatre Company, founded in 1979 and inhabiting the Almeida Theatre since 1981, had begun to establish a reputation for its innovative work and had also begun to acquire a reputation as arguably the most dynamic theatre in London.[127]

Party Time, for all its length, still did not suffice to calm the hostility of most reviewers. Charles Spencer, for example, noted: "Last night's disappointing premiere from our 'leading dramatist' . . . lasts almost 40 minutes. But *what pitiful unrewarding minutes they are.* Thirty years ago, when asked what his work was actually about, Pinter gnomically declared that it was about 'the weasel under the cocktail cabinet.' The weasel is still there. Instead of being a weasel of unspecified Pinteresque menace, however, it is now the weasel of state repression which, like many good left-wingers, Pinter clearly believes is due to arrive in this country at any minute, always assuming that it hasn't arrived already."[128] The loss of the inexplicit was mourned in a much more crude way by Benedict Nightingale, who perceived *Party Time* as lacking the richness of Pinter's earlier plays "composed in the 1960s and 1970s, none of which was specifically concerned with politics, [and which] presented us with elaborate tables and darkly hinted at an ugliness below. That is what made it original and haunting. But since he became a public crusader for liberal causes, his plays have got cruder as well as shorter and fewer. Both *One for the Road* and *Mountain Language,* well meant playlets decrying the abuse of human rights, *took the blood and vomit from beneath the table and shoved our noses in it.*"[129] Although Milton Shulman perceived Pinter's political plays as a continuation of his earlier work, he remarked cynically that the playwright "*has now acquired a political conscience.*"[130] A number of favorable reviews also pointed to familiar Pinteresque elements in the new production.[131] Terry Eagleton used Pinter's comment, "If you can't see that *The Birthday Party* and *The Caretaker* are political plays, . . . then you can't see much," as a basis for his own critical judgment of the new play: "It is as though the paranoia has now been defiantly justified in political terms, as a bunch of alarmingly realistic tortures takes over from the shadowily indeterminate predators of the earlier work."[132]

Alan Franks's "The Unmellowing of Harold Pinter" in the *Times Saturday Review* was published following the production of *Party Time.*[133] Franks found it ironic that while "20 years' worth of plays, from *The Birthday Party* in 1958 to *Betrayal* in 1978, should have vexed by seeming to hoard their meaning, their author now earns a comparable hostility by being utterly explicit." Franks implicitly expressed his critique of the view voiced by Shulman, among others, that Pinter has "acquired a conscience" and of the idea, expressed by Koenig, for example, that Pinter's "concern for the jailed and oppressed writers contains the desire to be sprung from his own silence, returned to his vocation from this present 'exile.'" Franks insisted that Pinter's political tendencies showed up as early as *The Hothouse*, written in 1959 but produced only 20 years later—that is, four years before *One for the Road*—clearly indicating that the playwright's political awareness existed in the earliest phases of his career.[134]

THE PLAYWRIGHT'S TURN

Moonlight, Pinter's next play, performed at the Almeida on September 7, 1993, and directed by David Leveaux, depicts a man on his deathbed and his complex family relationships: with his wife (attending to him), his estranged two sons (who remain in the distance), the ghost of their dead sister, and his mistress in the background. To the reviewers' great relief, this eighty-minute offering ("at last!") appeared to correspond to the Pinteresque construct. "You have to hand it to Harold Pinter," wrote Martin Hoyle. "The trouble is he hands it right back." Hoyle's next sentence is even more revealing: "Britain's greatest living playwright has come up with his first full-length play for 15 years and *it emerges as a collection of Pinterisms to order*: evasive gentility, shock four-letter words, mysterious codified exchanges, private games."[135] Spencer found it "a great relief to discover that [Pinter] has, at last decided to spare us his politics." Yet, as he pointed out the familiar Pinter attributes ("menacing," and "enigmatic"), Spencer worried about "moments here when *he seems to be offering a deliberate send-up of his own reputation for baffling an audience*."[136] Almost all the reviews were favorable and almost all of them celebrated Pinter's return (to his construct?) from his political exile: "Pinter is, so to speak, coming home to *The Homecoming*"; "*Moonlight* marks a genuine return to form."[137] Jeremy Kingstone approved of a Pinter who "calls on the Pinter styles of long ago."[138] Interestingly, the very few unfavorable reviews found the play's primary fault in its overtly Pinteresque nature.[139]

Moonlight ushered in a new round in Pinter's dialogue with critics of his work. In an interview with Jill Furmanovsky following the opening of *Moonlight*, the playwright admitted that this play had "been forced out of him in part by the recent spate of Pinterama." He further declared: "I want to put something on the record. . . . The record seems to imply that I haven't written anything since 1978. . . that I'd been blocked for fifteen years. I've actually written six short plays. . . . I've also written seven film scripts, . . . so that's seven and six. . . . It's about time that was recorded." The interviewer presented the playwright as "a man who made us redefine our attitude to communication, gave an adjective to the dictionary, and jolted our belief in a playwright's control over his creations." Addressing the political issue, she commented: "The change in Pinter's image is undoubtedly marked; when the first production of *No Man's Land* appeared in 1975 I wrote about a cool and 'unpolitical' writer at the time when there was much tub-thumping from younger Turks; the critic John Barber could pronounce at the same time that 'Man as social being has . . . [no] place in Pinter.' And yet, Pinter now describes his early plays, *The Dumb Waiter, The Birthday Party*, and *The Hothouse*, plays in which he developed a comedy of menace in which language was used as a weapon of aggression, evasion and even torture, as 'political.'"[140]

Pinter's insistence on presenting the political as rooted in his early plays, especially in view of the favorable reception of *Moonlight*, perceived as non-political, is doubly significant. It reflects and highlights the playwright's emergent tendency to present the political as an integral facet of his dramatic work. It is also compatible, however, with his ongoing practice as a dramatist, namely, challenging the perception of his drama as attached and restricted to clear-cut categories or a definite construct. Pinter's subsequent play, *Ashes to Ashes*, directed by the playwright and performed by the Royal Court Theatre at the Ambassadors Theatre on September 12, 1996, manifested both tendencies.

AN ACTIVE PARTICIPANT

If the reviewers seemed reluctant to legitimize the playwright's shift and repeatedly expressed their critique of his overtly political drama, academics have tended to address Pinter's dramatic move from an overview of his dramatic oeuvre. In the 1990s, studies of Pinter's work suggested that his development as a dramatist consisted of two primary, distinct phases: his early and midcareer phase, 1958–1982; and his later, politically engaged, phase, 1983–1991. Martin Esslin, a proponent of this view, comments on this distinction: "Whereas all his previous work was enigmatic, multilayered, relying on pauses, silences, and a subtext of far greater importance than what was actually being said, these later pieces operate unambiguously on the surface, even relying on voice-overs to make characters' thoughts crystal clear and proclaiming a message of blinding simplicity, a message which is a call to political action."[141]

Esslin's view exemplifies the common interpretation that the two phases in Pinter's writings differ with respect to the nature of the represented domain and to the degree of explicitness. The early/midcareer phase is seen to represent the private-personal domain and is distinguished by its inexplicitness (labeled Pinteresque), whereas the later phase represents the public-political domain and is marked by an explicit and direct dramatic mode.

Pinter challenged both reviewers and scholars with his 1996 play *Ashes to Ashes,* in which the verbal interaction consists of two contradictory discursive modes. For much of the play, the two major characters adhere to a different code of conversation as Devlin interrogates Rebecca about her former love relationships. The two apparently live together, and Rebecca supplies the information quite willingly. Her conversational pattern echoes the earlier Pinter, while Devlin's direct explicit style echoes the later Pinter in his overtly political phase, as seen in the following example.

> DEVLIN: You understand why I'm asking you these questions. Don't you? Put yourself in my place. I'm compelled to ask you questions. There are so many things I don't know. I know nothing . . . About any of this. Nothing. I'm in the dark. I need light. Or do you think my questions are illegitimate?
>
> REBECCA: What questions?
>
> DEVLIN: Look. It would mean a great deal to me if you could define him more clearly.
>
> REBECCA: Define him? What do you mean define him?[142]

The two conversational patterns are played one against another, producing a dialogue incompatible with either pattern, yet alluding to both. Moreover, in this play Pinter deploys readily identifiable, horrifyingly familiar references to the conduct of the Nazis, presented as fragmented images that constitute Rebecca's memories associated with her former lover. Collective memory ostensibly associated with a vast public domain is thus interlaced with one woman's personal memoirs.

In *Ashes to Ashes* Pinter poses an especially intriguing challenge. The play manifests the playwright's poetic response to the critical distinction between his two writing modes by activating the so-called early and later modes simultaneously. Challenging the clear-cut distinction between them, *Ashes to Ashes* is confusing. It does not deal distinctly with either the public or the private domains and, in encompassing both, turns out to belong to neither. Moreover, it is not fully compatible with Pinter's explicit or his inexplicit dramatic mode; it corresponds to both and thus to neither in particular. *Ashes to Ashes* conjoins, but does not resolve, two contrary, or very different, critical images of the playwright in a single play—that is, as a play in which Pinter seeks to incorporate and thus simultaneously converse with all the surrounding modes of critical discourse.

Ashes to Ashes left reviewers baffled, bewildered, and dissatisfied. Critical puzzlement, a routine reaction to Pinter's plays, in this case derived from the juxtaposition of the two incompatible modes upon which the play is constituted. *A Kind of Alaska* had surprised the reviewers yet they eventually endorsed it. *Moonlight*, which apparently stood outside the sequence of political plays, was perceived by reviewers as corresponding to the previous "Pinter" construct. But no comparable options were available for the reviewers of *Ashes to Ashes*. Unable to dismiss the personal context, they had difficulty ascribing a political theme to the play. At the same time, in view of the specific political associations it evokes, they were unable to perceive the play as merely the dissection of a couple's relationship. Eventually, they turned their inability to categorize *Ashes to Ashes* within either of the two Pinter phases or modalities into its major flaw. Embarking on the fourth option, emergency modes, they denounced this challenging play.

"It's About Nothing—and Everything," declares the headline of John Casey's review in the *Daily Telegraph*.[143] And Charles Spencer asserted: "*Ashes to Ashes* often comes across as a pale imitation of [Pinter's] own earlier—and better—work. . . . *The suspicion grows that this time the emperor really might not be wearing any clothes*." His seeming bafflement recalls reviewers' frustration with Pinter's first play: "A woman called Rebecca [is] describing how an unnamed sadistic lover came close to strangling her. A man called Devlin is quietly questioning her, trying to find out more. At first we wonder whether he is a psychotherapist; then her answers become so disjointed and inconsistent that we begin to suspect that we are in a mental hospital."[144] The confusion elicited by Rebecca's inconsistent account and the nature of the dialogue, adds to the confusion deriving from the blurring of boundaries of the two domains, the public/political and the private/personal. Unwilling to accept the blurring as intentional, Jack Tinker identified it as the source of the play's weakness: "Real or false? *Collective memory or more disconnected fantasy?*" He passed the problem on to "Michael Billington," who "will have the bother of supplying explanations to add to the footnotes of his Pinter biography. For that is all this play adds up to."[145]

Ashes to Ashes baffled the reviewers not only in the co-existence of opposing modes, but also in the juxtaposition of voices that echo other plays in the playwright's repertoire. The play thus offered a riddling map, with incompatible modes on the one hand, and countertraces on the other.[146] *Ashes to Ashes* can be viewed as Pinter's self-pronounced dramatic manifestation in the face of critical views, that is, a play that incorporates two only apparently mutually exclusive domains and modes of explicitness and hence showcases the coexistence of his multidramatic facets.

While Pinter had challenged critical views with his plays *Betrayal* and *Alaska,* his emphatic response to the categorization of his work goes back to his "return to form," as manifested by *Moonlight.* The shifts in his dramatic writings signaled to critics and audience alike that his work should not be restricted to clear-cut categories. What is highly significant, however, is that at the beginning of the phase, marked by *Moonlight* in 1993, Pinter seemed to re-define his position in the mediating endeavor, becoming an active participant in the process.

Specifically, Pinter employed a pincer-like move, gradually expanding his use of the diverse mediating channels accessible to him. He advanced his emergent policy through his dramatic writings, while simultaneously exploiting several other channels either by virtue of his capacities as an actor or director or by virtue of his acquired stature. Following his turn in *Moonlight,* Pinter juxtaposed his so-called opposing dramatic modes within the single play *Ashes to Ashes,* which he directed. Concomitantly, after *Moonlight,* he repeatedly addressed, in his responses to critics, journalists and interviewers, the issue of the political in his drama and the continuity of the political dimension of his work. This latter claim echoed, albeit with additional emphasis, past claims by the playwright, as well as a few recurrent critical responses.[147] Significantly, he exploited the stage given to him by helping devise the program for the first Pinter Festival, which would display the unity underlying his various dramatic facets.

The festival, at the Gate Theatre, Dublin, lasted for three weeks in May 1994. Notably, it was a sequel to a Beckett retrospective which had been staged at the Gate in 1991 to international acclaim. The Pinter Festival at the Gate thus celebrated the playwright's fame and status not only in its staging a season of his work (more usually a tribute to dead playwrights), but also by virtue of its association with his renowned predecessor, Samuel Beckett. Michael Billington, in his biography of Pinter, credits Michael Colgan, director of the Gate Theatre, with the bold idea of acknowledging a living playwright by celebrating his work, "to introduce Dublin audiences to some of the less familiar plays, and to put long and short pieces together in illuminating juxtaposition."[148] Colgan, in collaboration with Pinter, devised the program, which consisted of a double-bill production of *Betrayal* and *The Dumb Waiter*; a double-bill production of *Old Times* and *One for the Road*; *Landscape,* directed by the playwright; and *Moonlight,* restaged by Karel Reisz. The casts comprised both Irish and British actors.

Local critics on the whole expressed highly favorable views of the productions and, according to Billington, seemed to be less concerned with Pinter's politics than their British counterparts were.[149] The reviews of the festival in the *Observer,* the *Sunday Times,* and the *Financial Times* reflected the critics' recognition of the "essential unity of Pinter's imagination," a "point which the Festival has tended to bring home so powerfully."[150] The reviewers also tried to resolve the perceived dichotomy between incompatible modes or phases of Pinter's dramatic work by finding a unifying principle in both his early and his later plays. John Peter, for example, noted in the *Sunday Times* that "Pinter's plays have always been political in the sense that Ibsen's plays are political: they explore the private roots of power, the need to dominate and mislead, the terror of being excluded or enclosed, the comprising contagion of past actions, the compulsion to re-imagine the past." Peter's view of the political as unifying Pinter's dramas incorporated the facets of the playwright's work into a single "Pinter" construct.

The success of the first Pinter Festival led to the second Pinter Festival, held on January 23, 1997, which presented *The Collection* (with Pinter playing the role of Harry); *Ashes to Ashes*; *A Kind of Alaska* (directed by the playwright); and *No Man's Land.* The two Pinter Festivals at the Gate illustrate the mediatory function of theatre festivals in the enhancement of a playwright's reputation.

Another highly significant manifestation of Pinter's policy of actively participating in the mediation of his works at this stage is reflected in the publication of three books between 1994 and 1998, with all of which the playwright was directly involved. The first, a collection of conversations with Mel Gussow, comprises five conversations with Pinter between 1971 and 1993: two center on the early plays and three, which took place after the sequence of political plays—the last after the performance of *Moonlight*—deal with the later plays. This was followed by Michael Billington's biography of Pinter, with the playwright's full cooperation.[151] The third book, *Various Voices: Prose, Poetry, Politics, 1948–1998,* was by Pinter himself.

Several highly favorable reviews of *Various Voices* reflected the effect of the playwright's mediating policy.[152] This book, which reflects the playwright's view of his various voices, gradually came to be regarded by the critics as an integral component of his image, a reaction in line with the bi-directional dynamics underlying Pinter's interactions with the critics through the early phases of his career, namely, the incorporation of his own responses into the critical discourse centering on his work. On the cover of *Various Voices* appears the portrait of Pinter that was celebrated in 1992 as one of the new faces at the National Portrait Gallery.[153] The use of this portrait thus marked the author's canonicity and acquired standing. Furthermore, Pinter's image is highly familiar, not only as an actor, but also from the numerous photos of him, often dressed in black, that appear in the programs accompanying his plays, from reviews and press articles of his work, and from his appearance at public events and in television interviews. His portrait, then, alludes to yet another facet of his reputation—his emergence as an iconic figure.

The publication of *Various Voices* may have kicked off the journalistic profiles of the playwright that followed in the *Guardian*. That newspaper's extensive profile of Pinter, written by Stephen Moss, centered on the public image of the playwright, one that draws on his dramatic works as well as on his personality. Pinter declared to Moss that "*'to a great extent my public image is one that's been cultivated by the press. That's the Harold Pinter they choose to create.'*"[154] Pinter called considerable attention to his "created image," denouncing it to an extent, while actively intervening in its mediation by attempting to adjust it according to his own perception.

Pinter's next move displayed yet another strategy aimed at advancing the perception of his dramatic image as both unified and multifaceted: adopting the hitherto successful policy of juxtaposing early and late work, a policy he had endorsed in the program of the first Pinter Festival. Pinter's move this time was *to introduce* his new work in the same double-bill with his first written dramatic work. The double-bill performed at the Almeida on March 27, 2000, by now a venue that had come to be associated with his work, consisted of his play, *The Room*, and his new play *Celebration*, both directed by the playwright. *Celebration* is surprisingly comic. Set in a pricey restaurant, it satirically portrays three nouveau-riche couples in their slightly caustic relationships and their entertaining exchanges with the restaurant staff.

Most reviewers reacted favorably to Pinter's theatrical surprise at the Almeida, particularly to the singular combination of the early and new plays and the comic nature of *Celebration*.[155] Excluding Spencer's unfavorable view, the majority welcomed the production of *The Room* and the opportunity that it afforded them to revisit distinctly familiar Pinteresque territory. Sheridan Morley, for example, proclaimed: "What is intriguing here is the way *The Room* not only signals and foreshadows everything that we now mean by Pinteresque, but also the way that it has failed" to become dated,[156] while John Gross declared: "*The tone of voice is highly distinctive*; in retrospect, you can see that the piece contains a great deal of Pinter's later work in embryo."[157] Most reviews praised the entertaining *Celebration*, the playwright/director, cast, and set. Most also called attention to the similarity between the early and recent plays. "*Celebration* is a direct descendant of *The Room*; both are stories about power and intruders," remarked Susannah Clapp,[158] and Billington commented, "yet, for all their obvious contrasts, I was struck by a curious similarity between the two works."[159] These critical responses to *Celebration* show the success of Pinter's strategy of presenting an overview by combining his recent work with his earliest. In fact, *The Cambridge Companion to Harold Pinter*, published in 2001, depicts on its front cover two scenes: one from *The Room* and one from *Celebration*.[160]

Pinter's seventieth birthday, in 2000, again set off extensive press coverage. What now marked the articles, however, was a growing tendency to treat Pinter's political phase as an integral component of his writings. In contrast to their 1980s preoccupation with his growing political engagement, they devoted only a relatively short discussion to such issues, choosing instead to highlight Pinter's unique contribution as a dramatist. Kate Kellaway's article in the *Observer Review*, titled "Pinter Is 70. (Pause for Applause)," addressed the term "Pinteresque" and referred briefly to Pinter's political plays, emphasizing the similarities between the early and late Pinter.[161] Regarding the recent double-bill of *The Room* and *Celebration*, the journalist had found "an uncanny family likeness" between the two plays. Billington's article in the *Guardian* stressed the essential nature of the political in Pinter's work: "The kind of overtly political plays Pinter has been writing since 1985 . . . are often treated in Britain with patronizing condescension if not downright hostility. . . . But I would argue that *Pinter's political works are a crucial part of his oeuvre and the source of his continuing vitality*."[162] Bryan Appleyard chose to emphasize Pinter's "enormous tribute" to the theatre, highlighting all that is entailed by the term "Pinteresque"—which "has entered the language"— and listing the various revivals of the dramatist's plays performed around the world. In awe of Pinter's immense contribution, Appleyard asked,

"Garlanded with such international praise, can his Nobel Prize be much longer delayed?"[163]

Pinter's next step was to devise a program for yet another festival of his plays in 2001. First presented at the Gate Theatre in Dublin and subsequently at New York's Lincoln Center, the Pinter Festival (or Pinterfest, as it was also called) this time consisted of a broader range of double-bill combinations. *A Kind of Alaska* was paired with *One for the Road*; *The Room* with *Celebration*; *Mountain Language* with *Ashes to Ashes*. The festival also included *The Homecoming* and *Monologue*. Pinter himself acted the lead role in *One for the Road* and directed the double-bill production of *The Room* and *Celebration*. The same cast acted in both plays of the double-bills, *The Room* and *Celebration,* and *Mountain Language* and *Ashes to Ashes.* En route from Dublin to Lincoln Center, *One for the Road* was performed in London with the playwright in the lead role. Praising Pinter as playwright and actor, Susannah Clapp declared that "Pinter in Pinter is, as it should be, a double-strength occasion."[164] In 2002 Pinter became Companion of Honour, a distinction awarded by the Queen.[165]

In honor of Pinter's seventieth birthday, the BBC presented a three-week Pinter season. Starting on October 26, 2002, with a double episode of *Arena*, plus showings of *One for the Road* and *No Man's Land*, the season included *The Room* and *Celebration* and other one-act and full-length plays featuring a cast of star actors such as Laurence Olivier, John Gielgud, Ralph Richardson, Ian Holmes, Helen Mirren, Lindsay Duncan, and Alan Bates. The season included several of the films for which Pinter had written the screenplays, *The Servant* and *Accident* among them. In the *Times* preview report for this celebration, Benedict Nightingale commented: "I don't think any writer has received so much concentrated attention as BBC TV and radio is about to give Harold Pinter."[166]

The first broadcast of the retrospective, on BBC Two, comprised three parts: two *Arena* programs titled "Harold Pinter's Life, Work, and Political Passions" and a screening of his works. The *Arena* programs, prepared between 2000 and 2002, included several recent conversations with the playwright, interviews with actors and directors involved in productions of Pinter's plays, and an overview of his career and private life, integrating segments of interviews. The programs juxtaposed the playwright's enigmatic responses and the puzzlement generated by his work during the early years of his career with his direct and explicit responses in interviews during the later years, particularly with regard to political issues. In fact, Pinter amusedly admitted that he had become increasingly accessible to interviewers over the last decade, further confirming that his recognition of the political had underlined his dramatic work since the beginning of his career. The concluding part of this broadcast included a full screening of two dramatic works in which the playwright acted the lead role: his recent sketch *Press Conference* and *One for the Road*. *Press Conference,* first performed as part of an evening of Pinter sketches at the Royal National Theatre on February 8 and 11, 2002, is a satirical portrayal of a press conference with a new minister of culture who had formerly served as head of the secret police. Pinter acted the role of the minister with members of the company (the National Theatre) acting as the press. At the beginning of the sketch the Minister is asked by the press: "Do you find any contradiction between these two roles?" He answers: "None whatsoever. As head of Secret Police it was my responsibility, specifically, to protect and to safeguard our cultural inheritance against forces which were intent upon subverting it. We were defending ourselves against the worm. And we still are."[167]

The second broadcast, part of "Pinter at the BBC" and shown on BBC Four, October 30, 2002, was entitled "Politics and Pinter" and presented "the playwright's political thoughts and opinions." Throughout the rest of this season BBC Four showed plays by Pinter nightly. A third, earlier broadcast, on October 1, 2000, also transmitted as part of the "Pinter at the BBC" season, formed part of a fund-raising evening at the London Soho Theatre for the English PEN at which the members paid a special tribute to Pinter's activities as a member of International PEN.[168] The highlight of this evening was the reading of Pinter's early play *The Dumb Waiter* in which Pinter read the role of Gus, one of the two acting roles, a play clearly not seen in 1960 as a political work.

These television programs, broadcast within a close time-frame—*Arena*'s tribute to Pinter's unique contribution to the theatre, which concluded with two avowedly political plays, and the political event that honored the English branch of PEN, which incorporated an early play not formerly perceived as political—comprised a retrospective of this playwright that celebrated both the unity and the variety of his dramatic work.

A CONSTRUCT IN RETROSPECT

[Pinter] broke the contract between audience and playwright. Then he redefined it. . . . Almost nobody has ever done this. Almost everybody refines; almost nobody redefines. —Tom Stoppard on Pinter at 60.[169]

Harold Pinter's career, which began with critical rejection, culminated in his achieving a worldwide reputation. The stages of his career illuminate the mediating forces involved in a playwright's developmental trajectory, their modes of operation, the different channels they exploit, their interactions and altering configurations. In particular, Pinter's career exemplifies the policies endorsed by theatre reviewers in devising, employing, and modifying the playwright's construct, essential to their mediating function.

The reviewers' use of the construct indicates that they do not respond independently to each new play by the playwright in question but rather react in accordance with their overall perception of that playwright's distinctive theatrical expression. Moreover, the case of Pinter illustrates that the critics' operations in a dramatist's career constitute a continuous process through which a bi-directional interaction is established between playwright and mediators. This counters expectations that the process is one way only, that the playwright writes and the critics react. Rather, the bi-directional interaction affects and modulates the constructed image that critics devise with respect to a given playwright. Pinter's career demonstrates the role that a playwright can play in determining his own critical existence, through negotiating an implicit contract with these mediators of his work.

In the course of his career, Pinter first took an ambivalent position, consisting of both collaboration and evasion, in the face of those who judged his work (critics and audiences alike); thereafter he challenged the "Pinter" construct via his writings, subsequently assuming an active role in mediating his image by exploiting the diverse repertoire of channels available to him. Given Pinter's marked degree of intervention and the ongoing struggle for control among the mediators of his work, the interactions among the participants gradually became a battle of forces over the playwright's image. In 2005 the extent to which Pinter has succeeded in shaping the perception of his image was still open to interpretation.

On October 13, 2005, Harold Pinter was named as recipient of the Nobel Prize for Literature. Two extracts from the citation read: "He is generally seen as the foremost representative of British drama in the second half of the 20th century. That he occupies a position as a modern classic is illustrated by his name entering the language as an adjective to describe a particular atmosphere and environment in drama: 'Pinteresque'"; and "His drama was first perceived as a variation of absurd theatre, but has later more aptly been characterised as 'comedy of menace,' a genre where the writer allows us to eavesdrop on the play of domination and submission hidden in the mundane conversations."[170]

Commentaries on the award, which Pinter received during the week of his seventy-fifth birthday, appeared in the London press the following day.[171] In spite of the overall agreement that Pinter greatly deserves the Nobel laurels, several critics still denigrated his overtly political plays. Charles Spencer, for example, commented in the *Daily Telegraph*: "[I]n his early and mid-period plays, Pinter created an atmosphere of enigma by deliberately withholding information that most dramatists would regard as essential. . . . Since the 1980s, however, Pinter has become far more politicized. . . . Unfortunately, these adolescent politics have infiltrated his plays. His more recent offerings seem to me to show a talent in steep decline, missing all the richness and ambiguity of his greatest work."[172] The *Guardian* published David Hare's elaborate commentary, accompanied by Pinter's portrait from the National Portrait Gallery. Hare praised Pinter: "Like Arundhati Roy, [Pinter] has worked to begin to redefine the idea of what, in uniquely dangerous times, we may expect an artist to be. In doing so, he has blown fresh air into the musty attic of conventional British literature. We have among us just one writer who is certain to be performed in 50 years, and who may well be performed in 100. But beyond that, he has used his reputation for good. More power to him."[173] Another commentary in the *Guardian*, "In praise of . . . Harold Pinter," referred to the controversy over Pinter's politics: "Yet the award to Harold Pinter may not find universal acclaim. For though his early success was on the stage with plays such as *The Homecoming* and *The Caretaker*, now firmly enshrined in the canon, Mr. Pinter has never been afraid of using a wider arena—including the pages of this newspaper—to air his political views." The controversies over Pinter's overtly political plays have yet to be resolved, but the *Guardian* nonetheless asserted, "Here is a writer who from those first imponderable glories to late flowerings such as *Mountain Language* has grown more obviously politically engaged. The plays, even some of the poems, are part of a grand, often hidden tradition of dissent in English culture. Its proponents breathe something like divine fire into the literature of revolution. Bunyan had that fire. Milton had it. Auden had it, too. We are fortunate that another of their ilk should be living in our time."[174]

The playwright's first response to winning the Nobel Prize was bewilderment. "Why they've given me this prize I don't know. I hadn't seen the citation then. But I suspect that they must have taken my political activities into consideration since my political engagement is very much part of my work. It's interwoven into many of my plays. . . . I'm told I am required to make a forty-five-minute speech which is the longest speech I will ever have made. Of course, I intend to say whatever it is I think. I may well address the state of the world. I'll be interested myself to find out how I'm going to articulate the whole thing."[175]

Harold Pinter now had a lofty platform from which to state his own convictions to a worldwide audience, although frail health prompted him to delivered his Nobel Prize lecture, "Art, Truth, and Politics," in London rather than in Stockholm. Broadcast on Channel More4 on December 7, 2005,[176] his speech began:

"In 1958 I wrote the following: 'There are no hard distinctions between what is real and what is unreal, nor between what is true and what is false. A thing is not necessarily either true or false; it can be both true and false.' I believe that these assertions still make sense and do still apply to the exploration of reality through art. So as a writer I stand by them but as a citizen I cannot. As a citizen I must ask: What is true? What is false?"

Conclusion

THE MAGIC CIRCLE: THE FIGURES THAT "AUTHORIZE"

In his memoirs, Oscar Lewenstein recalls that when he suggested George Devine for the post of the first artistic director of the English Stage Company, he presented him as belonging to the "central magic circle." Lewenstein meant by this that Devine was a practical man of the theatre, familiar with and experienced in the London theatre—an insider—unlike the other members of the board of the newly founded company, who were outsiders. The metaphor of the magic circle can be applied to a number of figures who have appeared and re-appeared across the four cases discussed here, insiders who belonged to the central circle of mediation. These figures, who acquired their reputation as participants in theatre production, partook in the running of major theatrical enterprises (theatre companies or theatre centers) or were involved in producing major theatrical events, sustaining their key functions and roles through subsequent phases of their careers. (It is noteworthy that the key positions held by these insider figures were the result of a developmental process during which they pursued a different vision of the theatre than that prevailing at the time.) Devine clearly represents a salient figure, not only for his central role in founding and establishing the ESC as the first artistic director of the company, but also for his earlier involvement in the Old Vic Theatre Centre, together with Michel Saint-Denis and Glen Byam Shaw, two other insiders, which succeeded the London Theatre Studio, where he had collaborated with Saint-Denis. Devine, who had served as president of the Oxford University Dramatic Society, acquired his reputation as an actor and director, collaborating with the Shakespeare Memorial Theatre particularly during his years as a freelance practitioner. He also served as a member of the Arts Council Drama Panel. The success of the ESC under his directorship and the numerous writings on his career, including articles, interviews, and studies, all contributed to his being perceived as a representative artistic director. This phenomenon suggests that mediation processes, often also focusing on the key in-house mediators themselves, may result in the emergence of role models who eventually become the representatives of specific theatrical posts, such as artistic directors, directors, or producers.

Tony Richardson, another principal mediator who belonged to the magic circle, was a theatre director and critic throughout his Oxford years and had also served as president of the Oxford University Dramatic Society. Richardson began a professional collaboration with Devine while working at the BBC as a television director, subsequently joining the newly founded ESC as its first associate artistic director. In addition to his growing reputation as the director of various ESC productions, notably *Look Back in Anger*, Richardson pursued his early collaboration with Lindsay Anderson and Karel Reisz, launching the Free Cinema enterprise. Following the founding of the Woodfall Company with John Osborne, Richardson went on to become a prominent film director, producing Reisz's first feature film, among others. Lindsay Anderson too acquired his reputation as both a film and a stage director. He joined the ESC as assistant director, subsequently serving with William Gaskill and Anthony Page as artistic directors of this company. Anderson's articles on a variety of theatre and film issues and his reviews, such as those published in *Encore*, reflect another facet of his active and influential role as a mediator.

Yet another example is William Gaskill, who began directing at the Royal Court after working with Joan Littlewood in Theatre Workshop. In addition to directing various renowned ESC productions, Gaskill served as associate director of the company, succeeding Devine as the artistic director and subsequently becoming one of the three ESC artistic directors, with Anderson and Anthony Page. Gaskill also served as associate director of the National Theatre at the Old Vic after working for two seasons with the Royal Shakespeare Company at Stratford-upon-Avon. John Dexter, an insider too, directed renowned productions, particularly of Arnold Wesker's plays, at the Royal Court, serving also as associate director of the National Theatre at the Old Vic around the same years as Gaskill. Another principal figure who belonged to the central circle is John Bury, who worked with Joan Littlewood for over a decade as a stage designer for Theatre Workshop, where he also served as the artistic director of this company. Bury was subsequently chief designer at the Royal Shakespeare Company and thereafter head of design at the National Theatre. He served twice as a member of the Arts Council Drama Panel.

Oscar Lewenstein, a principal mediator too, was one of the major figures in the left-wing Unity theatre movement, general manager of the Glasgow Unity Theatre, manager of the Embassy Theatre in Hampstead, and an editor of Unity's *New Theatre* magazine. He served as the general manager of the Royal Court in the early 1950s, functioning as a connecting link between the founding members of the ESC (i.e., suggesting Devine for the post of artistic director to the members of the first ESC council), and he was a member of the first council and artistic committee of this company. Lewenstein, a prominent producer, presented, among other notable productions, Theatre Workshop's production of *Mother Courage,* the first production of a Brecht play in England, and he co-produced Brecht's *The Threepenny Opera* at the Court prior to the first season of the ESC. He served as chair of the ESC in the early 1970s and subsequently as artistic director until the mid 1970s, and he was the driving force behind four transfers of Theatre Workshop productions to the West End, leasing the Theatre Royal at Stratford East following Littlewood's departure in 1961.

Inevitably, only those insiders who were directly involved with the events recounted here, on the one hand, and those major enterprises relevant to the cases in question, on the other, have been the focus of scrutiny in this book. These exemplary cases, nevertheless, reveal that the key positions were shared among a fairly small number of specific figures. Moreover, the collaboration among principal figures involved in one enterprise often continued into the inauguration of another enterprise and structured ongoing collaborations and alliances.

Casting the argumentative net even further, the metaphor of the magic circle defines a second, wider circle of leading figures active in the mediation network at large. These figures practiced their mediation authority primarily as theatre reviewers, critics, authors of influential studies, or members of award committees or of funding bodies, at times simultaneously occupying several key institutional positions. Two examples are Kenneth Tynan and Martin Esslin.

Kenneth Tynan had already made his mark during his Oxford years—in the period immediately following the Second World War, when he and Tony Richardson dominated the Oxford theatre scene. Although Tynan directed and acted in a number of plays at the beginning of his career, he primarily acquired his reputation as a drama critic for the *Spectator,* the *Evening Standard,* the *Daily Sketch,* the *New Yorker,* and notably the *Observer,* becoming a leading critic during the postwar era. His frequent disagreement with Harold Hobson, another highly prominent critic, who worked for the *Sunday Times,* was well known. Tynan was a film critic for the *Observer,* a script editor for films, and an editor of television programs; he also devised the production *Oh! Calcutta!* and served for six years as literary manager of the National Theatre and for four years as its literary consultant. Pursuing his agenda to encourage innovative contemporary theatre, Tynan was a key proponent of Theatre Workshop from the company's early years at Stratford East and was an advocate of Littlewood's theatrical innovations. His review of *Look Back in Anger* has become one of the most famous reviews in British theatre history. Tynan also chaired drama conferences and was an active member of various influential committees. His numerous essays on theatre issues, some of which appeared in *Encore*, were subsequently published in a number of collections, and his life and work have been the subject of biographies and studies. Harold Hobson's career too has been the subject of several studies, and he has published books on the theatre in Britain and a number of collections of his reviews.

Martin Esslin, another prominent critic and the author of influential studies, notably *The Theatre of the Absurd*, published reviews and articles in *Encore*, was a steady contributor to *Plays and Players*, and established himself as a central authority on Harold Pinter's work. Esslin's powers as a cultural mediator also derived from his appointment as assistant head and subsequently head of the Drama Department of BBC radio. Esslin also served on the Drama Panel of the Arts Council. Other figures who belong to the wider circle of mediators include John Russell Taylor, Richard Findlater, Irving Wardle, and Simon Trussler, all of whom were not only prominent critics, but also authors of notable studies or editors of major theatre journals, as well as members of influential committees.

A few principal figures belong to both circles. Such, for example, is Charles Marowitz, who acquired his reputation simultaneously as critic, director, and playwright and eventually as editor of *Encore*. In fact, even the figures who are seen primarily as insiders generally wore more than one hat: they voiced their views on the theatre through various media channels and often extended their powers as members of external, influential committees. Prominent figures in the wider circle were at times also associated with a particular company or institution (e.g., serving as members of councils or boards). The significance of these two mediatory circles lies in the phenomenon of a fairly small number of theatrical figures who have acquired their authority by virtue of their key positions, constituting—in a seemingly game of musical chairs—a primary source of power that considerably influences developments in the theatre.

INTERACTIONS: PATTERNS AND EFFECT

The power of mediation on theatrical development not only resides in the key positions held by (and exchanged among) a limited number of major figures, but also stems from or is conditioned by the configuration that emerges from the interactions established among the parties operating in a given case. The reception of the English Stage Company's production of John Osborne's *Look Back in Anger* and of Theatre Workshop exemplify opposing instances with respect to mediatory configurations. The significance attributed to the ESC production of Osborne's play and its rise to fame demonstrate the consequence of one such all-powerful configuration of convergent mediating forces, reinforced by the contemporary favorable constellation in the socio-cultural arena and particularly in the theatrical field. The judgments surrounding this event have proven to be an influential factor in shaping the trajectories and reputations of the company, playwright, and play, leaving their impact too on assessments of modern British theatre made in the following decades. The ESC production of *Look Back in Anger* has been credited with a unique role in launching a new era in British theatre—the "breakthrough narrative," albeit a narrative modified or challenged by revisionist histories over the last two decades.

In contrast, the winding course and reputation of Theatre Workshop, as well as the shift in scholarly assessment in the last two decades of this company's theatrical contribution, show the effect that can result, both during the given era and over history, from divergent mediating forces. That is, first, Theatre Workshop's growing inability to reconcile its ideological agendas, location, and financial needs within a divided cultural arena, which led to its demise; and second, the subsequent assessments of this company and its key production, which repositioned both as major and defining contributions in theatrical history.

The careers of the two playwrights discussed—John Arden and Harold Pinter—exemplify yet other patterns of interactions that were established among the mediating parties and their effect. Arden's early career demonstrates the implications of a configuration of divergent forces: supportive in-house mediators, on the one hand, and hostile critical reception or controversy, on the other. Arden gained prominent standing when his plays became associated with established companies and institutions, whose backing, combined with the campaign pursued by his champions, seemed to outweigh the reviewers' vacillations concerning the particular construct to be attached to his plays. Subsequently, the gradually diminishing and eventual disappearance of support from the theatrical establishment, together with his own actions and choices, led to the undermining of Arden's acquired standing and his complete break with the London theatre.

Pinter, in contrast, gradually won the theatre critics over, subsequently rising to prominence through the convergence of mediating forces—critical and academic acclaim and growing support from established theatrical institutions—competing for authority over the playwright's emergent canon. Pinter's move through the later stages of his career to an overtly political drama divided this united front; a coalition of established theatrical institutions with the playwright then emerged that, together confronted the hostile theatre critics.

The career courses of both Arden and Pinter reveal that theatre reviewers have considerable weight through the early phases of a dramatist's career, particularly through what I call the process of the playwright's acceptance into the canon. Their influence, however, decreased once these dramatists were backed by established theatrical institutions—Arden acquired prominence and Pinter maintained his position. Their careers also reveal how a playwright's own position toward the mediation endeavor also comes into play.

The playwright's conduct has proven to be a significant factor in shaping the reception of his or her work and in affecting his or her constructed image. This book illustrates a range of positions taken and modes of engagement or collaboration employed by various playwrights, as well as the consequent outcomes. Brendan Behan, for example, became the darling of the media overnight. His conduct cultivated, albeit probably unintentionally, his constructed image as wild and non-conformist, contributing to the emergent narratives that revolved around the production process of his play *The Hostage.*

Throughout his career, John Osborne showed impressive aptitude in promoting, enhancing, and cultivating his image as an Angry (initially Young) Man. Shelagh Delaney's collaboration with the press contributed to her eventual image as the "English Françoise Sagan," further enhancing the aura of discovery which attached to her. John Arden's conduct, though seemingly cooperative in the early phases of his career, while also consistently singular and non-compromising, first heightened the controversy associated with his work, later contributed to the developing perception of his work as uniquely challenging and innovative, and thereafter effected his gradual distancing from the center of attention.

Pinter's initial conduct—simultaneously responsive and evasive—contributed to his emergent image as an enigmatic playwright, shifting later through that of the rebellious interlocutor into an active engagement with mediation, and further still as a dominant participant in the endeavor. His status as a performer, maintained throughout his diverse positioning and modes of engagement, also proved extremely effective in generating additional attention and intensifying mediatory operations. The critical responses to Pinter's overtly political plays illustrate that although a playwright's construct may undergo modifications, theatre reviewers, and to an extent academics too, maintain their own tactics, reluctant as they are in general to devise the construct anew. In citing Pinter for the Nobel Prize, for example, the Swedish Academy made little mention of his political views, noting only that he is known as a "fighter for human rights" whose stands are often "seen as controversial." However, in the presentation speech by the chair of the Nobel committee, Pinter's overtly political plays were already being described as an integral part of his developing poetics as a playwright. Presumably, critical responses to future revivals of these dramas and the views of his overall work in critical and historical studies to come will indicate the extent to which the "Pinter" construct may yet be altered.

The range of possible positions and reactions of the dramatists themselves toward the mediation processes of their work is clearly wider than that presented in this study, and the potential influence of the differing conducts of playwrights is consequently only partially dealt with here. Nonetheless, the exemplary cases demonstrate the possible effect that a dramatist's own conduct or role in the mediation endeavor may have on his or her career.

Mediators, whether individuals or organizations, motivated by diverse and at times contradictory agendas, often vie for authority over the evaluation of their subjects. The course of Theatre Workshop illustrates the continual struggle between two external mediating forces: the governmental authorities, particularly funding bodies, that declined to support this company and the prominent theatrical figures who championed its cause. Conflict over which play or playwright a company should support may also develop among rival in-house mediators driven by contradictory agendas. John Arden's early plays, for instance, were matters of dispute among the in-house mediators running the English Stage Company. Underlying the conflict over a particular subject is often a struggle for control or for position as the dominant cultural/theatrical authority, where in-house dynamics are concerned or with regard to the theatrical field at large. The early stages in the evolution of the English Stage Company illustrate the rivalry among in-house mediators over what subjects to support as inseparable from their primary struggle to control the company's policy, also manifested, for example, in their disputes over a repertoire or modes of advertisement. Inevitably, the struggle over a company's policy relates to the sort of theatre each mediator promotes.

The conflict of external mediators, either individuals or organizations, over the promotion or support of a particular company, playwright, production, or play appears to incorporate their underlying struggle to become an influential and perhaps dominant force in the cultural or theatrical field. Their goal is to accrue sufficient authority to determine the face of the evolving theatrical map or delimitation of the emergent canon, with positions assigned, niches ascribed, or constructs devised. The *Encore* campaigns, or the contrasting attitudes of the Arts Council toward the two theatre companies, are revealing examples of these driving agendas. Pinter's career illustrates the ongoing struggles among mediating forces, such as the rivalry that emerged between certain theatre reviewers and academics over the authority to judge new plays by this canonical playwright. Other instances of especially heated arguments among individual critics are exemplified in Charles Marowitz and Albert Hunt, who both exerted their power as mediators to claim the major contribution of John Arden's plays, fiercely attacking other theatre critics for downplaying his work; or Harold Hobson, whose laudatory review of Pinter's *The Birthday Party*—a work initially dismissed by the majority of theatre critics—reflected an exertion of his considerable powers to change the fortune of this production, albeit to no avail. These examples illustrate how, in seeking to defend or promote their subjects, critics often target other critics' perceived shortcomings. The competition to be perceived as the reigning authority is even more transparent when mediators profess agreement regarding, for example, the subject's unique contribution to theatre, as does John Russell Taylor in *Anger and After*, who then downplays Kenneth Tynan's seminal role in promoting Osborne's *Look Back in Anger*. A similar dynamic is at work in the underlying contest among such mediating forces as theatre reviewers, academics, and established institutions over the emergent Pinter canon.

One major difference between the case of a theatre company and that of an individual playwright derives from the greater number of mediators and consequent complexity of interactions in a theatre company. Moreover, some external forces of mediation, such as funding bodies, can prove crucial in affecting the developmental course of theatre companies—e.g., that of Theatre Workshop; while others, such as reviewers and critics, bring relatively heavier weight to bear in shaping the careers of individual playwrights—e.g., Pinter's career. Additionally, if the symbolic goods acquired by individual in-house mediators serve to influence the position and niche assigned to the company with which they are associated—e.g., the effect of Devine's reputation on the reception of the ESC—the placement assigned to the company becomes a significant factor in shaping the reception of a new playwright, and affects the criteria in the light of which the playwright or play will be evaluated—e.g., the critical reception of Angus Wilson's *The Mulberry Bush*, the first play performed by the ESC. Further, the company's structure, the relations obtaining among the various in-house mediators—e.g., conflict of agendas, frequent disagreements, rivalries or, alternatively, a united front—and their consequent impact on the interactions between in-house mediators and external ones can be significant factors in a company's evolution—e.g., the effect of Theatre Workshop's seeming unanimity regarding the company's agendas. The playwrights' own willingness and abilities to collaborate with either in-house or external mediators or both is also clearly effective in shaping their careers.

MEDIATION IN PROCESS

The processes of mediation that recur across the four cases examined here indicate that mediators affect other mediators. The chain reaction that evolved in the case of Theatre Workshop is one example. This company's success at their first Paris festival subsequently led to press coverage and to an invitation to another festival in Devon, increasing its visibility and eventually bringing more critical acclaim in a snowballing of recognition. The reassessment in the last two decades of Theatre Workshop's theatrical contribution also reveals an underlying chain reaction: a number of published histories and critical studies of the company or its productions, followed later by the publication of Littlewood's memoirs and wide media coverage that highlighted the innovation of both the founder-director and her company, and thereafter the consecutive publication of revisionist histories.

The emergence of both the Movement and the Angry Young Men cult demonstrates yet other examples of mediatory chain reactions. The media coverage of John Arden's *Pearl* illustrates the effect of favorable previews, followed by a television broadcast, on critical responses and subsequent recognition in the form of prizes and awards. The gradual build-up in the case of the ESC production of John Osborne's *Look Back in Anger* demonstrates the cumulative effect of association with a rising trend, a catchphrase, a television interview, critical acclaim, television broadcasts, and massive press coverage, and the manner in which all of these predispose a work to achieve awards and public recognition. Also apparent is the impact of a successful film version adapted from an acclaimed play, which in turn enhances the reputation of the playwright and of the original playscript or initial production. For example, the film version of Harold Pinter's *The Homecoming* also cultivated the fame of Peter Hall—the director of the stage and screen versions—and of the cast acting in both. Highly influential too, in establishing a reputation, are publications of critical and historical studies that present or assess the significance of a theatrical offering within the broader context either of a playwright's oeuvre, as did the numerous studies on *Look Back in Anger*, or of other theatrical developments, such as the many studies on the innovation of *Oh What a Lovely War* or John Russell Taylor's assessment of the significance of Osborne's play in his book *Anger and After*. An accumulation of academic studies eventually influences the position of a playwright, play, or company in the cultural or historical memory, as have the numerous studies dealing with the ESC, John Osborne, and *Look Back in Anger* on the position assigned to this company, playwright, production, and play. Still other factors contribute to building a reputation, among them a playwright's association with an established institution or acclaimed company, or a theatre company's or a playwright's association with particular venues of performance. An example is the association of the Pinter Festival at the Gate Theatre with the preceding, highly acclaimed Beckett retrospective. Reputation is also cultivated by virtue of association with a renowned producer, director, or star-cast; Pinter's *No Man's Land* and Arden's *Armstrong's Last Goodnight* are examples.

The stages in the development of recognition of a subject's theatrical merit or contribution are in general marked by typical modes employed by the mediators through the various mediatory channels. Press releases, previews, program notes, company brochures, press interviews, reviews, and articles can all play a role in introducing, promoting, or evaluating a newcomer or an established subject. Television interviews, especially those conducted by a renowned media figure such as Melvyn Bragg, appear to cultivate or confirm an already acquired theatrical standing—consider Malcolm Muggeridge's interviews with Osborne, Behan, and Littlewood, or Melvyn Bragg's interview with Arden. A press profile such as the *Observer*'s profile of Littlewood marks and enhances the reputation of a theatrical figure, just as emergent narratives elevate the status of a subject, such as those constructed around Osborne's *Look Back in Anger*, Brendan Behan's *The Hostage*, or Littlewood's work methods.

Several mediatory modes primarily serve to secure and maintain the attribution of canonicity to a play, a theatre company, or a playwright. This can be seen for instance in a season on television devoted to the plays of an individual playwright, such as the Pinter season at the BBC; a television program providing an overview of a playwright's career, exemplified by the *Arena* program on Pinter; a play serving as a set text in English literature syllabuses, notably John Arden's *Serjeant Musgrave's Dance*; festivals centered on plays by a single playwright, such as the Pinter festivals or Beckett retrospective at the Gate Theatre; conferences that center on the history of a particular theatre company, exemplified by the conference in Louisiana that engaged primarily with the legacies of the English Stage Company; or academic conferences that center on the works of an individual playwright, such as the international meeting at Ohio State University to celebrate Pinter's sixtieth birthday. Several singular means of mediation that reflect canonicity include the quotation of lines from an acclaimed play in a press article under the assumption of its familiarity to the general public—exemplified by the citation from Pinter's *No Man's Land*—as well as allusions to titles of works or to names of protagonists in various contexts, exemplified in the references to titles of works of the Angry Young Men as slogans and headlines, or to Littlewood's "lovely war."

A FINAL NOTE

There is no closure to the processes of mediation, for they are constantly in motion. During the last two years—from the end of 2004 to 2006—while I was in the advanced stages of writing this book, several key subjects discussed in this study underwent additional mediatory turns. Publication of the third volume of *The Cambridge History of British Theatre* in December 2004 set its seal on another turn in scholarly assessments of the developments in British theatre in the second half of the twentieth century. The Nobel Prize for Literature, awarded to Harold Pinter in October 2005, has bestowed the zenith of world recognition on this already highly acclaimed playwright. That year, which marked the fiftieth anniversary of the premier of Samuel Beckett's *Waiting for Godot* at the Arts Theatre, saw a special exhibit at the Theatre Museum in London, "Unleashing Britain: Theatre Gets Real, 1955–1964," and publication of a book of the same title, both of which traced the transformations in British theatre. The entrance space of the exhibit was divided among *Waiting for Godot, Look Back in Anger,* and plays performed by Joan Littlewood's Theatre Workshop. The display included program notes and other documents relating to the various plays, the original sets for both Beckett's and Osborne's plays, and a continuous screening of television interviews conducted with Peter Hall on *Waiting for Godot* and with Joan Littlewood, including the famous interviews from 1961 and 1994. In 2006, a biography of John Osborne by John Heilpern was published, followed by yet another mediatory turn centered on the impact of the 1956 ESC production of *Look Back in Anger,* the play, and the playwright. In 2006, too, the Royal Court celebrated its fiftieth anniversary with a special season that included readings of Osborne's plays, productions of new plays—for example, Tom Stoppard's *Rock 'n' Roll*—and the highly awaited and acclaimed production of Beckett's *Krapp's Last Tape,* with Harold Pinter. The tides of mediation still to come may well sweep over the theatrical past yet again, leaving unforeseen turns in their wake.

Notes

INTRODUCTION

1   See also Hayman 1979, 144–146, on the Off-Broadway influence on the fringe theatre in London.

2   See, for example, Taylor 1971; Hayman 1973 and 1979; Elsom 1976; Sinfield 1989; Lacey 1995; Rebellato 1999; Shellard 1999 and 2000b; Hewison 1995; Marwick 1998; Bull 2000 and 2004; Kershaw 2004; and Sandbrook 2005.

3   See Postlewait 1986 and Merritt 1990. See also Zarhy-Levo 1993; Shellard 1995b; and Zarhy-Levo 2001a.

4   See Beauman 1982 and Philip Roberts 1999. See also Goorney 1981.

5   See especially McConachie 1992.

6   See, for example, Wardle 1978a; Hunt and Reeves 1995; Fay 1995; and Shellard 1995a.

7   See, for example, Kathleen Tynan 1987; Shellard 2003, and Kustow 2005.

8   See Littlewood 1994 and Eyre 2003. See also Hobson 1978; Kazan 1988; Peter Hall 1993; and Brook 1999, as well as the memoirs of the prominent producer Oscar Lewenstein, who also served as artistic director (Lewenstein 1994).

9   Shrum 1996, 7.

10 See also the anthology of essays edited by Wagner (1999), which presents commentaries by leading English-Canadian theatre critics on the creation of Canadian national theatre and drama over two centuries (1829–1998).

11 See Wardle 1992 and Nightingale 1986. See also Hobson 1984 and Coveney 1994a.

12 See Hobson 1952 and Kenneth Tynan 1961a and 1967. See also Morley 1975 and 1990 and Fenton 1983.

13 See, for example, Gottfried 1963; Elsom 1976; Trussler 1981; and Lloyd-Evans 1985.

14 Hartnoll 1967, 91.

15 Hartnoll 1967, 92.

16 Kennedy 2003, 126. Note, also, the resemblance between the presentation of Beckett's renowned play in this entry (the 2003 edition of the *Oxford Encyclopedia*) and the entry for *Waiting for Godot*, in the 2001 edition of *The New Penguin Dictionary of the Theatre*. A few excerpts from this latter entry read: "Despite the bewilderment it initially caused critics and audiences, the play rapidly gained the status of a modern classic; . . . the enigmatic symbolism of the play has been much debated"; and, "in 1999 an international

poll of theatre professionals voted it the most significant play of the century"
(Law, Pickering, and Helfer 2001, 634).

17 Kennedy 2003, 128.

18 See, for example, the strikingly different emphasis in the entries for Brecht
in the second edition of *The Oxford Companion to the Theatre* (Hartnoll
1957, 84) and in the 2003 edition of *Oxford Encyclopedia of Theatre and Performance* (Kennedy 2003, 182–184).

19 See, in particular, Williams 1981, 36–56, on the variable relations (different
societies and different historical periods) among cultural producers and institutions.

20 See McConachie 1992.

21 Findlater 1952, 94–109.

22 Lewenstein's own standing as a producer undoubtedly also contributed to
the reception of Orton's play.

23 See Daneman and McCowen 1988. Paul Daneman played Vladimir in the
1955 London production.

1. CONVERGENT FORCES

1 See *The New Penguin Dictionary of the Theatre* (Law, Pickering, and Helfer
2001, 193); see also *Cambridge Paperback Guide to Theatre* (Stanton and Banham 1996) in which the entry on the ESC (110) refers the reader to the entry
on George Devine (96).

2 Philip Roberts 1999, xix.

3 Charles Landstone was associate drama director from 1942 to 1952.

4 Landstone 1953, 174.

5 Peter Lewis 1990, 11–13.

6 Regarding Quayle's intentions and the three-year plan, announced at the
end of 1952, see Beauman 1982, 211–214.

7 Wardle 1978a, 141–142; see also Philip Roberts 1999, 9.

8 Beauman 1982, 215.

9 Beauman 1982, 215. Prior to its name change in 1960, the RSC was known as
the company of the Shakespeare Memorial Theatre.

10 Jocelyn Herbert's interview with Philip Roberts (1999, 6); Roberts also traces
Devine's conception of a writers' theatre to 1948 (1999, 9).

11 Wardle 1978a, 161.

12 The OUDS also included such notable figures as Kenneth Tynan, Peter
Brook, and Peter Hall, who were all to become active and major participants
in the mediating network, eventually contributing to the changing theatrical scene during the 1950s and 1960s.

13 On Richardson and Devine's meeting with Elaine Brunner, see Richardson
1993, 87.

14 Lewenstein 1994, 6.

15　Philip Roberts 1999, 12–13.

16　Quoted in Philip Roberts 1999, 16.

17　Philip Roberts 1999, 13–15.

18　Lewenstein 1994, 10.

19　Philip Roberts 1999, 18.

20　Philip Roberts 1999, 8.

21　Philip Roberts 1999, 24.

22　See Philip Roberts 1999, 19–20.

23　Lewenstein 1994, 14; see also Wardle (1978a, 164), who quotes Devine's remark, "such an odd job lot that the company's bound to succeed."

24　Lewenstein 1994, 13–14.

25　Lewenstein 1994, 13–14.

26　Hugh "Binkie" Beaumont began his career in 1924 as assistant manager at Cardiff, under Howard and Wyndham. After serving as business manager at the Little Theatre and, in 1926, at the Duke of York, he joined Moss Empires, subsequently becoming a director, then managing director of the firm H. M. Tennent, Ltd. (a leading theatrical agency). He also served as a director of the Company of Four at the Lyric Hammersmith (1945), as a member of the governing body of the Shakespeare Memorial Theatre, Stratford-upon-Avon (1950), and as a member of the National Theatre board (1962). "Binkie" Beaumont dominated the West End during the 1940s (see Shellard 1999, 7–8). On the significant role of Binkie Beaumont and H. M. Tennent on the subsequent development of British theatre, see Shellard 2000b, especially 30–33.

27　Lewenstein 1994, 10.

28　Findlater 1981, 11.

29　Lewenstein 1994, 26.

30　Philip Roberts 1999, 21.

31　On Blond and Esdaile's hostile attitude toward Devine's agendas, see Philip Roberts 1999, 38.

32　Wardle 1978a, 166; see also Wardle (1978a: 165–166) on the sort of theatre Devine wished to build. The Royal Court is the theatre in which Granville Barker and George Bernard Shaw had great success introducing the new drama in 1904–1907. On the Court seasons of new drama, especially Shaw's, see Postlewait 2004, 45–46.

33　Browne 1975, 15.

34　On those included in the team see Wardle 1978a, 173–174.

35　Browne 1975, 13; Lewenstein 1994, 30. Lewenstein was appointed general manager of the Court in the autumn of 1956 (see Lewenstein [1994, 29] and also Philip Roberts [1999, 56]); as such Lewenstein's account of the financial state of the Company poses a major source.

36　See Philip Roberts (1999, 39) on the negotiation with Brecht regarding the Devine-Ashcroft production of his play *The Good Woman of Setzuan*.

37 The list of members of the Arts Council's Drama Panel is included in the records of the *Annual Reports of the Arts Council* located at the Victoria and Albert Museum, Study Room. Note that the posts served by the "support-ive" mediators indicated primarily their influential positions in the theat-rical field, since the grants awarded to the ESC during the company's first three years of operation were relatively small. The grants awarded to the ESC by the Arts Council increased slightly in 1959, and markedly from the beginning of the 1960s. This issue is discussed in chapter 2, dealing with the Theatre Workshop.

38 After six weeks at the Court, *The Threepenny Opera* was transferred to the Aldwych Theatre and later to the Comedy Theatre, where it ran for about six months.

39 Lewenstein's coproduction (with Wolf Mankowitz and Helen Arnold) of *The Threepenny Opera* (February 1956), one of the earliest productions of a Brecht play in Britain and one that preceded the first visit of the Berliner Ensemble in London (August 1956), is considered one of the signposts of the new theatrical era. Brecht's work was one of the major influences on new theatrical directions in Britain in the postwar era. The works performed by the Theatre Workshop were seen as highly influenced by Brecht's theatri-cal style. Brecht's influence was also apparent in the style of productions at the Court. Lewenstein as a producer and Devine as a director, were major promoters of Brecht's work in Britain (as was the critic Kenneth Tynan, who championed Brecht's work as early as 1954).

40 The version cited relies on the brochure of the English Stage Company, dated April 5, 1955. This brochure is included in the ESC Company file in the Study Room, Theatre Museum, London. Note that this early version of the bro-chure refers to the Kingsway Theatre rather than to the Royal Court Theatre. On the alterations to the Company's brochure see Philip Roberts 1999, 28.

41 *Plays and Players* 1956b; see also *Times* 1956b.

42 *Sunday Times* 1956.

43 In *Sunday Times* 1956; see also *Times* 1956a.

44 Worsley 1956a; see also Findlater 1956.

45 See *Stage* 1956.

46 P. G. 1956; see also Darlington 1956. Darlington claims: "This play still lacks the true theatrical thrust."

47 R. B. M. 1956; see also the review in the *Daily Telegraph* (1956), and Grainger 1956.

48 See Wardle (1978a, 179–180). Philip Roberts (1999, 46–47) also discuss Devine's uncharacteristic tampering with the play (cutting out one charac-ter), and Miller's ultimatum.

49 W. R. 1956.

50 Graham 1956.

51 *Daily Worker* 1956, April 16.

52 Tynan 1956d.

53 Wardle 1978a, 182–183.

54 On the ESC production of *The Good Woman of Setzuan*, its successful tour prior to its opening at the Royal Court, its unfavorable reception in London, and especially Harold Hobson's critique, see Browne 1975, 26–27.

55 *The Country Wife* was transferred to the Adelphi Theatre after sixty performances at the Royal Court (February 4, 1957) and later to the Chelsea Palace Theatre. See Wardle's account of the production (Wardle 1978a, 188–189).

56 Findlater 1981, 27; emphases in original.

57 Philip Roberts 1999, 47. According to Lewenstein (1994, 28), 675 plays were sent to the Court in response to the ESC's advertisement in the *Stage* in 1955.

58 In his autobiography John Osborne refutes the claim, repeated by many critics and historians, that *Look Back in Anger* was originally titled *On the Pier at Morecambe*. Osborne 1991, 35.

59 Wardle 1978a, 180.

60 According to John Osborne's autobiography the meeting took place in August 1955. See Osborne 1991, 4–7.

61 Philip Roberts 1999, 48.

62 Philip Roberts 1999, 38.

63 Philip Roberts 1999, 38.

64 Wardle 1978a, 181.

65 See Barber 1956; see also Worsley 1956b.

66 John Osborne 1991, 22.

67 Hobson 1956. Sir Harold Hobson (1904–1992), for many years the drama critic of the *Christian Science Monitor*, succeeded James Agates as drama critic of the *Sunday Times* (1947–1976). In 1971 he received the CBE and was knighted in 1977.

68 Kenneth Tynan 1956b.

69 The effective role of both Hobson and Tynan in changing the fortune of the first London production of a Beckett play, *Waiting for Godot* (August 3, 1955, at the Arts Theatre Club), reflects these critics' influence (especially when both were in agreement). On these critics' promotional reviews of *Waiting for Godot* in 1955 and their impact, see Daneman and McCowen 1988; see also the discussion of these reviews in Zarhy-Levo 2001a, 17–19.

70 John Osborne 1991, 20.

71 Terry Browne claims that "it excited the public interest. Receipts immediately rose to about sixty per cent of capacity" (Browne 1975, 15).

72 Philip Roberts 1999, 46, 236.

73 Ritchie (1988, 26, 222) refers to an article by Thomas Wiseman "Angry Young Man," which appeared in the *Evening Standard* (July 7, 1956), as the first mention by the press of Fearon's remark.

74 John Osborne 1991, 20.

75 Scott 1956.

76 Ritchie 1988, 27.

77 According to Philip Roberts, Blond wrote to Cecil Tennant of the BBC, who arranged the television excerpt (Philip Roberts 1999, 236n11).

78 The notice in *Radio Times*, for example, announced the broadcast, "introduced by the Earl of Harewood," as a "special performance before an invited audience, from the Royal Court" (1956).

79 The accounts vary on the length of the excerpt, ranging from five minutes (Wardle 1978a, 185), eighteen minutes (Philip Roberts 1999, 48) to twenty-five minutes (John Osborne 1991, 23). The data provided by the British Film Institute confirm the slot time of twenty-five minutes for the BBC excerpt. There are no available data at the British Film Institute as to the number of viewers who watched the broadcast.

80 Both Browne (1975, 26) and Wardle (1978a, 185) claim that the play became a box-office hit within three days of the broadcast. See also John Russell Taylor (1962, 35) on the play's box-office takings for the two weeks following the broadcast.

81 Philip Roberts 1999, 49.

82 John Osborne 1956.

83 The program *Play of the Week* was shown at peak viewing time (8 P.M.). The excerpt from the play (October 16, 1956) was shown at 9.30 P.M.

84 *TV Times* 1956.

85 The Television Audience Measurement (TAM) rating of 68 indicated the share of the viewing public who watched the program. The information cited is based on data supplied by the British Film Institute.

86 Aynsley 1956.

87 Lacey 1995, 23–24.

88 Ritchie 1988, 27–28. See also Morrison's study (1980), which challenges the perception that the Movement was largely the "creation" of literary critics.

89 On the role of the critics in the formation of the Absurd school, see Zarhy-Levo 2001a.

90 Ritchie 1988, 25.

91 On the reception and success of *The Outsider*, see also Sandbrook 2005, 164–169.

92 See Ritchie's amusing account of the first social encounter of Osborne and Hastings, arranged by Farson, and its disastrous results (1988, 27).

93 Hill 1997 [1986], 22.

94 Ritchie 1988, 28.

95 See Ritchie's critique of the attempts to equate the Angry Young Men with the beat generation (1988, 51). The term "beat" was first used by Jack Kerouac

in 1952 and picked up in a *New York Times* article by John Clellon Holmes that year. The Beats emerged partly in response to the election of Eisenhower in 1952, with the comfortable, suburban world of the 1950s as a convenient if reductive version of the era. See William Burroughs's *Junkie* (1953) and *Naked Lunch* (1959), Allen Ginsburg's *Howl* (1955), Lawrence Ferlinghetti's *Pictures from the Gone World* (1955), and Kerouac's *On the Road* (1957). Also the various publications of San Francisco's City Lights bookstore proved to be a touchstone. "Beatniks" became a very popular word. This movement was consolidated by the academics in the late 1950s and early 1960s (see Lipton 1959; Krim 1960). The mid-1950s is also the era that rock'n'roll emerged with Chuck Berry, Elvis Presley, Bill Haley and the Comets, Fats Domino, and so on.

96 Hill 1997, 22.

97 See Wiseman 1956.

98 See Ritchie's account on Osborne's various expressions of anger (1988, 128).

99 John Osborne 1957.

100 James Gordon 1958.

101 Ritchie 1988, 38.

102 Buchan 1956. "Look Back in Sorrow," *The Observer*, December 2.

103 Ritchie 1988, 32–33; Hill 1997, 21–24.

104 See Sandbrook's account of the New Wave in his historical study of Britain "from Suez to the Beatles [1956–1963]" (Sandbrook 2005, 178–218). Sandbrook remarks: "The idea of 'anger,' in fact, ran through much of New Wave writing, but it was never accompanied by any clear political programme." He further claims: "Political radicalism in the New Wave is the dog that did not bark. While railing against what they saw as the smug inertia of the fifties consensus, the new writers did not present any committed, coherent alternative to it, and their political impact was minimal." Sandbrook also comments that "the irony is that there were plenty of 'good, brave causes' in the fifties to which an idealistic young man might have dedicated himself: these were, after all, the years of the H-bomb, the early Cold War and the often bloody retreat from the Empire. Indeed, despite all its vehemence, masculine aggression and working class 'authenticity,' the New Wave illustrated not the weakness but the resilience, indeed the genuine contentment, of the post-war consensus" (2005, 186, 216, 217).

105 Wesker 1997, 188. Wesker's three renowned plays form a trilogy. *Chicken Soup with Barley* (1958), *Roots* (1959), and *I'm Talking about Jerusalem* (1960) were all directed by John Dexter and performed both at the Belgrade Theatre, Coventry, and at the Royal Court Theatre. The three plays were first performed as a trilogy at the Royal Court in June and July 1960, also directed by Dexter.

106 Wesker 1997, 188; emphasis in original.

107 Mashler 1957, 8. Note the similarity to Martin Esslin's statement regarding the Absurdist playwrights (1984 [1965], 7).

108 Ritchie 1988, 44.

109 On the critics' disenchantment with the AYM see Ritchie 1988, 46–47.

110 Weightman 1957.

111 Lacey suggests that within the New Wave the first "critical moment" in the early or middle years of the 1950s is that of Anger. "In that sense," Lacey comments, "*Look Back in Anger* is the only 'angry' play" (Lacey 1995, 7).

112 The name Woodfall was derived from a street off the King's Road where Osborne and Mary Ure, his second wife, had rented a house.

113 In his autobiography Osborne admits that although he was grateful to Tynan for recommending Kneale, since he himself had no experience in writing screenplays, he had objected, though apparently to no effect, to some of the changes Kneale had made in the film version of the play (1991, 108).

114 Hill 1997, 127.

115 The editors of *Sequence One* were John Boud and Peter Ericsson; *Sequence Two* was edited by Lindsay Anderson, Panelope Houston, and Peter Ericsson. The 1948 issue of *Sequence* was published in London, edited by Peter Ericsson and Gavin Lambert, with associate editors Lindsay Anderson and Panelope Houston.

116 *Sight and Sound*, established in the 1930s, was published by the British Film Institute. Anderson 1956.

117 Hill 1986, 128, 129. See also Lindsay Anderson's program notes for the Free Cinema's revival included in National Film Theatre notes, August 15, 1977, (British Film Institute National Library, London.)

118 See Lindsay Anderson 1997, 10, emphasis in original. On the aims of the Free Cinema, see also the interview conducted with Karel Reisz in 1992 (Reisz 1997). The interviews with both Anderson and Reisz appear in a collection of interviews with actors and filmmakers of British Cinema that is dedicated to the memory of Anderson, who died in 1994.

119 *Together*, originally known as *The Glass Marble*, was initially shot by the Italian director Lorenza Mazzetti, who did not complete its editing. Anderson agreed to take it on, completed the editing, produced the final takes, and changed the film's title.

120 On the forming of the Free Cinema see Murphy 1992, 11.

121 Walter Lassally, director of photography, who collaborated with Free Cinema directors in the late 1950s (at the beginning of their film-making careers), claimed in a 1994 interview: "The whole Free Cinema thing is often misunderstood these days. It was never a movement: it was a phrase coined by Lindsay for a group of films to be shown at the National Film Theatre. Then there was a 'manifesto,' a declaration signed by Lindsay, Karel, Tony,

myself, John Fletcher, and Lorenza Mazzetti. Lindsay particularly hoped that Free Cinema would have some influence on mainstream British cinema, and of course the influence was nil. Then out of the Free Cinema, with other film streams joining it, came the Woodfall company, which was really the key to the New Wave in Britain" (Lassally 1997, 348).

122 On censorship policy regarding the two films (especially *Room at the Top*), see Marwick 1998, 122–124.

123 See Welsh 1999, 3.

124 Quoted in "The Man behind the Angry Young Men," in *Films and Filming* 1959.

125 On the opening scene and the settings of the film, see Tibbetts 1999, 66–67.

126 Sinfield claims: "In *Look Back in Anger*, Jimmy's jazz trumpet helps to define an oppositional identity" (1989, 263; see also 158–161).

127 Gavin Lambert 1959.

128 Hart 1959.

129 On Richardson's view of the Free Cinema motto, see Walker 1974, 27.

130 The ESC profits, in effect, grew substantially following Woodfall's film *Tom Jones* in 1963, which was adapted by Osborne from Henry Fielding's eighteenth-century novel, directed by Richardson, and produced by United Artists.

131 See Findlater 1981, appendix 2.

132 Richardson 1993, 104–105. Richardson's memoirs have been published by his daughter, Natasha Richardson. According to Welsh (1999, 1) Richardson's London debut as stage director was an unsuccessful production of Thomas Middleton's *The Changeling* at Wyndham's Theatre, that opened and closed on May 16, 1954.

133 Richardson 1993, 105.

134 Richardson 1993, 105.

135 Kenneth Tynan 1956b.

136 Kenneth Tynan 1956b; see also Sinfield 1989, 240, 261.

137 Kenneth Tynan 1959.

138 John Russell Taylor 1962.

139 John Russell Taylor 1962, 9.

140 John Russell Taylor 1962, 31.

141 John Russell Taylor 1971, 9.

142 John Russell Taylor 1962, 34.

143 John Russell Taylor 1962, 33.

144 John Russell Taylor 1968b.

145 John Russell Taylor 1971, 7–11.

146 See Parmentier 1980, 435 and 448. Appendixes 1 and 2 list the circulation and readership of the main British newspapers in 1956.

147 On developments in cultural perceptions, attitudes, and policies in the

1940s and the 1950s, manifested in the education and the arts, see Hewison's extensive discussion (Hewison 1995, 88–122).

148 Referring to the end of the 1940s and beginning of the 1950s, Findlater (1952, 68) states: "For the first time in English history the state has undertaken the responsibility of providing the community with drama." On the Arts Council's financial support to the theatre, see Findlater 1952, 67–74. See also Hayman (1973, 227–233) on the objectives and policies of the Arts Council and their significance for the theatre.

149 The first magazine Dosse had published was *Dance and Dancers* (January 1950). The art magazines published by Dosse are regarded as a major contribution to postwar British cultural life.

150 Morgan 2001, 260; Hewison 1987, 278.

151 Morgan 2001, 234.

152 On Modernist texts and Modernism in English studies, see Sinfield 1989, 198.

153 Bull 2000, 83.

154 The first hardback edition of *Anger and After: A Guide to the New British Drama* had been published in 1962 by Methuen. The U.S. edition, *The Angry Theatre: New British Drama*, was published by Hill and Wang (1962) and reprinted in 1963, the year Penguin (Pelican Books) published the first paperback (revised) edition. 1969 saw the publication of the second hardback (revised) edition as well as a new paperback edition published by University Paperback.

155 Shellard 2000b, 30.

156 See the concluding section of chapter 2, which deals with the Theatre Workshop, for the views presented in revisionist histories of postwar British theatre published in the 1990s.

157 Note, however, that Tynan also acted as an in-house mediator of the National Theatre when he served under the direction of Sir Laurence Olivier as dramaturge and literary advisor (1963–1973).

158 "An Extract of Autobiography for Television," directed by Frank Cvitanovich, with Eileen Atkins as Mrs. Osborne and Alan Howard as Mr. Osborne. Transmitted on *ITV* July 1, 1985.

159 For example, the reviews of *A Better Class of Person* by Bennett 1981 and by Rissik 1985.

160 For example, Levin 1994 and *Guardian* 1994.

161 Billington 1994b.

162 Hare 1997, 194–195.

163 Hare 1997, 196.

164 Denison 1997.

165 Quigley 1997, 35.

166 Williams 1968, 318.

167 Trussler 1969a, 9.

168 Banham 1969, 1–5, 11–12.

169 Hayman claims that Kenneth Haigh, in the role of Jimmy Porter, "blazed the trail with the first of the 'angry' young heroes," and thereafter followed the success of actors such as Albert Finney, Peter O'Toole, Nicol William-son, Richard Harris, Tom Courtenay, and Robert Stephens (1969, 1–6).

170 Worth 1972, 67.

171 Quigley 1997, 52.

172 See Postlewait 1988, especially 306–307.

173 The conference, "The English Stage Company at the Royal Court Theatre: Production Practices and Legacies 1956–81," took place at Louisiana State University in October 7–10, 1981.

174 Doty and Harbin 1990, 8.

175 Doty and Harbin 1990, 31.

176 Doty and Harbin 1990, 31.

177 Wardle 1978a, 171.

178 Doty and Harbin 1990, 43.

179 Sinfield claims: "It wasn't the intention of the English Stage Company to promote left-wing plays. Its council tried to stop such plays (Osborne's *The Entertainer*, for instance) and the director, George Devine, distrusted politi-cal commitment and valued most his theatre's work with Samuel Beckett" (1989, 261).

180 In 1957 in "The Royal Court Theatre," Devine outlined his views on the ESC's policy and achievements and specified his principal concerns. Top-ping the list was the need to encourage new writers for the theatre.

181 Wardle 1978a, 198. See his description of the overall effect that the new play-wrights and plays performed at Royal Court had on the area (e.g., the young and vital atmosphere at Sloane Square).

182 Doty and Harbin 1990, 207.

183 Heilpern 2006a.

184 Edgar 2006, 8.

185 Heilpern's letter of response to Edgar's claims and critique was published in the next issue of *London Review of Books* (Heilpern 2006b).

186 Edgar refers to Hare's memorial eulogy of Osborne, as well as to a longer lecture first delivered in 2002, repeated on the stage of the Royal Court on the fiftieth anniversary of *Look Back in Anger*.

187 Edgar 2006, 10.

2. DIVERGENT FORCES

1 MacColl 1973, 61.

2 See later accounts by MacColl (1973, 60) and Goorney (1981, 5). Goorney, an actor, had worked with Littlewood between the years 1938 and 1968.

3   MacColl 1973, 62. Also see Clive Barker's later view cited in Goorney 1981, 5, 166. Clive Barker had joined Theatre Workshop as an actor in 1955. Following the company's demise he pursued an academic career, becoming a prominent scholar. Barker was coeditor, with Simon Trussler, of *New Theatre Quarterly*.

4   Goorney 1981, 8.

5   Goorney 1981, 7–8.

6   For the quotes see MacColl 1973, 62. On the issue of the group's studies and explorations, see also Paget 1995a, 214.

7   Moussinak's influence is discussed in Paget 1995a.

8   Paget 1995a, 218–220.

9   On the aims of Theatre Union see the group's Manifesto in MacColl 1986, ix, and also "Necessity and Aims of Theatre Union" (its second manifesto) in Goorney 1981, 26.

10 MacColl 1973, 67.

11 See the manifesto in Goorney 1981, 41.

12 Goorney 1981, 82–83.

13 See Lewenstein 1994, 83.

14 The company's short season at the Embassy Theatre in London could also have contributed to the decision.

15 See MacColl 1990, 265.

16 MacColl 1990, 265–266.

17 Goorney 1981, 88.

18 See MacColl's detailed account of the evolution of the company's revolutionary theatre style between 1930 and 1948 (MacColl 1986).

19 Goorney 1981, 91.

20 Goorney 1981, 92–93, and "Appendix: Finances" (215) for Local Authority Grants.

21 Paget 1990a, 245.

22 MacColl 1973, 66.

23 Paget 1995a, 212.

24 Goorney 1981, 97.

25 *Times*, 1953a and 1953b.

26 See Darlington 1954.

27 See Kenneth Tynan 1954 and Wiltshire 1954.

28 Note that Theatre Workshop had presented a production of *Richard II* a year earlier, on January 19, 1954.

29 See *Daily Mail* 1955.

30 See Hobson 1955a.

31 See *Daily Telegraph* 1955.

32 See Tynan 1955a.

33 *Times* 1955a. On the critical responses to Theatre Workshop's productions of Ben Jonson, as directed by Littlewood, see Schafer 1999, especially 160–167.

34 See Hobson 1955b.

35 Joan Littlewood 1994, 464.

36 *Sunday Times* 1955.

37 *Times* 1955c.

38 *Times* 1955b. Also see the highly favorable notices in the *Manchester Guardian* (Hope-Wallace 1955) and in the *Observer* (1955).

39 In the early 1950s Oscar Lewenstein, beginning his career as a producer, was highly impressed by Wolf Mankowitz's one-act play *The Bespoke Overcoat.* Several months later he formed a company with Mankowitz to produce plays. Their plan was that Lewenstein would work at the company full time while Mankowitz, continuing with his own work, would help with money-raising, advice, and ideas. Lewenstein perceived the forming of this company as the direct consequence of his success with the production of *Airs on a Shoestring* (see chapter 1). Their collaboration lasted until 1960. Mankowitz wrote novels, poems, plays, filmscripts, and journalistic pieces and was also an antiques dealer and businessman. After their company split up, Lewenstein formed a new company, Oscar Lewenstein Plays Ltd., whose shares were acquired by John Osborne, Tony Richardson, and the Americans Donald Flamms and Doris Abrahams (Lewenstein 1994, 8, 98–99).

40 On the developments surrounding Theatre Workshop's production of Brecht's play, see Goorney 1981, 102, and Lewenstein 1994, 24–25.

41 See Kenneth Tynan 1955b and Hobson 1955c.

42 Hobson 1984, 183–184.

43 Hobson 1984, 7.

44 See also Lewenstein's discussion of the 1955 Devon festival, in which he comments: "Whether we accept the view that the revolution started with *The Threepenny Opera* or *Look Back in Anger,* or Hobson's more eccentric view that it started with Joan's production of *Mother Courage,* I claim to have had an equal hand in it" (1994, 25).

45 Goorney 1981, 103.

46 See Tynan 1956a.

47 Lacey 1995, 48.

48 Lacey 1995, 49.

49 See Kenneth Tynan 1956c.

50 Goorney 1981, 105.

51 Littlewood 1994, 471, 472.

52 Goorney 1981, 153.

53 Note, in particular, Theatre Workshop's production of *Macbeth,* performed in Zurich on July 2–4, 1957; at Stratford East on September 3, 1957; and at the

Playhouse in Oxford on November 4, 1957. On Littlewood's interest in *Macbeth* and her innovative directorial approach to this play, see Schafer 2000, 149–161.

54 Kenneth Tynan 1957b. According to Shellard (2003, 202), in October 1957, Tynan—as part of his campaign for contemporary plays, which evidently gained grounds with the successful productions at the Royal Court and at Stratford East—had attempted to influence an increase in the government's support for the Arts. Especially alarmed by the financial state of Theatre Workshop, Tynan believed that if the Arts Council received a larger endowment, it would grant this worthy company a more appropriate subsidy.

55 Lindsay Anderson 1981a, 46. Anderson joined the ESC in 1957.

56 See for example *Daily Telegraph* 1958. See also Marwick (1998, 137), referring to the "strikingly original" nature of *A Taste of Honey* and remarking that "one aspect of Delaney's commercial appeal can be seen in the various nicknames she was given by the press: 'teenager of the week,' 'the Françoise Sagan of Salford,' and (of course) 'an angry young woman.'" See also Sandbrook (2005, 194–195), who refers to the new plays in the late 1950s that "fell under the heading of "kitchen sink' drama and reflected the intellectually fashionable interest in working-class life typified by the books of Hoggart and Williams." Sandbrook comments that "the grittiness of kitchen-sink drama owed much more to the working-class origins of the various writers associated with it," presenting Shelagh Delaney as "the most striking example." His other examples are Bernard Kops and Arnold Wesker.

57 See Shulman 1958b and Goring 1958.

58 See Kenneth Tynan 1958a.

59 Lindsay Anderson 1981b, 78 (Anderson's review was originally published in *Encore*, November 1958).

60 On the lack of sentimentality, see also *Times* 1958b.

61 Littlewood 1994, 250.

62 See "London: Pioneer Theatres," in the Arts Council of Great Britain, "Thirteenth Annual Report 1957–1958." The annual reports of the Arts Council are held at the National Art Library, Victoria and Albert Museum, London.

63 Holdsworth 1999, 6–8.

64 See Graham Greene's letter in the *Times*, June 28, 1958.

65 Goorney 1981, 109–110; Littlewood 1994, 525; and Holdsworth 1999, 7–8.

66 Holdsworth 1999, 7.

67 Goorney 1981, 110.

68 Milne 1981, 86.

69 Milne 1981, 86.

70 On the reasons possibly motivating the Arts Council's decision, see Holdsworth 1999, 8.

71 See *Times* 1958c.

72 Goorney 1981, 110–111.

73 Hobson 1958b.

74 See Kenneth Tynan 1958b; for the quotes see Tynan 1961a, 218–219 and 220.

75 Lewenstein 1994, 89–90.

76 Littlewood 1994, 538.

77 Goorney 1981, 111.

78 See Goring 1959.

79 Lewenstein (1994, 192) describes his own involvement in the film version of *A Taste of Honey* as having "assisted the producer on the preparation but not credited." See also Marwick (1998, 137–198) on the censorship problems with the film.

80 See, for example, Darlington 1959a.

81 See Croft 1959.

82 Croft 1959.

83 See *Observer* 1959.

84 See the letter by J. L. Hodgkinson (1959), drama director, Arts Council of Great Britain, published in the *Observer* on March 22 (Hodgkinson 1959), and the *Observer*'s response published the same date.

85 Mallory 1959.

86 *Variety*'s awards were given to Frances Cuka as the most promising new West End actress and Murray Melvin as the second-most promising new actor (both for *A Taste of Honey*); Joan Littlewood as number two among producers (Jerome Robbins was first for *West Side Story*); and Shelagh Delaney as the third most promising new playwright in the West End, after Peter Schaffer for *Five Finger Exercise* and Willis Hall for *The Long and the Short and the Tall*.

87 See *Daily Telegraph* 1959.

88 See, for example, *Daily Telegraph* 1961b and *Evening Standard* 1961.

89 Lewenstein 1994, 90–91.

90 Robert Hollis 1959.

91 Goorney 1981, 116.

92 See Shulman 1959; the *Times* 1959a; Darlington 1959b; and Wilson 1959a.

93 Wall 1959 and Wilson 1959c.

94 In his memoirs, Lewenstein further comments on the Arts Council's reluctance to provide the Theatre Workshop with an adequate subsidy, lamenting the departure of Peter Brook for France and the disintegration of Joan Littlewood's company: "When will we learn to cherish genius rather than buildings?" (1994, 93–94).

95 Arts Council of Great Britain, "Fourteenth Annual Report 1958–1959," 30.

96 John Bury served twice on the Arts Council's drama panel, 1960–1968 and 1975–1985.

97 Arts Council subsidies to Theatre Workshop and to the English Stage Com-

pany are compared in Goorney (1981, 214). See also Shellard's comparison of subsidies awarded to these companies (1999, 63).

98 Littlewood 1994, 547.

99 See, for example, Darlington 1960; the *Times* 1960a; Pryce-Jones 1960; and Shulman 1960.

100 See for example, Levin 1961 and *Daily Herald* 1961.

101 See Holdsworth 1999, 8–9 and her account of the consequent forming of Theatre Workshop (Stratford) Ltd. (9).

102 Littlewood 1994, 558.

103 See *Reynolds News* 1960.

104 Goorney 1981, 121.

105 Hutchinson 1961.

106 Nathan 1961.

107 See *Daily Mail* 1961a.

108 See Shulman 1961.

109 See Hastings 1961.

110 See *Times* 1961.

111 Littlewood 1994, 580.

112 The subsidy awarded the Theatre Workshop by the Arts Council for 1960–1961 was 2000 pounds; in addition the group received annual support from ten borough councils, amounting to 1,450 pounds and the grant of 1,500 pounds from the London County Council (LCC). The offer for 1961–1962 repeated these amounts. See Arts Council, "Sixteenth Annual Report, 1960–1961." For these same years the Arts Council had awarded the English Stage Company 8,000 pounds.

113 See Goodwin and Milne 1960.

114 See Goodwin and Milne 1960, 9–10; emphasis mine.

115 Goodwin and Milne 1960, 19–20.

116 *Daily Telegraph* 1961a.

117 See, for example, Driberg 1961 and *Daily Mail* 1961b.

118 *Daily Mail* 1961c.

119 Goorney 1981, 123–124.

120 See Mark Cleveland's interview with Oscar Lewenstein, 1962.

121 Littlewood 1981, 133.

122 See Kenneth Tynan 1961b. In his book *Tynan Right and Left*, the essay appears under the title "A Breakthrough Breaks Down: 1961" (1967, 82–84).

123 Levin 1963a.

124 See Hastings 1963.

125 See especially Paget 1990b, and also Paget 1996.

126 Marowitz 1963, 50. New York-born Charles Marowitz established his reputation as a theatre director following his work with Peter Brook on the Royal Shakespeare Company 1962 production of *King Lear* and the 1964 production

of Peter Weiss's *Marat/Sade* and its accompanying Theatre of Cruelty Season. Marowitz is associated with modern adaptations of Shakespeare's plays, with the Absurd (via Artaud), with alternative theatre, and above all, with experimental theatre. He joined Clive Goodwin and Tom Milne as a coeditor of *Encore* in 1962 (July–August, Vol. 9, No. 4).

127 Marowitz 1963, 50.

128 See *Daily Mail* 1963 and *Daily Telegraph* 1963a.

129 See, for example, the highly favorable reviews of the film in the *Sunday Times* (Powell 1969) and in the *Daily Mail* (Wilson 1969) and the more reserved reviews in the *Observer Review* (Allsop 1969) and the *Morning Star* (Hibbin 1969).

130 On the impact of *Oh What a Lovely War*, see Paget 1990b, Paget 1990c, and Paget 1995b.

131 According to Chilton in an interview by Derek Paget, the front page of Theatre Workshop's program for the production originally read: "A musical entertainment based on the idea of Charles Chilton." This program is enclosed in the production file documented at the Study Room, Theatre Museum, London; however, "as soon as the show was perceived as a 'success,'" the posters and program publicizing the production "were changed to read 'Joan Littlewood's Musical Entertainment'" (Paget 1990b, 260). See also notes 11 and 12 in Paget 1990b, 260, on the lawsuits against Theatre Workshop.

132 Frances Cuka recalls that at Stratford East the production ended with Victor Spinetti's cynical speech, which "was quite frightening and you were left crying your heart out," but when the play was performed at the West End, after the speech "the entire cast came on singing 'Oh, What a Lovely War' followed by a reprise of the songs. All frightfully hearty and calculated to send the audience home happy." To the explanation "the Management didn't take kindly to a down ending," Cuka comments: "As far as I knew Joan and Gerry were the Management, having rented the theatre from Donald Albery" (quoted in Goorney 1981, 127). On the significant differences between the two productions (the original at Stratford East and the West end transfer), see also Paget 1990b, 244.

133 MacColl calls the aftereffect of the production—"the audience feeling nice and comfy"— a clear-cut failure. "Theatre," he claimed, "when it is dealing with social issues, should have heart; you should leave the theatre feeling furious. It was at this point we could say farewell to the dream of creating working-class theatre" (quoted in Goorney 1981, 127–128).

134 See Clive Barker's view cited in Goorney 1981, 181.

135 On the Arts Council's funding policy and the subsidies given to Theatre Workshop between 1965 and 1975, see Holdsworth 1999, 10, 12–14.

136 For the issue of censorship see, for example, Goorney 1981, 118–19 and Coren 1985, 51.

137 See Clive Barker's view of the changes taking place in the company's work in Goorney 1981, 180–181.

138 Littlewood was most notably involved in the production of *Mrs. Wilson's Diary*, by John Wells and Richard Ingrams, on September 21, 1967, which transferred to the Criterion Theatre and ran about eight months, and in the production of *The Marie Lloyd Story*, by Daniel Farson and Harry Moore, music by Norman Key, on November 28, 1967. On Littlewood's final productions between 1964 and 1973, see Holdsworth 2006, 38–42.

139 On Littlewood's ideas and plans for Fun Palace, see Holdsworth 2006, 32–36.

140 Holdsworth 1999, 10. For a detailed account of the Fun Palace project and the financial problems it entailed, see also Holdsworth 1999, 10–12.

141 Markowitz was reviewing Lionel Bart's musical *Twang!*, a disastrous affair, one of the final projects with which Littlewood had been involved.

142 See Marowitz 1965c.

143 Coren 1985, 58.

144 Holdsworth 1999, 15.

145 The issue of Littlewood's "free" attitude toward the dramatic text is much debated in accounts of her work. Whereas some, such as Taylor, see her rewriting of texts as a problem (if not a defect) in Littlewood's theatrical policy, others, such as Goodwin and Milne (1960, 14–15), present revision as an aspect of her directorial innovation.

146 See chapter 1 for the impact of Taylor's work of the sixties on John Osborne's career, as well as on the developmental course of the English Stage Company. See John Russell Taylor 1969, 119, 120.

147 On the subject of classics, compare John Russell Taylor 1969, 119, with Goodwin and Milne 1960, 9–10.

148 John Russell Taylor 1969, 123.

149 John Russell Taylor 1969, 120; and see Clive Barker's view (cited in Goorney 1981, 138), which sheds light on suspicious attitudes toward Littlewood's "seemingly unstructured" way of working.

150 Goorney 1981, 124.

151 *Daily Mail* 1961a.

152 John Russell Taylor 1969, 121.

153 On the conference, which Tynan organized with John Calder, the publisher, see Shellard 2003, 281–282.

154 See Tynan 1967, 316, 317.

155 See Rebellato 1999, 63 and also 229–230, note 31.

156 In my review of the assessments of the two companies and their key productions that appear in accounts published in the decades following the 1960s, I do not imply that these companies, or more particularly the two productions—

the ESC production of Osborne's play and Theatre Workshop's production of *Oh What a Lovely War*—were the only events competing for a reputation as the crucial turning point in modern British theatre (if indeed a particular event can be defined as a turning point). The review of these assessments (or reassessments) primarily serves to illustrate further the construction process of the historical explanations and narratives over the last five decades.

157 Elsom 1976, 74.
158 Elsom 1976, 83.
159 Elsom 1976, 100.
160 Elsom 1976, 100–103.
161 Elsom 1976, 81.
162 See Hayman 1979, 131–132, 134–136.
163 See Marowitz 1963; for the quote, see Hayman 1979, 136, 137.
164 Hayman 1979, 135.
165 Hayman 1979, 9–10.
166 Hayman 1979, 35–38.
167 See Courtney 1982, preface.
168 Courtney 1982, 281; the reference is to Tynan 1958b.
169 Courtney 1982, 254, 255.
170 Courtney 1982, 257.
171 Brown 1982, 4.
172 Brown 1982, 25.
173 Brown 1982, 25, 26.
174 Brown 1984b, 3.
175 Goorney 1981, xi. See also Goorney 1986 on the contribution of the prewar work of Theatre Workshop to the evolution of political and popular theatre in Britain.
176 See Farson 1981; *Guardian Women* 1984.
177 Coren 1985, 60.
178 Sinfield 1989, 261, 262.
179 See, for example, Wells 1994; Lewis 1994; and *Observer* 1994.
180 For the press coverage, see *Observer* 1994; Coveney 1994b; and Peter 1994.
181 The documentary appeared on *Omnibus*, BBC-1, produced by John Hough, April 19, 1994.
182 See Mackenzie 1995.
183 See the epigraph to this segment (*Times* 1995).
184 See, for example, Mackenzie 1995.
185 Paul Taylor 1998.
186 Kingstone 1998.
187 Thorpe 2002. See also Eyre 2002.
188 Paget 1990b, 244; emphasis in original.

189 John Russell Taylor 1962, 1. Whether or not one agrees with Paget's statement (which also implies that there was one particular starting point for the revolution in postwar English theatre), is irrelevant here. What is significant is that Paget's assertion exemplifies the pronounced shift in scholarly evaluations of the two events (and companies).

190 Paget 1990b, 244, 245.

191 Paget 1990c.

192 Paget 1990c, 118.

193 Paget 1990c, 119, 120. In the concluding remark of this essay, Paget asserts, "The Great War has become something of a staple for both English studies and History, a fact which has much to do with *Oh What a Lovely War*'s popularising of the 'new' history in the sixties" (1990c: 127).

194 Paget 1995a, 212.

195 Innes 1992, 74.

196 Lacey 1995, 3.

197 Lacey 1995, 17–23, 44–48.

198 Lacey 1995, 53.

199 Lacey 1995, 43.

200 Lacey 1995, 48, 49.

201 Lacey 1995, 6, 51, 60.

202 The title alludes to *1066 and All That*, a well-known parody of the history of England as taught to children during their school years.

203 Rebellato 1999, 2, 9.

204 Rebellato 1999, 38.

205 Rebellato 1999, 66.

206 Rebellato 1999, 67.

207 Rebellato 1999, 63.

208 Rebellato 1999, 67.

209 Rebellato 1999, 67–68.

210 Rebellato 1999, 68.

211 Shellard 1999, 64.

212 Shellard 1999, 65.

213 Shellard 1999, 96.

214 See Shellard 1999, 63 and also Goorney 1981, 214–215.

215 Reading's letter to Shellard, quoted in Shellard 1999, 70.

216 Shellard 2000b, 30.

217 See Holdsworth 1999, 6–8.

218 Holdsworth 1999, 3.

219 This term, as used by Kershaw, became current only much later.

220 Kershaw 2004, 310.

221 Kershaw 2004, 322.

222 Kershaw 2004, 325.

223 Shellard 1999, 190.

224 Kershaw 2004, 300. Kershaw is also the author of *The Politics of Performance* (1992) and of *The Radical in Performance* (1999).

225 Bull 2004, 336; emphasis in original.

226 Bull 2004, 336.

227 Paget 2004, 397.

228 Paget 2004, 397–398.

229 Paget 2004, 399.

230 Paget 2004, 409.

231 Paget 2004, 411.

232 Barnes 1986, 141, emphasis in original. Barnes does not supply an entry for the Theatre Workshop, but rather refers to the entry for Joan Littlewood.

233 Kenneth Tynan 1967, 316.

234 Kenneth Tynan 1967, 317.

3. JOHN ARDEN

1 Both citations are from an unpublished interview I conducted with John Arden and Margaretta D'Arcy on September 12, 2001, at their house in County Galway, Corrandulla, Ireland, hereafter cited as either Arden interview or D'Arcy interview.

2 Margaretta D'Arcy, Irish born, acted in several of Arden's early plays. Many of their collaborative plays and projects relied on D'Arcy's experience as an actress. Arden's contribution as a writer ranges from stage and radio plays to novels, short stories, and essays. This account centers on the London phase of Arden's career.

3 Regarding the subhead, Albert Hunt begins his study on John Arden: "From the beginning of his career as a playwright, John Arden has been at the centre of controversy" (1974, 17).

4 Arden interview.

5 "Margaretta encouraged me to stop working at the office—well, I wasn't really enjoying it very much. I wasn't terribly good at the work" (Arden interview).

6 Wardle 1978a, 199.

7 See Arden's interview with Tom Milne and Clive Goodwin (Arden 1961b), followed by replies to further questions put by Simon Trussler in 1966 (Marowitz and Trussler 1968, 36–57, 44, and Arden 1968).

8 Hunt 1974, 53.

9 Arden 1968, 40, 44.

10 Arden 1967, 193.

11 *Times* 1957.

12 *Daily Telegraph* 1957.

13 Kenneth Tynan 1957c.

14 Wilson 1957.

15 *Times* 1958d.

16 *Illustrated London News* 1958.

17 *Sunday Times* 1958.

18 Wilson 1958b.

19 Hobson 1959.

20 *Times* 1959b.

21 Barker 1959.

22 Darlington 1959c.

23 Hope-Wallace 1959.

24 Wilson 1959b.

25 Brahms 1959, 106–107.

26 Muller 1960b.

27 Frank Lewis 1960.

28 Hunt 1974, 22.

29 Gray 1982, 3–4.

30 Gray 1982, 4, 11.

31 On the major role of theatre reviewers in the admission of a new playwright into the theatrical canon, see Zarhy-Levo 2001a.

32 Gray 1982, 1.

33 Philip Roberts 1999, 73.

34 Roberts 1999, 77.

35 Roberts 1999, 76.

36 Devine is cited in Roberts 1999, 56–57.

37 Peter Roberts 1961.

38 Pryce-Jones 1959.

39 Philip Roberts 1999, 73.

40 Hunt 1974, 17.

41 The leaflet is included in the file of the Royal Court production of *Serjeant Musgrave's Dance* (1959), in the archives of the Theatre Museum, London.

42 Shorter 1959.

43 Hobson 1965b. See Lewis 1965 for another favorable notice of *Serjeant Musgrave's Dance*.

44 The program note is included in the file of the National Theatre production of *Serjeant Musgrave's Dance* (1981), in the archives of the Theatre Museum, London.

45 Stewart 1981.

46 Trewin 1981.

47 Barber 1981. Both Barber and Trewin wrote their notices based on previews of the production.

48 Billington 1984.

49 Wardle 1984.

50 Kitchin 1962, 119.

51 See, for example, the student edition published by Methuen (edited by Glenda Leeming) in 1982.

52 Hayman 1980.

53 Mallory 1960. Leslie Mallory's long article on Joan Littlewood (1959) is discussed in chapter 2.

54 Arden's earlier essays were published in *Encore*; his later essays on the theatre and those written in collaboration with Margaretta D'Arcy were published in Arden 1977.

55 Hunt 1974, 17.

56 Arden 1960b.

57 Arden 1968, 28, 30, 26, 27, 34.

58 The 1965 interview is an edited version of one published in *Peace News*, 1963.

59 Arden 1965, 13, 14, 15, 16, 18.

60 Hunt 1960, 26–27.

61 Hunt 1960, 28.

62 Wardle 1963.

63 Marowitz 1965a, 52.

64 Marowitz 1965a, 54.

65 *Serjeant Musgrave's Dance* was published by Methuen in 1960. *Live Like Pigs* (1961), *The Happy Heaven* (1962), and *The Waters of Babylon* (1964) were published by Penguin Books.

66 *Ironhand* was first produced at the Bristol Old Vic, November 12, 1963, directed by Val May.

67 Beauman 1982, 271–273.

68 On the aims of the experimental season, see the interview Simon Trussler conducted with Peter Brook, "Private Experiment in Public" (Trussler 1964).

69 Beauman 1982, 273.

70 Milne 1965c, 12.

71 Hunt 1974, 115. See "'The Theatre of Cruelty' as a salute to Antonin Artaud" in Brook 1999, 134–141; and see Brook 1988, 40–41, 56–60.

72 Hope-Wallace 1965.

73 Shulman 1965.

74 Darlington 1965a; see also Levin 1965b.

75 Nightingale 1965.

76 Nightingale 1965.

77 See Arden's early 1966 letter to Lord Willis about the curious amendments imposed by the censor, illustrated in the case of *Armstrong's Last Goodnight* (quoted in Findlater 1968, 210–212).

78 William Gaskill joined the ESC in 1957, after working with Joan Littlewood in the Theatre Workshop. After two seasons (1961–1962) with the RSC at

Stratford-upon-Avon, Gaskill became associate director of the National Theatre at the Old Vic (1963–1965), returning to the Royal Court as artistic director of the ESC (1965–1972). John Dexter, who began his career as a television and radio actor, started directing at the Royal Court in 1957. He is especially known for his collaboration with Arnold Wesker, whose trilogy he had directed. Dexter served as associate director of the National Theatre at the Old Vic from 1963 to 1966 and 1971 to 1975.

79 Milne 1965c, emphasis in original.

80 The program note is kept in the study room at the Theatre Museum, London.

81 Darlington 1965b.

82 *Daily Telegraph* 1965.

83 John Russell Taylor 1974, 3.

84 John Russell Taylor 1974, 3.

85 See *Encore*, September-October 1965 (editors: Tom Milne, Charles Marowitz, Michael Kustow, and Simon Trussler). This issue includes an introduction by Simon Trussler, an essay by Albert Hunt, a revised edition of Arden's talk with Hunt on *The Workhouse Donkey*, an interview with William Gaskill about his production of *Armstrong's Last Goodnight*, an article written by Albert Hunt and Geoffrey Reeves on their experiences in directing Arden's plays, and Tom Milne's article on *Armstrong's Last Goodnight*.

86 See Marowitz 1965b.

87 Hunt 1974, 128. See his discussion of the play on 128–143; particularly 138–141.

88 Kustow joined Goodwin, Milne, and Marowitz as editor of *Encore* in 1964, beginning with the March-April issue.

89 See Kustow 1965, and in particular his emphasis on history and politics.

90 On the playwrights' quarrel with the management, see their preface to the printed text (Arden and D'Arcy 1969).

91 See Hunt 1974, 139.

92 See Trussler 1969b, 181.

93 Trussler 1969b, 186.

94 See Hunt's response to Trussler's argument (1974, 140).

95 Trussler's assessment: "Arden is a loner not only instinctively but artistically. His early plays were the products of an individual dramatic consciousness of strong intellectual sinews, sure technical insight, and increasing emotional maturity. That he has never achieved the instant success of Osborne or Pinter emphasizes that he is also a much more difficult dramatist to come to terms with—and if this implies that his audience will always be an elite, this does not condemn him to writing for a coterie but to the discovery of a new particularized or localized elite for each successive play" (Trussler 1969b, 190).

96 Hunt 1974, 141.

97 Hunt (1974, 157) notes that although he wrote the greater part of his book prior to the RSC production, "the story of the production illustrates the thesis of the book—that the revolutionary content of Arden's play makes stylistic demands that are outside of the normal range of the established British theatre."

98 J. W. Lambert wrote the introduction to the first published edition of *Live Like Pigs* in 1961, whereas Arden wrote most of the introductory notes to his later published plays.

99 John Russell Taylor 1967, 10.

100 John Russell Taylor 1962, 72; John Taylor 1963, 72; John Taylor 1969, 84.

101 John Russell Taylor 1963, 91.

102 John Russell Taylor 1969, 104.

103 John Russell Taylor 1969, 105.

104 John Russell Taylor 1969, 375.

105 See Trussler 1965, 4–5.

106 See Arden 1994, 375.

107 Arden 1994, 375.

108 Gray 1982, 67. Ronald Hayman's interview with John Arden, "The Conversation of John Arden," aired on BBC Radio 3 in 1980. See Hayman 1980.

109 Gray 1982, 67.

110 Quoted in Page 1985, 62.

111 Gaston 1991, 165.

112 Gray 1982, 26.

113 Gray 1982, 85–86.

114 See Michael Anderson 1976.

115 Michael Anderson 1976, 51–52, 60.

116 Arden interview.

117 D'Arcy interview.

118 On *The Ballygombeen Bequest*, see Hunt 1974, 152–156 and Gray 1982, 89–91; also Gavin Richards's account on the production of this play in Wroe 2004. John McGrath formed the 7:84 Theatre Company in 1971, aiming to set a "truly revolutionary theatre" in "opposition to bourgeois theatre" (Itzin 1980, 120). The name of the company alluded to the fact that 7 percent of the worldwide population owned 84 percent of the wealth.

119 Arden interview and D'Arcy interview.

120 *Time Out* 1972.

121 D'Arcy interview.

122 Gardner 1972.

123 Michael Anderson 1976, 52.

124 *Guardian* 1978.

125 See the printed edition of *Pearl*, published by Methuen in 1979.

126 Arden 1979. See also Guralnick's instructive study of *Pearl* (1997, 152–189),

especially the view she develops that this play is "about" *The Bagman*, "a radio-play-about-theatre about a radio-play-about-theatre" (1997, 152).

127 *Times*, June 21, 1978.

128 Billington 1978a.

129 In the preview Billington recounts that a *Yorkshire Post* journalist who had heard Arden's first radio play told the playwright during an interview that Alfred Bradley would love to have another. The result was *Pearl*.

130 See also Michael Billington's (1994a) favorable review of the revival of Arden's *Armstrong's Last Goodnight* at the Royal Lyceum Theatre, Edinburgh.

131 Reynolds 1978.

132 See also the highly favorable review by Anthony Curtis (1978).

133 Arden 1977, 177.

134 See Itzin 1980, 24–27.

135 Itzin 1980, 28, emphasis in original.

136 Itzin 1980, 33.

137 See Kershaw 1992, 110.

138 D'Arcy interview.

139 In his conclusion to his study of Arden's plays (1969), Ronald Hayman laments the fact that the playwright had not worked regularly with one company, which could have been of benefit to him.

140 In a telephone interview Harriet Devine, George Devine's daughter conducted with Arden on April 27, 2005, the playwright recounted the circumstances involved in the production of several of his plays, admitting, regarding directors: "That was one of the problems. I did very well with different people but I never stuck with one of them" (Arden 2006, 27).

141 See, for example, *New Theatre Quarterly* issues between March 1975 and 1976 and Malik 1986, including the introductory editorial note to Malik's article.

142 Wike 1995.

143 Susan Bennett 1995, 74.

4. HAROLD PINTER

1 Gussow 1994, 25.

2 "A Birthday Card from His Friends" (Kellaway 2000).

3 This event was part of the *Arena* program, "Harold Pinter's Life, Work, and Political Passions," broadcast on BBC Two, October 26, 2002.

4 Pinter 1977 [1961], 11.

5 Pinter 1976 [1962], 11.

6 Quigley (1975, 47–48), for example, alludes to the milk bottle event, recounted by Pinter in his famous interview with Lawrence Bensky (1966, 31). The playwright's account of the biographical event serves Quigley's explanation of the unique nature and effect of the dialogue in Pinter's plays.

7 See Zarhy-Levo 2001a.

8   See Zarhy-Levo 1998b.

9   See Zarhy-Levo, 2001c.

10 See, for example, Darlington 1958: "It turned out to be one of those plays in which an author wallows in symbols and revels in obscurity," and *Times* 1958a: "Mr. Harold Pinter's effects are neither comic nor terrifying: they are never more than puzzling and after a little while we tend to give up the puzzle in despair."

11 *The Birthday Party* was performed successfully on the tour that preceded the first London production of the play. The reviews of the London production did not refer to this earlier successful run. The possible explanations for the negative reactions of the London critics, as opposed to the favorable critical responses outside of London, are discussed in Stevenson 1984, 55.

12 See Hobson 1958a.

13 For a detailed discussion of the attitude of *Encore*'s critics to Pinter's plays, see Stokes 2001.

14 These two sketches, in the review *One to Another*, were performed at the Lyric Theatre, Hammersmith on July 15, 1959.

15 These three sketches, in the review *Pieces of Eight*, were performed at the Apollo Theatre on September 23, 1959.

16 *The Room* and *The Dumb Waiter*, directed by Pinter, were performed at Hampstead Theatre Club on January 21, 1960 and transferred to the Royal Court on March 8, 1960.

17 The "baffling mixture" (see Wilson 1958a) was newly perceived as a "unique blend" and as "a special brand," highly recommended (*Observer* 1960). In contrast to reviews of the first London production of a Pinter play (see *Times* 1958a, note 10), only two years later Pinter was said to have an "extraordinary gift for comic dialogue, and an ability to keep an audience at once puzzled and intent" (*Daily Telegraph* 1960).

18 *The Caretaker* was performed at the Arts Theatre Club on April 27, 1960, and transferred to the Duchess on May 30, 1960, directed by Donald McWhinnie.

19 See Quigley's (1975, 11) comment on this transformation in the critics' attitudes.

20 Muller 1960a; emphases mine.

21 Muller 1960a. See also Gibbs 1960: "Mr. Pinter is to be admired for having mastered so thoroughly the precarious art of mystifying an audience and entrancing them at the same time."

22 The reviewers compared Pinter's first play to Ibsen's plays, on the one hand, and to those of Osborne, Beckett, and Ionesco, on the other. See, for example, Shulman 1958a; *Times* 1958a; and Trewin 1958.

23 See, for example, Rossely 1960 and also Kenneth Tynan 1960, who proclaimed: "The piece is full of those familiar overtones that seem to be inseparable from much of avant-garde drama."

24 See Schroll, who perceives the first production of *The Caretaker* in April
1960 as the one that "probably marked the opening phase of the Pinter fashion" (1971, 18).

25 See, for example, Muller 1960a: "This is a play and a production which no
one who is concerned with the advance of the British drama can afford to
miss. This is theatre."

26 *Plays and Players* 1960.

27 John Russell Taylor 1963, 217–218.

28 Hayman 1973, 138.

29 Eyre and Wright 2000, 227–228.

30 Eyre and Wright 2000, 227–228.

31 On the BBC productions of Beckett's plays, including *All That Fall, Embers,
Words and Music,* and *Cascando,* see Worth 1981.

32 The interview with John Sherwood was broadcast on the BBC European
service in the series *The Rising Generation* on March 3, 1960, and the interview with Kenneth Tynan in the series *People Today* was broadcast on BBC
on October 28, 1960.

33 An example is Pinter's reported reply, published November 28, 1967 in the
Daily Mail, to the woman who asked him to explain *The Birthday Party.*
This reply has been frequently cited by critics (Esslin 1973, 37–38; Dukore
1982, 11–12). The woman's letter and Pinter's reply are also quoted in the lead
paragraph of a later Pinter interview (Moss 1999).

34 The Bensky interview of Pinter was first published in the *Paris Review,* Fall
1966, reprinted in *The Paris Review Interviews: Writers at Work,* third series,
by Viking Press in 1967, and after several more reprints was published under
the title *Harold Pinter* by Penguin (1977) George Plimpton, ed., 347–368.

35 Esslin 1970, 33–34.

36 The letter appears in Pinter 1998c. "Writing for the Theatre" appears as the
introduction to *Harold Pinter: Plays: One* (1976).

37 See Esslin 1970, 33–34. See also Ganz, who suggests that Pinter placed the
note in the program intending to "defend the plays' obscurity" (1972b, 3).

38 Pinter's unique mode of explanation is manifested in his letter to Peter
Wood, director of the first production of *The Birthday Party* (see Pinter
1998b [1958]).

39 Note, for example, the following statements by Pinter: "The more acute the
experience the less articulate its expression" (1976, 11); "Language, under
these conditions, is a highly ambiguous business. So often, below the word
spoken, is the thing known and unspoken" (1976, 13); "One way of looking at speech is to say that it is a constant strategem to cover nakedness"
(1976, 15).

40 See *Sunday Times* 1962.

41 On *The Collection,* which began the collaboration between Peter Hall and

Harold Pinter, see Peter Hall interviewed by Catherine Itzin and Simon Trussler in *Theatre Quarterly* in 1974 (reprinted in Smith 2005, 33–36).

42 *Times* 1963.

43 *Sunday Times* 1962.

44 Levin 1963b.

45 Darlington 1963.

46 On July 1, 1963, the film version of *The Caretaker* won one of the Silver Bears at the Berlin film festival. On September 30, 1963, the Joan Kemp-Welch production of *The Lover* won the Prix Italia for television drama at Naples. On November 23, 1963, the script and leading performances in *The Lover* received awards from the Guild of British Television Producers and Directors. On March 2, 1964, Pinter won the British Screenwriters' Guild Award for his screenplay of *The Servant*, which was directed by Joseph Losey, who thereafter collaborated with Pinter on two other films.

47 See, for example, *Times* 1964, and Darlington 1964.

48 Levin 1964.

49 The Pinteresque label exemplifies the strategy of name-giving; see a discussion of this strategy in Zarhy-Levo 2001a, 100–101.

50 Schroll 1971, 7, 77.

51 Barry Norman (1965) recounted that the U.S. impresario Roger Stevens, who read Pinter's first play *The Birthday Party* and liked it immensely, gave the playwright (who was "quite broke" at the time) financial support to carry on writing in return for obtaining U.S. rights to his next three plays "at obviously advantageous terms." Pinter, according to the journalist, did not complain, perceiving Stevens's act as "a remarkable gesture."

52 See, for example, Shorter 1965 and Levin 1965a. Harold Hobson's review (1965a) dealt with the ambiguity in the play, by turning it around to prove "that Mr. Pinter tricks his audience into believing that he is writing a play about the homecoming of a son." Hobson's claim that Pinter disguises his intentions echoes his review of *The Birthday Party* (1958a). In both reviews Hobson praised Pinter's dramatic talent, presenting the negative reactions to the plays as reflecting the critics' shortcomings, rather than Pinter's.

53 See, for example, *Times* 1965: "Several *familiar* Pinter motives are involved in this," or "at this stage in the play Pinter shows all *his old cunning* in twisting clichés and formal phrases into unexpected freshness" (emphases mine). See also Trewin 1965.

54 The majority of reviews of *The Homecoming* expressed reservations, also acknowledging and stating a belief in Pinter's powers as a dramatist.

55 See especially Hope-Wallace 1963, Shulman 1963, and *Daily Telegraph* 1963b.

56 In this context, a Pinter remark from October 1989 is especially amusing: "I made a terrible mistake when I was young, I think, from which I've never recovered. I wrote the word 'pause' into my first play" (Gussow 1994, 82).

57 This claim is corroborated by the reviews of Joe Orton's first produced play in London, *Entertaining Mr. Sloane,* in 1964, that pointed out Pinteresque aspects in Orton's drama: "Do you think you've inspired any imitation? Have you ever seen anything in a film or theatre which struck you as, well, Pinteresque?" Pinter replied: "That word! These damn words and that word 'Pinteresque' particularly—I don't know what they're bloody well talking about! I think it's a great burden for me to carry, and for other writers to carry" (Bensky 1977, 365–366).

58 The Censor had asked Pinter to amend a play earlier in his career. Findlater (1968, 197) reports that Pinter was not allowed to use the word "arse" in his 1960 play *The Caretaker,* "although it had been licensed in *My Fair Lady* the year before."

59 Kathleen Tynan 1968.

60 Hobson 1969. On Peggy Ashcroft in *Landscape* see also Cave (1989, 6–8).

61 *Evening Standard* 1969.

62 On Pinter's role in the success of Joyce's *Exiles* see Zarhy-Levo 1998b.

63 Hobson 1971. Vivien Merchant was married to Pinter from 1956 to 1980.

64 Billington 1975b.

65 Peter Hall recounts in his diaries: "The press for *No Man's Land* is good but careful. And maddeningly patronising: 'Surely not one of his best plays'; 'the Pinter Puzzle'; 'the Pinter enigma.' None of them actually gets to grips with what the play means" (Hall 1983, 160).

66 Billington 1975a.

67 Shulman 1975.

68 Wardle 1975.

69 Barber 1975.

70 Trewin 1975.

71 De Jongh 1975.

72 On Esslin's promotion of Pinter in the three editions of *Theatre of the Absurd* (1961, 1968, 1980), see Zarhy-Levo 1993, 532–534.

73 Esslin 1970. Esslin also served as head of BBC drama (radio), beginning in 1963.

74 Among the critical studies dealing with Pinter's drama published by the 1970s are: Lois Gordon 1969; James Hollis 1970; Burkman 1971; Schroll 1971; Lahr 1971; Ganz 1972a; Worth 1972; Trussler 1973b; Hinchcliffe 1975; Michael Anderson 1976; Dukore 1976; and Gale 1977.

75 Verdaasdonk discusses the reviewers' reactions to a new publication by an established author, claiming that their heavy reliance on "drawing analogies in judging recent publications suggests that the perception of [literary] books is strongly context bound. Linking a particular title to other items of the same category affects the way it is perceived and valued" (1994, 386).

76 *Betrayal* was first produced in Germany and directed by Peter Wood, who directed the first production of Pinter's *Birthday Party*.

77 Page 1993, 54; emphases mine.

78 Billington 1978b; emphases mine.

79 Billington 1991.

80 Wardle 1978b.

81 See *Sunday Times* 1978. This critic, like several others (such as J. C. Trewin in *Punch* and Paul Johnson in the *Evening Standard*), linked Pinter's *Betrayal* with Stoppard's new play *Night and Day*, first performed a week earlier at Phoenix. Neither play apparently complied with the playwrights' devised constructs.

82 Morley 1978.

83 Cushman 1978. Robert is the deceived husband in the play. Note also J. C. Trewin's review, written a few months later, which tries to calm the anxiety evoked by the playwright's "deviant" play, insisting that it bears the Pinter signature. Trewin claimed "We can be creatures of habit: if a writer has succeeded in one style we want him to go on repeating himself. [. . .] Pinter has been labeled as the dramatist of ambiguity and we ought not to come from the theatre knowing, without argument, what he means. [. . .] Really there is no cause to be troubled: Pinter in the past has been perfectly lucid. [. . .] All will agree that the new Pinter . . . could hardly be by anyone else (1979)." Peter Hall recounts in his diaries Pinter's reaction to the unfavorable reviews of *Betrayal:* "Harold said he had risen above the daily critics, but when *all* the weekend critics had had a go too he began to wonder. Then came a pile of mail from people he respects, and from members of the public, all praising the play. So he concluded that the object was the same for them as for the critics; it depends from which point of view you were looking at it" (1983, 392, emphasis in original).

84 *A Kind of Alaska* was published with *Victoria Station* and *Family Voices* in *Other Places* (Pinter 1983).

85 Barber 1982.

86 Cushman 1982.

87 See Nightingale 1982.

88 Sacks 1973, 74–87.

89 See Zarhy-Levo 2001a, 95–101.

90 Wardle 1982; emphases mine.

91 Nightingale 1982; emphases mine.

92 Morley 1982; emphases mine.

93 See *Country Life* 1982; Shulman 1982; Cushman 1982; Barber 1982; Coveney 1982.

94 Pierre Bourdieu contends that academies, "claiming a monopoly over the

consecration of contemporary producers, are obliged to combine tradition and tempered innovation" (1985a, 2).

95 Burkman and Kundert-Gibbs 1993.

96 See also Katherine Burkman's earlier study (1986, 153) in which she perceives Deborah's awakening state in the context of modern existence, that is, she views Deborah's disorientation as akin to that of the characters in Beckett's *Waiting for Godot*.

97 For a further discussion of these three studies, as well as of Burkman's 1986 study, see Zarhy-Levo 2001b, 89–92.

98 Almansi and Henderson 1983, 101; emphases mine.

99 *Precisely* was performed at the Apollo Victoria Theatre, in *The Big One* (anti-nuclear performance).

100 *One for the Road* was performed at the Lyric Hammersmith Studio.

101 Chaillet 1984; emphases mine.

102 Carne 1984; emphases mine.

103 Coveney 1984; emphases mine.

104 Shorter 1984; emphases mine.

105 Hudson 1984.

106 This triple-bill production, entitled *Other Places,* included the plays *Victoria Station* and *One for the Road*, directed by Kenneth Ives, March 7, 1985.

107 Billington 1985; emphases mine.

108 Wardle 1985; emphases mine.

109 Muller 1960a.

110 See Peter 1985.

111 The first edition of *One for the Road* was published by Methuen in 1984.

112 Pinter 1985, 11.

113 Pinter 1985, 12.

114 See the interview Anna Ford conducted with Pinter on *Mountain Language* and *One for the Road*, "Radical Departures," which aired on *Omnibus* on BBC TV (Ford 1988). A reprint of the transcript of Pinter's interview was published in Smith 2005, 79–89.

115 See Billington 1988.

116 See especially Shulman 1988; Conway 1988; Tinker 1988; and Charles Osborne 1988.

117 Toynbee 1990.

118 Peter 1990.

119 See Pinter 1981, 153.

120 See Koenig 1990, where she also writes: "Since 1978, when *Betrayal* opened to notices as dismissive as the pans of *The Birthday Party* 20 years before, Pinter has not written a full-length play. His energies have gone into directing. . . , writing short dramatic pieces, and, increasingly, engaging in political protest."

121 *New World Order* was performed at the Royal Court Theatre Upstairs.

122 *Party Time* was performed at the Almeida Theatre in a double bill with *Mountain Language.*

123 See Pinter on *Party Time* in his interview with Mireia Aragay and Ramon Simo at the Universitat de Barcelona, December 6, 1966 (Smith 2005, 91–92). The interview is titled "Writing, Politics, and *Ashes to Ashes.*"

124 McAfee 1991; emphases mine.

125 See Spencer 1991a; emphases mine.

126 Nightingale 1991a; emphases mine.

127 The acquired standing of the Almeida Theatre is mostly credited to Jonathan Kent and Ian Mcdiarmid, who became joint artistic directors in 1990.

128 Spencer 1991b.

129 Nightingale 1991b; emphases mine.

130 Shulman 1991; emphases mine.

131 See, for example, Edwards 1991 and Coveney 1991.

132 Eagleton 1991.

133 Franks 1991.

134 In his 1988 interview with Anna Ford on *Omnibus*, Pinter explicitly acknowledged that he perceives *The Birthday Party, The Dumb Waiter,* and *The Hothouse* to be political plays (Smith 2005, 85).

135 See Hoyle 1993; emphases mine.

136 Spencer 1993; emphases mine.

137 Nightingale 1993.

138 Kingstone 1993.

139 See, for example, de Jongh 1993.

140 Furmanovsky 1993, 18.

141 Esslin 1993, 27. On Pinter's shift to overtly political drama, see also the extensive discussion in Merritt 1990, 171–186.

142 Pinter 1996, 12.

143 See Casey 1996.

144 Spencer 1996; emphases mine.

145 Tinker 1996; emphases mine.

146 For a detailed discussion of this play, see Zarhy-Levo 1998a.

147 See Pinter's view on his political inclination at the beginning of his playwriting career in his October 1989 conversation with Mel Gussow (Gussow 1994, 82).

148 Billington 1996, 354.

149 Billington 1996, 354.

150 This citation from the review written by Fintan O'Toole in the *Observer*, appears in Billington 1996, 355. See also other citations of reviews of this festival in Billington (354–355).

151 Billington's biography, which concludes with *Ashes to Ashes*, draws on many

conversations with the playwright (on Pinter's cooperative attitude, see Billington 1996, ix). The biography covers the wide range of Pinter's dramatic activities and promotes the playwright's political engagement.

152 See especially Macaulay 1998: "By this point in the book, Pinter has reconciled his various voices, demonstrated the considerable journey he has taken as a writer over 50 years, and taken the reader on that journey, too. It is a journey of heart, mind and spirit." See also Scannell 1999 and the interview John Walsh conducted with Pinter in 1999. Walsh describes Pinter's plays as "famously filled with threat and menace and lurking violence that lies in families, marriages and political systems" (Walsh 1999).

153 Pinter's portrait, an oil on canvas, was painted by Justin Mortimer. See *Independent on Sunday* 1999.

154 See Moss 1999; emphases mine.

155 On the effect achieved by presenting *Celebration* with *The Room*, as well as on the reviewers' responses to this production, see Raby 2001a, especially 57–61.

156 Morley 2000.

157 Gross 2000; emphases mine.

158 Clapp 2000.

159 Billington 2000a (emphases mine); see also Nightingale 2000 and Hagerty 2000.

160 In addition to *The Cambridge Companion* (Raby 2001b), which covers various facets of this playwright's work and career, Routledge in the same year published a study that presents an overview of the playwright's work (Lois Gordon 2001).

161 Kellaway 2000.

162 Billington 2000b; emphases mine.

163 Appleyard 2000.

164 Clapp 2001; see also Allen 2001.

165 In 1995, Pinter received the David Cohen British Literature Prize for lifetime achievement in literature and in 1996 the Laurence Olivier award for lifetime achievement in theatre. In 1996, he turned down a knighthood offered by John Major, then Britain's Prime Minister.

166 Nightingale 2002a; see also Nightingale 2002b.

167 See Pinter 2002 (first page of sketch).

168 The evening included accounts by writers formerly imprisoned in Iran, Turkey, and South America and by family members of writers who did not survive, all of whom expressed their gratitude to Pinter for his active and influential involvement in the campaign to free them.

169 Quoted in Peter 1990.

170 Nobel Prize extracts cited in *Daily Telegraph* 2005.

171 On October 10, 2005, Pinter's seventy-fifth birthday, his new work *Voices*, a twenty-nine minute musical-dramatic collaboration with the composer James Clarke, was broadcast on BBC Radio Three. In an interview for the *Independent* conducted with the playwright and composer about the new radio play, Alice Jones reported that "for *Voices*, Pinter has reworked five of his later plays—*One for the Road, Mountain Language, The New World Order, Party Time* and *Ashes to Ashes*—into a fragmented narrative on cruelty, torture and oppression, which is interrupted, accompanied and complemented by Clarke's mercurial score, performed by the BBC Symphony Orchestra, the soprano Eileen Aargaard and an Azeri singer, Fatma Mehrralieva, among others. Nine actors, including Douglas Hodge, Anastasia Hille, Roger Lloyd Pack and Pinter himself have reprised the roles they performed previously at various London theatres" (Jones 2005).

172 Spencer 2005.

173 See Hare 2005.

174 *Guardian* 2005b.

175 *Guardian* 2005a; Pinter was talking to Michael Billington.

176 The broadcast, which included Pinter's speech and then a screening of *The Homecoming*, was billed as "Harold Pinter's Speech Live from Stockholm," although it was prerecorded in London several days before the broadcast. The program was initiated and produced by Michael Kustow.

Bibliography

Allen, Keith. 2001. "Pinter Storms the Yanks." *Daily Telegraph*, August 4.

Allen, Walter. 1979 [1954]. "Review of *Lucky Jim*." In *Protest*, ed. Gene Feldman and Max Gartenberg, 339–341. London: Souvenir Press.

Allsop, Kenneth. 1969. "War Game Comparisons." *Observer Review*, April 13.

Almansi, Guido, and Simon Henderson. 1983. *Harold Pinter*. London: Methuen.

Anderson, Lindsay. 1956. "Stand Up! Stand Up!" *Sight and Sound* 26, 2: 63–69.

———. 1981a [1957]. "Vital Theatre?" In *New Theatre Voices of the Fifties and Sixties: Selections from Encore Magazine 1956–1963*, ed. Charles Marowitz, Tom Milne, and Owen Hale, 41–47. London: Eyre Methuen.

———. 1981b [1958]. Review of *A Taste of Honey*. In *New Theatre Voices of the Fifties and Sixties: Selections from Encore Magazine 1956–1963*, ed. Charles Marowitz, Tom Milne, and Owen Hale, 78–80. London: Eyre Methuen.

———. 1997. "Interview." In *An Autobiography of British Cinema: By the Actors and Filmmakers Who Made It*, ed. Brian McFarlane, 8–16. London: Methuen.

Anderson, Michael. 1976. *Anger and Detachment: A Study of Arden, Osborne, and Pinter*. London: Pitman Publishing.

Appleyard, Bryan. 2000. "Comment." *Sunday Times*, November 5.

Arden, John. 1960a. *Serjeant Musgrave's Dance*. London: Methuen.

———. 1960b. "Telling a True Tale." *Encore*, May–June, 22–26.

———. 1961a. *Live Like Pigs*. Harmondsworth: Penguin.

———. 1961b. "Building the Play: An Interview with John Arden." *Encore*, July–August, 22–41.

———. 1962. *The Happy Haven*. Harmondsworth: Penguin.

———. 1964. *The Waters of Babylon*. Harmondsworth: Penguin.

———. 1967. "Author's Note." In *Three Plays*, 193–194. Harmondsworth: Penguin.

———. 1968. "Interviews with Tom Milne and Clive Goodwin, and with Simon Trussler." In *Theatre At Work: Playwrights and Productions in the Modern British Theatre*, ed. Charles Marowitz and Simon Trussler, 36–57. New York: Hill and Wang.

———. 1977. *To Present the Pretence: Essays on the Theatre and Its Public*. London: Methuen.

———. 1979. *Pearl*. London: Methuen.

———. 1994 [1971]. "A Few Historical Facts." In *Plays: Two*, 374–381. London: Methuen.

———. 2006. "Interview with Harriet Devine." In *Looking Back: Playwrights at the Royal Court, 1956–2006,* interviews by Harriet Devine, 21–28. London: Faber and Faber.

———. and Margaretta D'Arcy. 1969. "An Asymmetrical Authors' Preface." In *The Hero Rises Up,* 5–8. London and Reading: Cox & Wayman.

Aynsley, Cyril. 1956. "Stage Play Explodes on Screens." *Daily Express,* November 29.

Banham, Martin. 1969. *Osborne.* Edinburgh: Oliver and Boyd.

Barber, John. 1956. "This Bitter Young Man—Like Thousands." *Daily Express,* May 9.

———. 1975. "Richardson and Gielgud in Fine Partnership." *Daily Telegraph,* April 24.

———. 1977. "Adamant Ardent Ardens." *Daily Telegraph,* January 7.

———. 1981. Review of *Serjeant Musgrave's Dance. Daily Telegraph,* May 29.

———. 1982. Review of *A Kind of Alaska. Daily Telegraph,* October 16.

Barker, Felix. 1959. "A Slow Fuse, But What An Explosion!" *Evening News,* October 23.

Barnes, Philip. 1986. *A Companion to Post-War British Theatre.* Australia: Croom Helm.

Beauman, Sally. 1982. *The Royal Shakespeare Company: A History of Ten Decades.* Oxford: Oxford University Press.

Bennett, Alan. 1981. "Bad John (a review of *A Better Class Of Person*)." *London Review of Books,* December 22, 3–16.

Bennett, Susan. 1995. "Brecht—Britain—Bakhtin: The Bridge of Armstrong's Last Goodnight." In *John Arden and Margaretta D'Arcy: A Casebook,* ed. Jonathan Wike, 67–81. New York: Garland Publishing.

Bensky, Lawrence M. 1966. "The Art of the Theatre III: Harold Pinter: An Interview." *Paris Review* 10 (Fall): 13–37.

Billington, Michael. 1975a. "*No Man's Land.*" *Guardian,* April 24.

———. 1975b. Review of *No Man's Land. Guardian,* June 25.

———. 1978a. "Pearl of Great Praise." *Guardian,* July 1.

———. 1978b. Review of *Betrayal. Guardian,* November 16.

———. 1984. Review of *Serjeant Musgrave's Dance. Guardian,* May 25.

———. 1985. Review of *A Kind of Alaska. Arts Guardian,* March 8.

———. 1988. Review of *Mountain Language. Guardian,* October 22.

———. 1991. "Friends vs. Lovers." *Guardian,* January 23.

———. 1993. Review of *Moonlight. Guardian,* September 8.

———. 1994a. "Piece Keepers." *Guardian,* September 5.

———. 1994b. "A Prisoner of Dissent." *Guardian,* December 27.

———. 1996. *The Life and Work of Harold Pinter.* London: Faber and Faber.

———. 2000a. Review of *The Room* and *Celebration. Guardian,* March 23.

———. 2000b. "Angry Old Man." *Guardian,* October 14.

Bold, Alan, ed. 1984. *Harold Pinter: You Never Heard Such Silence*. London: Vision.

Bourdieu, Pierre. 1980a. "Mais qui a Créé le Créateur." In *Questions de Sociologie*, 207–221. Paris: Edition de Minuit.

———. 1980b. "La Metamorphose des Gouts." In *Questions de Sociologie*, 161–173. Paris: Edition de Minuit.

———. 1980c. "The Production of Belief: Contribution to an Economy of Symbolic Goods." In *Media, Culture and Society* 2: 261–293.

———. 1985a. "The Market of Symbolic Goods." *Poetics* 14: 13–44.

———. 1985b. "The Social Space and the Genesis of Groups." In *Theory and Society* 14: 723–744.

Brahms, Caryl. 1959. "Lines of Communication." *Plays and Players*, December: 106–107.

Brook, Peter. 1988. *The Shifting Point: Forty Years of Theatrical Exploration, 1946–1987*. London: Methuen.

———. 1999. *Threads of Time: A Memoir*. London: Methuen.

Brown, John Russell. 1982. *A Short Guide to Modern British Drama*. London: Heineman Educational Books.

———, ed. 1984a. *Modern British Dramatists*. Englewood Cliffs, N.J.: Prentice-Hall.

———. 1984b. "Introduction." In *Modern British Dramatists*, ed. John Russell Brown, 1–12. Englewood Cliffs, N.J.: Prentice-Hall.

Browne, Terry. 1975. *Playwrights' Theatre: The English Stage Company at the Royal Court*. London: Pitman.

Buchan, Alastair. 1956. "Look Back in Sorrow." *Observer*, December 2.

Bull, John. 2000. "Looking Back at Godot." In *British Theatre in the 1950s*, ed. Dominic Shellard, 82–94. Sheffield, England: Sheffield Academic Press.

———. 2004. "The Establishment of Mainstream Theatre, 1946–1979." In *The Cambridge History of British Theatre. Vol. 3: Since 1985*, ed. Baz Kershaw, 326–348. Cambridge: Cambridge University Press.

Burkman, Katherine H. 1971. *The Dramatic World of Harold Pinter: Its Basis in Ritual*. Columbus: Ohio State University Press.

———. 1986. *The Arrival of Godot*. London: Associated University Presses.

———. 1993. "Deborah's Homecoming in *A Kind of Alaska*: An Afterword." In *Pinter at Sixty*, ed. Katherine H. Burkman and John L. Kundert-Gibbs, 193–199. Bloomington: Indiana University Press.

———, and John L. Kundert-Gibbs, eds. 1993. *Pinter at Sixty*. Bloomington: Indiana University Press.

Callow, Simon. 1997. *The National: The Theatre and Its Work, 1963–1997*. London: Nick Hern, in association with Royal National Theatre.

Carne, Rosalind. 1984. Review of *One for the Road*. *New Statesman*, March 23.

Carpenter, Humphrey. 1998. *Dennis Potter: A Biography*. London: Faber and Faber.

Casey, John. 1996. Review of *Ashes to Ashes. Daily Telegraph*, September 18.

Cave, Richard Allen. 1989. *New British Drama in Performance on the London Stage: 1970–1985*. Gerrards Cross: Colin Smythe.

Chaillet, Ned. 1984. Review of *One for the Road. Wall Street Journal*, March 23.

Chambers, Colin, and Mike Prior. 1987. *Playwrights' Progress: Patterns of Postwar British Drama*. Oxford: Amber Lane Press.

Childers, Joseph, and Gary Hentzi, eds. 1995. *The Columbia Dictionary of Modern Literary and Cultural Criticism*. New York: Columbia University Press.

Clapp, Susannah. 2000. Review of *The Room* and *Celebration. Observer*, March 26.

———. 2001. "The Road to Somewhere." *Observer*, July 8.

Cleveland, Mark. 1962. "Littlewood and After." *Reynolds News*, February 4.

Cohen, Michael. 1985. "The Politics of the Earlier Arden." *Modern Drama* 28: 198–210.

Conway, Lydia. 1988. Review of *Mountain Language. What's On*, November 2.

Coren, Mike. 1985. *Theatre Royal: 100 Years of Stratford East*. London: Quartet Books.

Review of *A Kind of Alaska*. 1982. *Country Life*, November 25.

Courtney, Richard. 1982. *Outline History of British Drama*. Totowa, New Jersey: Littlefield, Adams.

Coveney, Michael. 1982. Review of *A Kind of Alaska. Financial Times*, October 15.

———. 1984. Review of *One for the Road. Financial Times*, March 16.

———. 1991. Review of *Party Time. Observer*, November 10.

———. 1993. Review of *Moonlight. Observer*, September 12.

———. 1994a. *The Aisle Is Full of Noises: A Vivisection of the Live Theatre*. London: Nick Hern.

———. 1994b. "Mother Courage." *Observer*, March 27.

Croft, Michael. 1959. "The Inside Story." *Observer*, February 22.

Curtis, Anthony. 1978. "Deep in the Forest of Arden." *Financial Times*, July 1.

Cushman, Robert. 1978. "Thanks for the Memory." *Observer*, November 19.

———. 1982. Review of *A Kind of Alaska. Observer*, October 17.

Daily Herald. 1961. "More Fings Ain't What They Used t'Be." February 13.

Daily Mail. 1955. "It's That Age Again." January 18.

———. 1961a. "London Becomes Broadway's Test Bench." June 29.

———. 1961b. "Curtain Down." July 10.

———. 1961c. "Joan Littlewood Tells Me All . . ." July 11.

———. 1963. "Royal Surprise." April 6.

Daily Telegraph. 1955. "Bicycle in Ben Jonson: *Volpone* Revival." March 4.

———. 1956. Review of *The Mulberry Bush*. April 3.

———. 1957. "Play without Style." October 21.

———. 1958. "Girl Emulates Rattigan: *A Taste of Honey*." May 28.

———. 1959. "Behan Play's Paris Award: Italian Prize for Producer." July 18.

———. 1960. Review of *The Dumb Waiter* and *The Room*. January 22.

———. 1961a. "'Old Ladies' of Arts Council." July 25.

———. 1961b. "Big Ovation for Behan." September 22.

———. 1963a. "Musical Gets 10 West End Offers." March 23.

———. 1963b. Review of *The Lover* and *The Dwarfs*. September 19.

———. 1965. "An Expression of Our Age." October 13.

———. 2005. "Extracts from the Citation." October 14.

Daneman, Paul, and Alec McCowen. 1988. "Still Waiting for Godot."
    Drama 1: 13–15.

Darlington, William A. 1954. Review of *The Fire Eaters*. *Daily Telegraph*,
    March 31.

———. 1956. "Repertory at Royal Court." *Daily Telegraph*, April 3.

———. 1958. Review of *The Birthday Party*. *Daily Telegraph*, May 20.

———. 1959a. "Pungent Soho Characters." *Daily Telegraph*, February 18.

———. 1959b. "Market Musical a Success." *Daily Telegraph*, October 20.

———. 1959c. "Recruiting All Awry." *Daily Telegraph*, October 23.

———. 1960. "Songs Strong Point of Soho Musical." *Daily Telegraph*,
    February 12.

———. 1963. "Pinter at His Most Pinteresque." *Daily Telegraph*, September 19.

———. 1964. Review of *The Birthday Party*. *Daily Telegraph*, June 19.

———. 1965a. "Drowned in Floods of Verbiage." *Daily Telegraph*, June 16.

———. 1965b. "Credit Goes to Albert Finney." *Daily Telegraph*, October 13.

de Jongh, Nicholas. 1975. Review of *No Man's Land*. *Guardian*, 25 June.

———. 1993. Review of *Moonlight*. *Evening Standard*, September 8.

Denison P. D., ed. 1997. *John Osborne: A Casebook*. New York: Garland.

Devine, George. 1957. "The Royal Court Theatre: Phase 1." In *International
    Theatre Annual*, No. 2, ed. Harold Hobson, 152–162. London: John Calder.

Devine, Harriet. 2006. *Looking Back: Playwrights at the Royal Court, 1956–2006*.
    London: Faber and Faber.

Doty, Gresdna A. and Billy J. Harbin, eds. 1990. *Inside the Royal Court Theatre,
    1956–1981: Artists Talk*. Baton Rouge: Louisiana State University Press.

Driberg, Tom. 1961. "Genius Quits." *Reynolds News*, July 10.

Dukore, Bernard F. 1976. *Where the Laughter Stops: Pinter's Tragic-Comedy*.
    Columbia: University of Missouri Press.

———. 1982. *Harold Pinter*. London: Macmillan.

Eagleton, Terry. 1991. Review of *Party Time*. *Times Literary Supplement*,
    November 15.

Edgar, David. 2006. "Stalking Out." *London Review of Books*, July 20.

Edwards, Jane. 1991. Review of *Party Time. Time Out*, November 13.

Elsom, John. 1976. *Post-War British Theatre*. London: Routledge and Kegan Paul.

English, John W. 1979. *Criticizing the Critics*. New York: Hastings House.

Esslin, Martin. 1961. *The Theatre of the Absurd*. Garden City, N.Y.: Doubleday.

———. 1968. *The Theatre of the Absurd* Rev. and enlarged ed. Harmondsworth: Penguin.

———. 1970. *The Peopled Wound: The Work of Harold Pinter*. New York: Doubleday.

———. 1980. *The Theatre of the Absurd* Rev. ed. Harmondsworth: Penguin.

———, ed. 1984 [1965]. *Absurd Drama*. Harmondsworth: Penguin.

———. 1993. "Harold Pinter's Theatre of Cruelty." In *Pinter at Sixty*, ed. Katherine H. Burkman and John L. Kundert-Gibs, 27–36. Bloomington: Indiana University Press.

Evening Standard. 1961. "Behan on Broadway 'Wild and Welcome.'" September 21.

———. 1969. "Pinter Comes Up with a Disaster." July 3.

Eyre, Richard. 2002. "Oh, What a Lovely Woman." *Guardian*, September 25.

———. 2003. *National Service: Diary of a Decade at the National Theatre*. London: Bloomsbury.

———. and Nicholas Wright. 2000. *Changing Stages: A View of British Theatre in the Twentieth Century*. London: Bloomsbury.

Farson, Daniel. 1981. "Where Is Joan Littlewood." *Sunday Telegraph*, May 24.

Fay, Stephen. 1995. *Power Play: The Life and Times of Peter Hall*. London: Hodder and Stoughton.

Fenton, James. 1983. *You Were Marvelous: Theatre Reviews from the "Sunday Times."* London: Jonathan Cape.

Findlater, Richard. 1952. *The Unholy Trade*. London: Victor Gollancz.

———. 1956. "Selling Themselves to Satan (in London, S.W.3)." *Tribune*, April 13.

———. 1968. *Banned! A Review of Theatrical Censorship in Britain*. London: Panther.

———. 1977. Interview with Pinter. In *Harold Pinter: Plays Two*, 9–12. London: Methuen.

———, ed. 1981. *At the Royal Court*. New York: Grove Press.

Ford, Anna. 1988. "Radical Departures." *Listener*, October 27.

Franks, Alan. 1991. "The Unmellowing of Harold Pinter." *Times Saturday Review*, October 19.

Furmanovsky, Jill. 1993. "HP Source." *Time Out*, September 15–22.

Gale, Steven H. 1977. *Butter's Going Up: A Critical Analysis of Harold Pinter's Work*. Durham, N.C.: Duke University Press.

Ganz, Arthur, ed. 1972a. *Harold Pinter: A Collection of Critical Essays*. Englewood Cliffs, N.J.: Prentice-Hall.

———. 1972b. "Introduction." In *Harold Pinter: A Collection of Critical Essays*, ed. Arthur Ganz, 1–19. Englewood Cliffs, N.J.: Prentice-Hall, Inc.

Gardner, Raymond. 1972. "Exit Stage: Left." *Guardian*, November 28.

Gaston, George. 1991. "An Interview with John Arden." *Contemporary Literature* 32: 147–170.

Gibbs, Patrick. 1960. Review of *The Caretaker*. *Daily Telegraph*, April 28.

Godzich, Wlad. 1978. "Afterword: Religion, the State, and Post(al) Modernism." In Samuel Weber, *Institution and Interpretation*. 153–164. Minneapolis: University of Minnesota Press.

Goodwin, Clive, and Tom Milne. 1960. "Working with Joan." *Encore*, July-August, 9–20.

Goorney, Howard. 1981. *The Theatre Workshop Story*. London: Methuen.

———. 1986. "Epilogue." In *Agit-Prop to Theatre Workshop*, ed. Howard Goorney and Ewan MacColl, 199–205. Manchester: Manchester University Press.

———, Ewan MacColl, eds. 1986. *Agit-Prop to Theatre Workshop*. Manchester: Manchester University Press.

Gordon, Lois. 1969. *Stratagems to Uncover Nakedness: The Dramas of Harold Pinter*. Columbia: University of Missouri Press.

———, ed. 2001. *Pinter at 70: A Casebook*. New York: Routledge.

Gordon, James. 1958. "A Short Directory to *Angry Young Men*." *Good Housekeeping*, January, 93.

Goring, Edward. 1958. "Honey? It's More Like a Marmalade." *Daily Mail*, May 28.

———. 1959. "What a Difference a Year Makes: The 'Factory Sagan' Tastes the Honey of Success." *Daily Mail*, October 9.

Gottfried, Martin. 1963. *Opening Nights: Theatre Criticism of the Sixties*. New York: G. P. Putnam's Sons.

Graham, Paul. 1956. "This Is the Best Play for Years." *Daily Worker*, April 16.

Grainger, Derek. 1956. "*The Mulberry Bush*." *Financial Times*, April 3.

Gray, Frances. 1982. *John Arden*. London: Macmillan.

Greene, Graham. 1958. Letter in the *Times*, June 28.

Gross, John. 2000. Review of *The Room* and *Celebration*. *Sunday Telegraph*, March 26.

Guardian. 1978. "Arden Must Live." May 26.

———. 1994. "Appreciation 4/5." December 27.

———. 2005a."Harold Pinter Nobel Laureate in His Own Words." October 14.

———. 2005b. "Comment and Debate: In Praise of … Harold Pinter." October 14.

Guardian Women. 1984. "Oh What a Lovely." June 25.

Guralnick, Elissa S. 1997. "The Stage: John Arden's *Pearl*, and *The Bagman, Too.*" In *Sight Unseen: Beckett, Pinter, Stoppard, and Other Contemporary Dramatists on Radio*, 152–189. Athens: Ohio University Press.

Gussow, Mel. 1994. *Conversations with Pinter.* London: Nick Hern.

Hagerty, Bill. 2000. Review of *The Room* and *Celebration. News of the World*, March 23.

Hall, Ann C. 1993. *A Kind of Alaska: Women in the Plays of O'Neill, Pinter, and Shepard.* Carbondale: Southern Illinois University Press.

Hall, Peter. 1983. *Peter Hall's Diaries: The Story of a Dramatic Battle.* Ed. John Goodwin. London: Hamish Hamilton.

———. 1993. *The Autobiography of Peter Hall: Making an Exhibition of Myself.* London: Sinclair-Stevenson.

Ham, Moonyoung C. 1993. "Portrait of Deborah: A Kind of Alaska." In *Pinter at Sixty*, ed. Katherine H. Burkman and John L. Kundert-Gibbs, 185–192. Bloomington: Indiana University Press.

Hare, David. 1997. "Eulogy for John Osborne." In *John Osborne: A Casebook*, ed. P. D. Denison, 193–196. New York: Garland.

———. 2005. "In Pinter You Find . . ." *Guardian*, October 14.

Hart, Henry. 1959. "Review of *Look Back in Anger.*" *Films* 10 (October): 491.

Hartnoll, Phyllis, ed. 1957. *The Oxford Companion to the Theatre* 2d ed. London: Oxford University Press.

———, ed. 1967. *The Oxford Companion to the Theatre* 3d ed. London: Oxford University Press.

Hastings, Ronald. 1961. "Allegory for Sherlock Holmes." *Daily Telegraph*, June 29.

———. 1963. "Sketches Aid 1914–18 War Songs." *Daily Telegraph*, March 20.

Hayman, Ronald. 1968. *John Osborne.* London: Heinemann.

———. 1969. *John Arden.* London: Heinemann Educational.

———. 1973. *The Set-Up: An Anatomy of the English Theatre Today.* London: Eyre Methuen.

———. 1979. *British Theatre since 1955: A Reassessment.* Oxford: Oxford University Press.

———. 1980. "Arts Values." *Listener*, September 4.

Heilpern, John. 2006a. *John Osborne: A Patriot for Us.* London: Chatto and Windus.

———. 2006b. "Thrillingly New." *London Review of Books*, August 3.

Hern, Nicholas. 1985. "A Play and Its Politics: A Conversation between Harold Pinter and Nicholas Hern." In *One for the Road*, by Harold Pinter, 5–23. London: Methuen.

Hewison, Robert. 1987. *Too Much: Art and Society in the Sixties, 1960–75.* New York: Oxford University Press.

————. 1995. *Culture and Consensus: England, Art, and Politics since 1940.* London: Methuen.

Hibbin, Nina. 1969. "'Oh, What a Lovely War' Is Just a Bit Too Lovely." *Morning Star*, April 9.

Hill, John. 1997 [1986]. *Sex, Class and Realism: British Cinema, 1956–1963.* London: British Film Institute.

Hilton, Julian. 1984. "The Court and Its Favours: The Careers of Christopher Hampton, David Storey, and John Arden." In *Modern British Dramatists*, ed. John Russell Brown, 50–75. Englewood Cliffs, N.J.: Prentice-Hall.

Hinchcliffe, Arnold P. 1975. *Harold Pinter.* New York: Twayne.

Hobson, Harold. 1952. *Verdict at Midnight: Sixty Years of Dramatic Criticism.* London: Longmans, Green.

————. 1955a. Review of *Richard II. Sunday Times*, January 23.

————. 1955b. "Paris Angry." *Sunday Times*, May 8.

————. 1955c. "Try Again." *Sunday Times*, July 3.

————. 1956. "A New Author." *Sunday Times*, May 13.

————. 1958a. Review of *The Birthday Party. Sunday Times*, May 25.

————. 1958b. "Triumph at Stratford East." *Sunday Times*, October 19.

————. 1959. Review of *Serjeant Musgrave's Dance. Sunday Times*, October 25.

————. 1965a. Review of *The Homecoming. Sunday Times*, June 6.

————. 1965b. " The Soldier's Tale." *Sunday Times*, December 12.

————. 1969. "Paradise Lost." *Sunday Times*, July 6.

————. 1971. "Remembrance of Things Past." *Sunday Times*, June 6.

————. 1978. *Indirect Journey: An Autobiography.* London: Quality Book Club.

————. 1984. *Theatre in Britain: A Personal View.* Oxford: Phaidon Press.

Hodgkinson, J. L. 1959. "Theatre Workshop." *Observer*, March 22.

Holdsworth, Nadine. 1999. "'They'd Have Pissed on My Grave': The Arts Council and Theatre Workshop." *New Theatre Quarterly* 53: 3–16.

————. 2006. *Joan Littlewood.* London: Routledge.

Hollis, James H. 1970. *Harold Pinter: The Poetics of Silence.* Carbondale: Southern Illinois University Press.

Hollis, Robert. 1959. "The Woman Who Is Shaking Up the Theatre." *John Bull*, June 13.

Hope-Wallace, Philip. 1955. "'Le Workshop' Scores a Success in Paris." *Manchester Guardian*, July 23.

————. 1959. "Something Short of a Great Play." *Manchester Guardian*, October 24.

————. 1963. Review of *The Lover* and *Dwarfs. Guardian*, September 19.

————. 1965. Review of *Left Handed Liberty. Guardian*, June 16.

Hoyle, Martin. 1993. Review of *Moonlight. Mail on Sunday*, September 12.

Hudson, Christopher. 1984. Review of *One for the Road. Standard*, March 19.

Hunt, Albert. 1960. "*Serjeant Musgrave* and the Critics." *Encore*, January-February, 26–28.

———. 1965. "On Comedy: John Arden Talks to Albert Hunt about *The Workhouse Donkey.*" *Encore*, September–October, 13–19.

———. 1974. *Arden: A Study of His Plays.* London: Eyre Methuen.

———, and Geoffrey Reeves. 1965. "Arden, Professionals and Amateurs." *Encore*, September-October, 27–37.

———, eds. 1995. *Peter Brook.* Cambridge: Cambridge University Press.

Hutchinson, Tom. 1961. "Miss Theatre Angers playwright." *Daily Express*, January 26.

Illustrated London News. 1958. Review of *Serjeant Musgrave's Dance.* October 18.

Independent on Sunday. 1999. "The Sitter's Tale: Harold Pinter." April 25, Culture section.

Innes, Christopher. 1992. *Modern British Drama: 1890–1990.* Cambridge: Cambridge University Press.

Itzin, Catherine. 1980. *Stages in the Revolution: Political Theatre in Britain since 1968.* London: Methuen.

Jones, Alice. 2005. "Menace Set to Music." *Independent*, October 7.

Kazan, Elia. 1988. *A Life.* London: Andre Deutsch.

Kellaway, Kate. 2000. "Pinter Is 70. (Pause for Applause)." *Observer*, September 24.

Kennedy, Dennis, ed. 2003. *Oxford Encyclopedia of Theatre and Performance.* Oxford: Oxford University Press.

Kershaw, Baz. 1992. *The Politics of Performance: Radical Theatre as Cultural Intervention.* London: Routledge.

———. 2004. "British Theatre, 1940–2002: An Introduction." In *The Cambridge History of British Theatre Vol. 3: Since 1985*, ed. Baz Kershaw, 291–325. Cambridge: Cambridge University Press.

Kingstone, Jeremy. 1993. Review of *Moonlight. Times*, September 8.

———. 1998. "Lest We Forget." *Times*, August 18.

Kitchin, Laurence. 1962. *Mid-Century Drama.* London: Faber and Faber.

Koenig, Rhoda. 1990. "Past Master of the Pregnant Silence." *Independent*, October 7.

Krim, Seymour, ed. 1960. *The Beats.* Greenwich, Conn.: Fawcett.

Kustow, Michael. 1965. Review of *Left Handed Liberty. Encore*, July-August, 39–41.

———. 2005. *Peter Brook: A Biography.* New York: St. Martin's Press.

Lacey, Stephen. 1995. *British Realist Theatre: The New Wave in Its Context, 1956–1965.* London: Routledge.

Lahr, John. 1971. *A Casebook on Harold Pinter's "The Homecoming."* New York: Grove Press.

Lambert, Gavin. 1959. "Review of *Look Back in Anger.*" *Film Quarterly* 12: 39–41.

Lambert, Jack W. 1961. "Introduction." In *John Arden: Live Like Pigs,* 7–15. Harmondsworth: Penguin.

Landstone, Charles. 1953. *Off Stage: A Personal Record of the First Twelve Years of State Sponsored Drama in Great Britain.* London: Elek.

Lassally, Walter. 1997. "Interview." In *An Autobiography of British Cinema: By the Actors and Filmmakers Who Made It,* ed. Brian McFarlane, 346–351. London: Methuen.

Law, Jonathan, David Pickering, and Richard Helfer, eds. 2001 [1998]. *The New Penguin Dictionary of the Theatre.* London: Penguin.

Leeming, Glenda. 1974. *John Arden.* Ed. Ian Scott-Kilvert. Harlow: Published for the British Council by Longman Group.

———, ed. 1982. *Serjeant Musgrave's Dance.* London: Methuen.

Lehman, Engel. 1976. *The Critics.* New York: Macmillan.

Levin, Bernard. 1961. "Q: Why Did the Censor Do a Double Take? A: Because There's a New Man Nudging His Elbow." *Daily Express,* February 14.

———. 1963a. "Perhaps (Success!) the Audience Will Walk Out on This." *Daily Mail,* March 20.

———. 1963b. "And My Index Finger Itches." *Daily Mail,* September 19.

———. 1964. Review of *The Birthday Party. Daily Mail,* June 19.

———. 1965a. Review of *The Homecoming. Daily Mail,* June 4.

———. 1965b. "In Memory of Magna Carta, Arden's Theme." *Daily Mail,* June 16.

———. 1994. "How His Genius Struck Me." *Times,* December 27.

Lewenstein, Oscar. 1994. *Kicking against the Pricks: A Theatre Producer Looks Back: The Memoirs of Oscar Lewenstein.* London: Nick Hern.

Lewis, Frank. 1960. Review of *The Happy Haven. Sunday Despatch,* September 18.

Lewis, Peter. 1965. Review of *Serjeant Musgrave's Dance. Daily Mail,* December 10.

———. 1990. *The National: A Dream Made Concrete.* London: Methuen.

———. 1994. "Stage Prescience." *Independent Magazine,* March 26.

Lipton, Lawrence. 1959. *The Holy Barbarians.* New York: Julian Messner.

Littlewood, Joan. 1981 [1961]. "Goodbye Note from Joan." In *New Theatre Voices of the Fifties and Sixties: Selections from Encore Magazine 1956–1963,* ed. Charles Marowitz, Tom Milne, and Owen Hale, 132–134. London: Eyre Methuen.

————. 1994. *Joan's Book: Joan Littlewood's Peculiar History as She Tells It.* London: Methuen.

Lloyd-Evans, Gareth, and Barbara Lloyd-Evans, eds. 1985. *Plays in Review: 1956–1980.* London: Batsford Academic and Educational.

Macaulay, Alastair. 1998. "Rage and Rhetoric, Onstage and Off." *Financial Times,* November 28/29.

MacColl, Ewan. 1973. "Theatre Workshop Story Part 1: Grass Roots of Theatre Workshop." *Theatre Quarterly* 3: 56–69.

————. 1986. "Introduction: The Evolution of a Revolutionary Theatre Style." In *Agit-Prop to Theatre Workshop,* ed. Howard Goorney and Ewan MacColl, ix–lvii. Manchester: Manchester University Press.

————. 1990. *Journeyman: An Autobiography.* London: Sidwick & Jackson.

Mackenzie, Suzie. 1995. "Oh What a Lovely Rude Joan." *Evening Standard,* June 9.

Malik, Javed. 1986. "The Polarized Universe of the *Island of the Mighty*: The Dramaturgy of Arden and D'Arcy." *New Theatre Quarterly* 2: 38–53.

Mallory, Leslie. 1959. "A Kiss for Miss Littlewood." *News Chronicle,* April 9.

————. 1960. "Another Victim of the Violence of Angry *Old* Men." *News Chronicle,* September 20.

"The Man behind the Angry Young Men." *Films and Filming* (February 1959): 9.

March, Paddy. 1975–1976. "Easter at Liberty Hall: In the Ardens' *Non- Stop Connoly Show,* How the Irish Hero Was Remembered—in a Twenty-Six Hour Play." *Theatre Quarterly* 5: 133–143.

Marowitz, Charles. 1961. "A Cynic's Glossary of Theatre Terms." *Encore,* May–June, 31–33.

————. 1963. "Littlewood Pays a Dividend." *Encore,* May-June, 48–50.

————. 1965a. "The Workhouse Donkey." *Encore,* March–April, 52–54.

————. 1965b. "What Happened to *Encore.*" *Plays and Players* 12: 3.

————. 1965c. Review of *Twang! Plays and Players* 13: 7.

————, and Simon Trussler, eds. 1968. *Theatre At Work: Playwrights and Productions in the Modern British Theatre.* New York: Hill and Wang.

————, Tom Milne, and Owen Hale, eds. 1981. *New Theatre Voices of the Fifties and Sixties: Selections from Encore Magazine, 1956–1963.* London: Eyre Methuen.

Marwick, Arthur. 1998. *The Sixties: Cultural Revolution in Britain, France, Italy, and the United States, c. 1958–c. 1974.* Oxford: Oxford University Press.

Mashler, Tom, ed. 1957. *Declaration.* London: Macgibbon and Kee.

McAfee, Annalena. 1991. "The New World Order." *Evening Standard,* July 23.

McConachie, Bruce A. 1992. "Historicising the Relations of Theatrical Production." In *Critical Theory and Performance,* ed. Janelle G. Reinelt and Joseph R. Roach, 168–178. Ann Arbor: University of Michigan Press.

Merritt, Susan Hollis. 1990. *Pinter in Play: Critical Strategies and the Plays of Harold Pinter.* Durham, N.C.: Duke University Press.

Milne, Tom. 1965a. "Armstrong's Last Goodnight." *Encore,* September–October, 37–40.

———. 1965b. "Cruelty Cruelty." *Encore,* January–February, 8–12.

———. 1965c. "Producing Arden: An Interview with William Gaskill." *Encore,* September-October, 20–27.

———. 1981 [1958]. "Art in Angel Lane." In *New Theatre Voices of the Fifties and Sixties: Selections from Encore Magazine, 1956–1963,* ed. Charles Marowitz, Tom Milne, and Owen Hale, 80–86. London: Eyre Methuen.

Morgan, Kenneth O. 2001 [1990]. *Britain since 1945: The People's Peace.* Oxford: Oxford University Press.

Morley, Sheridan. 1975. *Review Copies: Plays and Players in London, 1970–74.* Totowa: Rowman and Littlefield.

———. 1978. "Death in Venice." *Punch,* November 29.

———. 1982. Review of *A Kind of Alaska. Punch,* October 27.

———. 1990. *Our Theatre in the Eighties.* London: Hedder and Stoughton.

———. 2000. Review of *The Room* and *Celebration. Spectator,* April 1.

Morrison, Blake. 1980. *The Movement: English Poetry and Fiction in the 1950s.* Oxford: Oxford University Press.

Moss, Stephen. 1999. "Under the Volcano (Profile: Harold Pinter)." *Guardian,* September 4.

Muller, Robert. 1960a. Review of *The Caretaker. Daily Mail,* April 30.

———. 1960b. "Pointless and Macabre." *Daily Mail,* September 15.

Murphy, Robert. 1992. *Sixties British Cinema.* London: British Film Institute.

Nathan, David. 1961. "Why I 'Tinker' with New Plays." *Daily Herald,* January 27, 1961.

Nightingale, Benedict. 1965. "The Theatre of Bewilderment." *Guardian,* July 6.

———. 1982. Review of *A Kind of Alaska. New Statesman,* October 22.

———. 1986. *Fifth Row Center: A Critic's Year On and Off Broadway.* New York: Times Books.

———. 1991a. Review of *The New World Order. Times,* July 22.

———. 1991b. Review of *Party Time. Times,* November 7.

———. 1993. Review of *Moonlight. Times,* September 8.

———. 2000. Review of *The Room* and *Celebration. Times,* March 24.

———. 2002a. "Pinter Comes Home." *Times,* October 16.

———. 2002b. "Old Times." *Times,* October 26.

Norman, Barry. 1965. "Five Desperate Years of Harold Pinter." *Daily Mail,* March 9.

Observer. 1955. "A Notice on the Paris Festival." May 29.

———. 1959. "The Observer Profile: Theatre Worker." March 15.

———. 1960. Review of *The Dumb Waiter* and *The Room.* January 24.

———. 1994. "Joan's Lovely War." March 13.

Osborne, Charles. 1988. Review of *Mountain Language*. *Daily Telegraph*, October 22.

Osborne, John. 1956. "The Things I Wish I Could Do ... by the Theatre's Bright Boy." *Daily Express*, October 18.

———. 1957. "You Have Fallen for the Great Swindle." *News Chronicle*, February 27.

———. 1981. *A Better Class of Person*. London: Faber and Faber.

———. 1991. *Almost a Gentleman: 1955–1966, An Autobiography*. Vol. 2. London: Faber and Faber.

———. 1999. *Looking Back: Never Explain, Never Apologise*. London: Faber and Faber.

P. G. 1956. "Skeletons in the Cupboard." *Daily Worker*, April 4.

Page, Malcolm. 1985. *Arden on File*. London: Methuen.

———. 1993. *File on Pinter*. London: Methuen Drama.

Paget, Derek. 1990a. *True Stories? Documentary Drama on Radio, Screen and Stage*. Manchester: Manchester University Press.

———. 1990b. " 'Oh What a Lovely War': the Texts and Their Context." *New Theatre Quarterly* 6: 244–260.

———. 1990c. "Popularising Popular History: *Oh What a Lovely War* and the Sixties." *Critical Survey*, 2: 117–127.

———. 1995a. "Theatre Workshop, Moussinac, and the European Connection." *New Theatre Quarterly* 11: 211–224.

———. 1995b. "Thoughts on Reading Joan's Book." *Speech and Drama* 44: 29–34.

———. 1996. "Remembrance Play: *Oh What a Lovely War* and History." In *Acts of War: The Representation of Military Conflict on the British Stage and Television since 1945*, eds. Tony Howard and John Stokes, 82–97. Aldershot, England: Scolar Press.

———. 2004. "Case Study: Theatre Workshop's *Oh What a Lovely War*, 1963." In *The Cambridge History of British Theatre, Vol. 3: Since 1985*, ed. Baz Kershaw, 397–411. Cambridge: Cambridge University Press.

Parmentier, Guillaume. 1980. "The British Press in the Suez Crisis." *Historical Journal* 23: 435–448.

Peter, John. 1985. "Victims in No-Man's Land." *Sunday Times*, March 10.

———. 1990. "Harold Pinter: The Poet of No-Man's-Land." *Sunday Times*, October 7.

———. 1994. "The Play's the Thing." *Sunday Times*, March 27.

Pinter, Harold. 1976 [1962]. "Writing for the Theatre." In *Harold Pinter, Plays: One*, 9–16. London: Methuen.

———. 1977 [1961]. "Writing for Myself." In *Harold Pinter, Plays: Two*, 9–12. London: Methuen.

———. 1981 "No Man's Land." In *Harold Pinter, Complete Works: Four,* 73–155. New York: Grove Press.

———. 1983. *Other Places.* New York: Grove Press.

———. 1984. *One for the Road.* London: Methuen.

———. 1996. *Ashes to Ashes.* London: Faber and Faber.

———. 1998a. *Various Voices: Prose, Poetry, Politics, 1948–1998.* London: Faber and Faber.

———. 1998b [1958]. "On *The Birthday Party* I." In *Various Voices,* 8–11. London: Faber and Faber.

———. 1998c [1958]. "On *The Birthday Party* II." In *Various Voices,* 13–15. London: Faber and Faber.

———. 2002. *Press Conference.* London: Faber and Faber.

Plays and Players. 1956a. "Personality of the Month." March.

———. 1956b. "On the English Stage Company." March.

———. 1960. "Personality of the Month." March.

Postlewait, Thomas. 1986. *Prophet of the New Drama: William Archer and the Ibsen Campaign.* Westport, Conn.: Greenwood Press.

———. 1988. "The Criteria for Periodization in Theatre History." *Theatre Journal* 40: 299–318.

———. 2004. "The London Stage, 1895–1918." In *The Cambridge History of British Theatre Vol. 3: Since 1985,* ed. Baz Kershaw, 34–59. Cambridge: Cambridge University Press.

———, and Bruce A. McConachie, eds. 1989. *Interpreting the Theatrical Past.* Iowa City: University of Iowa Press.

Powell, Dilys. 1969. "I Could Not Restrain My Tears." *Sunday Times,* April 13.

Pryce-Jones, Alan. 1959. "Return to Arden." *Observer,* November 1.

———. 1960. "When East Moves West." *Observer,* February 11.

Quigley, Austin E. 1975. *The Pinter Problem.* Princeton, N.J.: Princeton University Press.

———. 1997. "The Personal, the Political, and the Postmodern in Osborne's *Look Back in Anger* and *Dejavu.*" In *John Osborne: A Casebook,* ed. P. D. Denison, 35–61. New York: Garland.

R. B. M. 1956. "*The Mulberry Bush* at the Royal Court." *Stage,* April 5.

Raby, Peter. 2001a. "Tales of the City: Some Places and Voices in Pinter Plays." In *The Cambridge Companion to Harold Pinter,* ed. Peter Raby, 57–72. Cambridge: Cambridge University Press.

———. ed. 2001b. *The Cambridge Companion to Harold Pinter.* Cambridge: Cambridge University Press.

Radio Times. 1956. 133 (October 12), 27.

Rebellato, Dan. 1999. *1956 and All That.* London: Routledge.

Reisz, Karel. 1997. "Interview." In *An Autobiography of British Cinema: By the*

Actors and Filmmakers Who Made It, ed. Brian McFarlane, 475–479. London: Methuen.

Reynolds, Gillian. 1978. "Best of British Drama." *Daily Telegraph*, July 5.

Reynolds News. 1960. "SNUBBED by the Critics—but Hailed by All FRANCE." October 23.

Richardson, Tony. 1993. *The Long-Distance Runner: An Autobiography*. New York: William Morrow.

Rissik, Andrew. 1985. "Cross Fire." *New Statesman*, July 12.

Ritchie, Harry. 1988. *Success Stories: Literature and the Media in England, 1950–1959*. London: Faber and Faber.

Roberts, Peter. 1961. "Contemporary Father." *Plays and Players*, February, 127.

Roberts, Philip. 1999. *The Royal Court Theatre and the Modern Stage*. Cambridge: Cambridge University Press.

Rossely, John. 1960. Review of *The Caretaker*. *Guardian*, April 27.

Sacks, Oliver. 1973. *Awakenings*. New York: Harper Collins.

Sandbrook, Dominic. 2005. *Never Had It So Good: A History of Britain from Suez to the Beatles*. London: Abacus.

Scannell, Vernon. 1999. "Pauses for Thought." *Sunday Telegraph*, January 3.

Schafer, Elizabeth. 1999. "Daughters of Ben." In *Ben Jonson and Theatre: Performance, Practice and Theory*, ed. Richard Cave, Elizabeth Schafer, and Brian Wooland, 154–178. London: Routledge.

———. 2000 [1998]. *Ms-Directing Shakespeare: Women Direct Shakespeare*. New York: St. Martin's Press.

Schroll, Herman T. 1971. *Harold Pinter: A Study of His Reputation, 1958–1969*. Metuchen, N.J.: Scarecrow Press.

Scott, George. 1956. *Time and Place*. London: Staples Press.

Shellard, Dominic. 1995a. *Harold Hobson: Witness and Judge*. Keele, Staffordshire: Keele University Press.

———. 1995b. "A Magnificent Obsession: Harold Hobson and *Waiting for Godot*." *Theatre Notebook* 50: 68–78.

———. 1999. *British Theatre since the War*. New Haven, Conn.: Yale University Press.

———, ed. 2000a. *British Theatre in the 1950s*. Sheffield, England: Sheffield Academic Press.

———. 2000b. "1950–54: Was It a Cultural Wasteland?" In *British Theatre in the 1950s*, ed. Dominic Shellard, 28-40. Sheffield, England: Sheffield Academic Press.

———. 2003. *Kenneth Tynan: A Life*. New Haven, Conn.: Yale University Press.

Shorter, Eric. 1959. "Whirligig of Chaos in Arden Play." *Daily Telegraph*, December 10.

———. 1965. Review of *The Homecoming*. *Daily Telegraph*, June 4.

———. 1984. Review of *One for the Road*. *Daily Telegraph*, March 16.

Shrum, Wesley Monroe, Jr. 1996. *Fringe and Fortune: The Role of Critics in High and Popular Art*. Princeton, N.J.: Princeton University Press.

Shulman, Milton. 1958a. Review of *The Birthday Party*. *Evening Standard*, May 19.

———. 1958b. "A Good Try, Miss Delaney, But I Couldn't Believe It." *Evening Standard*, May 28.

———. 1959. "Mankowitz Comes Up with a Brash and Breezy Musical." *Evening Standard*, October 20.

———. 1960. "Not One for the Matinee Set . . ." *Evening Standard*, February 12.

———. 1961. "An Attack Completely out of Range." *Evening Standard*, June 29.

———. 1963. Review of *The Lover* and *The Dwarfs*. *Evening Standard*, September 19.

———. 1965. "It's Unorthodox, Mr. Arden, But Virile and Mature." *Evening Standard*, June 16.

———. 1975. "Word Game Made for Two . . ." *Evening Standard*, April 24.

———. 1982. "Review of *A Kind of Alaska*." *Evening Standard*, October 15.

———. 1988. Review of *Mountain Language*. *Evening Standard*, October 21.

———. 1991. Review of *Party Time*. *Evening Standard*, November 7.

Sinfield, Alan. 1989. *Literature, Politics, and Culture in Postwar Britain*. Oxford: Basil Blackwell.

Smith, Ian, ed. 2005. *Pinter in the Theatre*. London: Nick Hern.

Smurthwait, Nick. 1993. "Out of the Sink into the Shadows." *Sunday Telegraph*, October 17.

Spencer, Charles. 1991a. Review of *The New World Order*. *Daily Telegraph*, July 22.

———. 1991b. Review of *Party Time*. *Daily Telegraph*, November 7.

———. 1993. Review of *Moonlight*. *Daily Telegraph*, September 9.

———. 1996. Review of *Ashes to Ashes*. *Daily Telegraph*, September 20.

———. 2005. "Happy Birthday Party for Harold Pinter." *Daily Telegraph*, October 14.

Stage. 1956. "Limelight." April 5.

Stanton, Sarah, and Martin Banham. 1996. *Cambridge Paperback Guide to Theatre*. Cambridge: Cambridge University Press.

Stevenson, Randal. 1984. "Harold Pinter—Innovator?" In *Harold Pinter: You Never Heard Such Silence*, ed. Alan Bold, 29–60. London: Vision.

Stewart, Ian. 1981. "Action Within and Without." *Country Life*, June 18.

Stokes, John. 2001. "Pinter and the 1950s." In *The Cambridge Companion to Harold Pinter*, ed. Peter Raby, 28–44. Cambridge: Cambridge University Press.

Sunday Times. 1955. "A Notice on the Paris Festival." June 26.

———. 1956. "Plays and Players." March 25.

———. 1958. Review of *Serjeant Musgrave's Dance*. October 5.

————. 1962. "Pinter between the Lines." March 4, 25.

————. 1978. Review of *Betrayal*. November 19.

Taylor, John Russell. 1962. *Anger and After: A Guide to the New British Drama*. London: Methuen.

————. 1963. *Anger and After: A Guide to the New British Drama*. Rev. ed. Harmondsworth: Penguin.

————. 1967. "Introduction." In *John Arden: Three Plays*, 7–15. Harmondsworth: Penguin.

————, ed. 1968a. *John Osborne:* Look Back in Anger: *A Casebook*. London: Macmillan.

————. 1968b. "Introduction." In *John Osborne:* Look Back in Anger: *A Casebook*, ed. John Russell Taylor, 10–22. London: Macmillan.

————. 1969. *Anger and After: A Guide to the New British Drama*. Rev. ed. London: Methuen.

————. 1971. *The Second Wave: British Drama for the Seventies*. London: Methuen.

————. 1974. "John Arden." British Council Feature Articles Service, press release.

————. 1978. *Anger and After: A Guide to the New British Drama*. Rev. ed. London: Eyre Methuen.

Taylor, Paul. 1998. "Oh What a Lovely Coup for Milton Keynes. "*Independent*, April 4.

Thorpe, Vanessa. 2002. "Littlewood, First among Radicals, Leaves Stage." *Observer*, September 22.

Tibbetts, John C. 1999. "Breaking the Proscenium: Tony Richardson, the Free Cinema, the Royal Court, and Woodfall Films (*Look Back in Anger* [1959] and *The Entertainer* [1960])." In *The Cinema of Tony Richardson: Essays and Interviews*, eds. James M. Welsh and John C. Tibbetts, 49–79. Albany: State University of New York.

Time Out. 1972. On *The Island of the Mighty*. December 8–12.

Times. 1953a. Review of *A Christmas Carol*. December 10.

————. 1953b. Review of *Treasure Island*. December 28.

————. 1955a. Review of *Volpone*, March 4.

————. 1955b. "*Arden of Faversham* in Paris: A Popular Success." May 25.

————. 1955c. "A City of Plays: The Drama of Many Countries, Taking Stock of the Paris Festival." June 9.

————. 1956a. "On the English Stage Company." March 31.

————. 1956b. "Modern Plays in Repertory; The Court Venture." April 2.

————. 1957. "Review of *The Waters of Babylon*." October 21.

————. 1958a. Review of *The Birthday Party*. May 20.

————. 1958b. "*A Taste of Honey*: Exhilarating Occasion for Theatre Workshop." May 28.

———. 1958c. "Original Written in Irish." September 25.

———. 1958d. "Half an Hour too Long." October 1.

———. 1959a. "Sardonic Humour of Street Market Musical." October 20.

———. 1959b. "Sergeant Musgrave's Punitive Expedition." October 23.

———. 1960. "West End's Best Produced Musical." February 12.

———. 1961. "Lead in the Souffle." June 29.

———. 1963. "Mr. Pinter Pursues an Elusive Reality." Review of *The Dwarfs*. September 19.

———. 1964. Review of *The Birthday Party*. June 19.

———. 1965. "A World Out of Orbit." June 4.

———. Notice announcing program for recording process of Arden's *Pearl*. June 21.

———. 1995. "St. Joan's Lovely War with the Theatre." June 21.

Tinker, Jack. 1988. Review of *Mountain Language*. *Daily Mail*, October 21.

———. 1996. Review of *Ashes to Ashes*. *Daily Mail*, September 20.

Toynbee, Polly. 1990. "Master of Strident Silences."*Guardian*, September 29.

Trewin, John C. 1958. Review of *The Birthday Party*. *Illustrated London News*, May 31.

———. 1965. Review of *The Homecoming*. *Illustrated London News*, June 19.

———. 1975. "Arranging the Features." *Illustrated London News*, June 25.

———. 1979. "Backwards and Forwards." *Illustrated London News*, January.

———. 1981. "Review of *Serjeant Musgrave's Dance*." *Times*, June 11.

Trussler, Simon. 1964. "Private Experiment in Public." *Plays and Players*, February, 178–183.

———. 1965. "Arden: An Introduction." *Encore*, September-October, 4–8.

———. 1969a. *John Osborne*. London: Longmans, Green.

———. 1969b. "Political Progress of a Paralyzed Liberal: The Community Dramas of John Arden." *Drama Review* 13: 181–192.

———. 1973a. *John Arden*. New York: Columbia University Press.

———. 1973b. *The Plays of Harold Pinter: An Assessment*. London: Gollancz.

———. 1981. *New Theatre Voices of the Seventies*. London: Methuen.

TV Times. 1956. "Play of the Week." 5 (November 23): 19.

Tynan, Kathleen. 1968. "In Search of Harold Pinter: Part Two." *Evening Standard*, April 26.

———. 1987. *The Life of Kenneth Tynan*. London: George Weidenfeld and Nicolson.

Tynan, Kenneth. 1954. Review of *The Good Soldier Shweik*. *Observer*, November 14.

———. 1955a. Review of *Volpone*. *Observer*, March 6.

———. 1955b. "Dimmed Debut." *Observer*, July 3.

———. 1956a. Review of *Edward II*. *Observer*, April 24.

———. 1956b. "The Voice of the Young." *Observer*, May 13.

———. 1956c. "The End of the Noose." *Observer,* May 27.

———. 1956d. "Long-Run Habit in the London Theatre." *Scotsman,* June 6.

———. 1957a. "Theatre and Living." In *Declaration,* ed. Tom Mashler, 108–129. London: Macgibbon and Kee.

———. 1957b. "Debit Account." *Observer,* October 13.

———. 1957c. "The Ego Triumphant." *Observer,* October 27.

———. 1958a. "Lennie Laughton." *Observer,* June 1.

———. 1958b. "New Amalgam." *Observer,* October 19.

———. 1959. "Look behind the Anger." *Observer,* December 27.

———. 1960. Review of *The Caretaker. Observer,* June 5.

———. 1961a. *Curtains.* New York: Atheneum.

———. 1961b. "The Breakthrough That Broke Down." *Observer,* October 1.

———. 1967. [1964]. *Tynan Right and Left.* New York: Atheneum.

Verdaasdonk, H. 1994. "Analogies as Tools for Classifying and Appraising Literary Texts." *Poetics* 22: 373–388.

W. R. 1956. "Witch Hunt." *West London Press,* May 4.

Wagner, Anthon, ed. 1999. *Establishing Our Boundaries: English-Canadian Theatre Criticism.* Toronto: University of Toronto Press.

Walker, Alexander. 1974. *Hollywood UK.* New York: Stein and Day.

Wall, Michael. 1959. "Laughter in Portobello Road." *Guardian,* December 18.

Walsh, John. 1999. "That Nice Mr. Pinter." *Independent,* February 8.

Wardle, Irving. 1958. "Comedy of Menace." *Encore,* September-October, 28–33.

———. 1963. "Arden: Talking about His Way of Writing Plays." *Observer,* June 30.

———. 1975. "In a Land of Dreams and Actuality." *Times,* April 24.

———. 1978a. *The Theatres of George Devine.* London: Eyre Methuen.

———. 1978b. "Pinter, Master of Ambiguity, Offers a Blank Statement of the Obvious." *Times,* November 16.

———. 1982. Review of *A Kind of Alaska. Times,* October 15.

———. 1984. Review of *Serjeant Musgrave's Dance. Times,* May 25.

———. 1985. Review of *A Kind of Alaska. Times,* March 8.

———. 1992. *Theatre Criticism.* London: Routledge.

Weightman, J. G. 1957. "Out of the Mouths." *Twentieth Century,* December, 535.

Wells, John. 1994. "Joan Littlewood." *Independent Magazine,* February 28, 46.

Welsh, James M. 1999. "Introduction: Running the Distance." In *The Cinema of Tony Richardson: Essays and Interviews,* ed. James M. Welsh and John C. Tibbetts, 1–22. Albany: State University of New York Press.

Wesker, Arnold. 1997. "A Memory of John Osborne." In *John Osborne: A Casebook,* ed. P. D. Denison, 187–191. New York: Garland.

Wike, Jonathan, ed. 1995. *John Arden and Margaretta D'Arcy: A Casebook.* New York: Garland.

Williams, Raymond. 1968. *Drama from Ibsen to Brecht.* London: Hogarth Press.

———. 1981. *Culture*. London: Fontana.

Wilson, Cecil. 1957. "It's Hazy and Promising." *Daily Mail*, October 21.

———. 1958a. Review of *The Dumb Waiter* and *The Room*. *Daily Mail*, May 20.

———. 1958b. "Savage, Brutish, Squalid: And a Great New Talent." *Daily Mail*, October 1.

———. 1959a. "Make-believe? It's Murk Now." *Daily Mail*, October 20.

———. 1959b. "Time for THAT Play Mr. Arden." *Daily Mail*, October 23.

———. 1959c. "From East to West with a Big Bang." *Daily Mail*, December 17.

———. 1969. "A Weapon to End All Wars . . ." *Daily Mail*, April 9.

Wiltshire, Maurice. 1954. Review of *The Good Soldier Schweik*. *Daily Mail*, November 10.

Wiseman, Thomas. 1956. "My Top Ten of 1956." *Evening Standard*, December 22.

Worsley, Thomas C. 1956a. "The Arts and Entertainment." *New Statesman*, March 24.

———. 1956b. "Review of *Look Back in Anger*." *New Statesman*, May 19.

Worth, Katherine. 1972. *Revolutions in Modern English Drama*. London: G. Bell and Sons.

———. 1981. "Beckett and the Drama Medium." In *British Radio Drama*, ed. John Drakakis, 191–217. Cambridge: Cambridge University Press.

Wroe, Nicholas. 2004. "Britain's Brecht." *Guardian*, January 3.

Zarhy-Levo, Yael. 1993. "The Theatre Critic as a Cultural Agent: Esslin, Marowitz and Tynan." *Poetics* 21: 525–543.

———. 1998a. "The Riddling Map of Harold Pinter's *Ashes to Ashes*." *Journal of Theatre and Drama* 4: 133–146.

———. 1998b. "Theatrical Success: A Behind-the-Scene Story." *Theatre History Studies* 17: 61–70.

———. 2001a. *The Theatrical Critic as Cultural Agent: Constructing Pinter, Orton and Stoppard as Absurdist Playwrights*. New York: Peter Lang.

———. 2001b. "Critical Modes and the 'Rebellious' Playwright: Pinter's *Alaska* and Stoppard's *Arcadia*." *Journal of Dramatic Theory and Criticism* 16: 81–99.

———. 2001c. "Pinter and the Critics." In *The Cambridge Companion to Harold Pinter*, ed. Peter Raby, 212–230. Cambridge: Cambridge University Press.

Index

external mediators, 10, 11, 12, 13, 215–217

Eyre, Richard, 6, 166

Farson, Daniel, 39

Fearon, George, 24, 33, 35, 37, 39, 52, 54

Fenn, Charles, 70

festivals, theatre, 2, 13, 22, 24, 88, 138, 145, 167–168, 219; Chichester Festival Theatre, 134, 141; Devon festival, 73, 74, 75; Edinburgh Festival, 7, 54, 72, 105–106, 120, 150; International Theatre Festivals, 72–73, 79; International Youth Festival in Moscow, 39; London International Festival of Theatre (LIFT), 194; Paris festival, 75, 88, 93, 101, 104; Pinter Festival, 200–201, 202, 204, 218, 219

Financial Times, 201

Findlater, Richard, 15, 23, 26, 31, 55, 167, 212, 230n148, 250n58

Finney, Albert, 130, 142–143

Franks, Alan, 195, 196

Free Cinema, 44, 45, 46, *47*, *48*, 49, 50, 210, 228n121

funding bodies. *See* mediation, process of

Furmanovsky, Jill, 196

Gambon, Michael, 191

Gardiner, Gerald, 79

Gardner, Raymond, 153–154

Gaskill, William, 50, 59–60, 121, 141, 210, 243n78

Gaston, George, 148–149

Gate Theatre, Dublin, 200, 204, 218, 219

Genet, Jean, 5

Gielgud, John, 101, 173, 175, 204

Goldman, James, 94

Goodwin, Clive, 55, 83, 96, 134

Goorney, Howard; on Arts Council, 83, 110; on Devon festival, 74; on Fun Palace, 102; on *The Hostage*, 84, 86; on leadership, 70; on Littlewood, 66, 98; on *Make Me an Offer*, 90–91, 92; on *The Quare Fellow*, 77; on *Sparrers Can't Sing*, 93; and Stratford East location, 68, 97; on *A Taste of Honey*, 87; on *They Might Be Giants*, 94; on *Uranium 235*, 67; on West End transfers, 79

Goring, Edward, 81

Graham, Paul, 29

Granada Television, 52, 97

Gray, Frances, 123, 124, 148, 149, 157

Greene, Graham, 83

Griffith, Robert E., 94

Griffiths, Trevor, 149

Gross, John, 203

Guardian, 12, 140–141, 153, 155, 160, 202, 203, 207

Guardian Women, 110

Gunn, Tom, 37

Gussow, Mel, 161, 201

Haigh, Kenneth, 25, 32, 231n169

Hale, Owen, 55

Hall, Ann, 185

Hall, Peter; and *Betrayal*, 177, 251n83; and censorship defense, 79; and *The Collection*, 168; and *Encore*, 55; and *The Homecoming*, 169, 218; and *A Kind of Alaska*, 180; and *Landscape*, 170, 172; and *No Man's Land*, 173, 175, 250n65; and Oxford University Dramatic Society (OUDS), 222n12; and Pinter, 161, 175; and Royal Shakespeare Company, 5; and *Silence*, 170, 172; and Theatre of Cruelty, 139; and *Waiting for Godot*, 220

Hall, Stuart, 55

producers, 2, 10, 11. *See also specific individuals*

Pryce-Jones, Alan, 126

Quayle, Anthony, 18–19, 20–21

Quigley, Austin, 57, 58, 162, 175, 246n6

Raffles, Gerry, 66, 67, 68, 70, 73, 75, 80, 88, 89, 92, 94, 97, 99, 102, 103. *See also* Theatre Workshop

Rattigan, Terence, 80

Reading, Jack, 115

Rebellato, Dan, 6, 16, 106, 107, 114

Redgrave, Michael, 67, 101, 128, 130

Redgrave, Vanessa, 101

Reisz, Karel, 44, 45, 46, 50, 128, 201, 210. *See also* Free Cinema

Reynolds, Gillian, 156

Reynolds News, 96, 98

Richards, Gavin, 150, 245n118

Richardson, Miranda, 191

Richardson, Ralph, 18, 101, 173, 175, 204

Richardson, Tony, 19–20, 46, 49, 50, 87, 159, 210; and English Stage Company, 17, 24, 25, 28; and Free Cinema, 44, 45; and *Look Back in Anger*, 31, 32, 35, 37, 43–44, 51–52, 58; and Woodfall Company, 87

Ritchie, Harry, 35, 38–39, 41, 42

Roberts, Philip, 6, 17, 18, 20–21, 22, 29, 31–32, 33, 35, 36, 59, 124–125, 222n10

Rock 'n' Roll (Stoppard), 220

Room at the Top, 44, 46

Round House, 144, 145, 146

Royal Court Theatre, 5, 6, 17–18, 19, 20, 21, 31, *34*, 37, 39, 51, 59, 60–61, 107, 110, 114, 117, 120–125, *127*, 194, 197, 220, 223n32

Royal Shakespeare Company, 5, 6, 12, 21, 61, 66, 101, 138, 139–140, 146, 150,

151, 152–154, 155, 156, 160, 169, 170, *171*, 172, 210, 222n9

Sacks, Oliver, 180, 182–183, 184, 188

Saint-Denis, Michel, 18, 19, 21, 28, 125, 209

Salzman, Harry, 33, 43

Sartre, Jean-Paul, 5

Schroll, Herman, 169

Scott, George, 35

Scott, J. D., 38

Sequence, 44, 46, 228n115

7:84 Theatre Company, 150, 157, 245n118

Shakespeare, William; *Richard II*, 70, 71, 73; *Twelfth Night*, 67; *Wars of the Roses*, 139; *As You Like It*, 67

Shakespeare Memorial Theatre at Stratford-upon-Avon, 18–19, 25, 28, 222n9

Shall, Andrew, 155

Shaw, George Bernard, 223n32

Shaw, Glen Byam, 18, 26, 28, 43, 209

The Sheep Well (De Vega), 65–66

Shellard, Dominic, 6, 16, 56, 107, 114–115, 116, 234n54

Sherwood, John, 167, 248n32

Shorter, Eric, 128, 187

Shrum, Wesley, 6, 7

Shulman, Milton, 81, 94, 140, 173, 195

Sight and Sound, 44

Sillitoe, Alan, 50

Simpson, N. F., 60, 128, 164

Sinfield, Alan, 110, 231n179

Smith, Maggie, 101

Smurthwait, Nick, 160

Soyinka, Wole, 60, 105

Spencer, Charles, 194, 195, 199, 207

Spinetti, Victor, 91, 93, 237n132

Stage, 28, 29, 96

Stanislavsky, Konstantin, 69

STUDIES IN THEATRE HISTORY AND CULTURE